This book guides you to build a quality campaign from the ground up to compete on the highest level.

—Ping Jen, Product Manager, Bing Ads

The title of this book isn't pulling any punches; it really is the "ultimate guide" to pay-per-click advertising. Whether you're just getting started with PPC or if you're an old pro, this book is not only "ultimate" but it is also essential. Each chapter is filled with timeless information that can serve as the bedrock of your PPC campaign foundation. The strategies in this book will improve your PPC performance and ultimately grow your business. This content will deliver value for years to come. Your ROI on buying this book is off the charts!

—Joseph Kerschbaum, Midwest Account Director, 3Q Digital

Brilliant insights. Advanced material. Don't think, just buy it. Rich is one of those guys that makes you sit up and listen closely. His knowledge of the data behind AdWords is quite literally unparalleled. (Outside a few people in Google. Maybe.) He digs in deep and makes you smirk in awe at the clever ways all that data can help you improve your account. A must read.

—Mike Rhodes, CEO, WebSavvy.com.au

Just buy this one. Stokes writes the one PPC book to own in 2014. Great for beginners, required reading for those in the know. Up-to-the-moment fresh for 2014.

—Rob Sieracki, Co-founder, Ox Optimal PPC Consultancy

Since reading *Ultimate Guide to Pay-Per-Click Advertising* I no longer feel I'm at the foot of an impossibly long learning curve. This book reveals the inner workings of the search ad networks without using tea leaves and crystal balls. Instead, it focuses on the few strategic metrics that make a difference, and backs them up with valid data from real campaigns. It's the first book I've read that made me feel I could take data-driven action to improve my search advertising campaigns. Most importantly, I now know something that other search marketers don't, and that gives me the edge in this competitive ad marketplace.

—Brian Massey, Author of *Your Customer Creation Equation*

If you or anyone on your team needs to learn or get refreshed with the fundamentals of paid search marketing, this is the book for you. Clean, simple, and very actionable.

—Rob Griffin, EVP, Havas Media

Rich Stokes has turned mountains of data into meaningful and actionable insights into how Search Engine Marketing really works. This is required reading for any online marketer who wants to be in the 1 percent of successful Search Engine Marketers. With my eight years of experience in optimizing for Keyword Coverage and Impression Share, I know that what Richard says is right on the money and has led my own clients to realize 3X to 5X sales growth in a matter of months on mature campaigns that had been 'optimized' and managed previously by other agencies.

—Kevin Milani, VP of Digital Marketing, Virtual Marketing Staff LLC

Entrepreneur
MAGAZINE'S

ULTIMATE

GUIDE TO

Pay-Per-Click

ADVERTISING

Second Edition

- Master advanced Search Engine strategies
- Employ secrets used by the top 1% of search marketers to **capture sales from 99% of the competition**
- Completely revised, including new insights on Product Listing Ads, Ad Extensions, Mobile and more

Entrepreneur
PRESS®

RICHARD STOKES

Entrepreneur Press, Publisher
Cover Design: Andrew Welyczko
Production and Composition: Eliot House Productions

This publication is designed to provide accurate and authoritative information in regard to the
subject matter covered. It is sold with the understanding that the publisher is not engaged in
rendering legal, accounting or other professional services. If legal advice or other expert assistance is
required, the services of a competent professional person should be sought.

Library of Congress Cataloging-in-Publication Data
Stokes, Richard L., 1971–
    [Entrepreneur magazine's ultimate guide to pay-per-click advertising]
    Ultimate guide to pay-per-click advertising / by Richard Stokes.—Second edition.
        pages   cm.
        ISBN-13: 978-1-59918-534-7 (alk. paper)
        ISBN-10: 1-59918-534-2 (alk. paper)
    1. Internet marketing. 2. Internet advertising. I. Entrepreneur (Santa Monica, Calif.) II. Title.
    HF5415.1265.S753 2014
    659.14′4—dc23   2013042629

Printed in the United States of America

18 17 16   10 9 8 7 6 5 4 3

Dedicated to Kelly, Brendan, Brittain,
and my latest conversion, Brooks

Contents

CHAPTER 29

Mobile Search and Enhanced Campaigns 265

CHAPTER 30

Conclusion. 283

About the Author 285

Index. 287

Acknowledgments

Many thanks go out to my contributors: Perry Marshall (author, *Ultimate Guide to Google AdWords*), Ping Jen (product manager, Bing Ads), Jon Rise (CEO, Rise Interactive), Noam Dorros, Matt Van Wagner of Find Me Faster, and Howie Jacobson (author, *AdWords for Dummies*) for their contributions. These are some of the finest search marketers in the world, and anyone interested in PPC advertising would do well to follow their advice closely.

This book would not be possible without the talented folks at AdGooroo. It's hard to believe it has been ten years. Thank you for an exciting decade.

I would like to acknowledge the wonderful people at Kantar Media, who had the vision to see a great thing and make it greater: Terry Kent, Amy Silverstein, Joel Pacheco, and Jeff Krentz.

I am also very grateful to the team at Entrepreneur Press for their vision and assistance during the preparation of this work.

I'd like to express my thanks to Rick Carlson, CEO of Surf Secret, and Dave Gobel and Roger Holzberg, both executive members of the Methuselah Foundation, for sharing their marketing data with me for use in this book.

This book would not have been possible without the patience of my family—Kelly, Brendan, Brittain, and Brooks—throughout many months of marathon writing sessions. And finally to my parents: Persistence paid off.

Foreword to the Second Edition by Perry Marshall

"If you want to win at pay-per-click today, you MUST know stuff everyone else doesn't know."

I have yet to have a single conversation with Richard Stokes that didn't reveal something fascinating.

Rich is a data geek in the best sense of the term, but he's more than that. He is fascinated, intrigued and absorbed in what it <u>means</u>, not just what it <u>says</u>.

I attribute this to the fact that Richard started out as an affiliate marketer ten years ago, buying ads on Google, selling products and living by his wits. As I recall, he quit his job when he started making north of $50,000 per month.

Well, the list of people in the world who have actually done that is not a very big one.

Now there is also a group of people in the world who make their living by studying gargantuan amounts of data and telling you what it means. This is also not a very big list of people.

But the number of people who have done all of the above—been a bootstrapping entrepreneur, wolverine marketer, and junkie of delicious data—is absolutely tiny. Perhaps you can count them on one or two hands, and that's it.

Richard Stokes is one of those precious few.

And he is the *only* one who's writing books, freely sharing their discoveries.

And that's why I like Rich so much. It's why I had him speak at my Maui AdWords Elite Master's Summit two years in a row,;ee what might tumble out; it's why so many Fortune 500 companies come to him and his company, AdGooroo, when they must decide how to optimally position themselves in the Google advertising landscape.

Outside the Googleplex, there may not be anyone else who knows more than Richard about how the Google AdWords algorithm actually works.

Add to that the fact that he's founded an impressive company—AdGooroo itself is a study in successful business building—you have all the makings of a great business book. If you're spending tens of thousands of dollars on clicks, you're not gonna want to put it down.

Warning: Pay-per-click is trickier than it looks. As Richard says, just 1 percent of Google's advertisers generate 80 percent of Google's paid search revenue. It has become one of those things that can be made to appear very simple and easy but in reality demands well-honed chops, close attention to trends, and a good bit of art and intuition.

Juggling these things is a lot harder if you're not even quite sure how Google's machine works in the first place. Google won't tell you nearly as much as Richard will.

Like I said, every conversation I've ever had with Richard has been a fascinating tour of insider information. You will find the same to be true of every chapter of this book.

Wherever you are in your pay-per-click journey and your evolution as an entrepreneur or marketing professional, I wish you the very best of success. You've already done more than most people will do: You've picked up an excellent book by a world-class expert. So you deserve it.

Now sit at Richard's feet, and hear what wisdom he has to share.

—Perry Marshall
Chicago, Illinois

Preface to the Second Edition

In the early 2000s, after many stops and starts, I hit my first major-league home run on the internet with an antivirus software review website I created as a side project while working full-time at a well-known, global advertising agency.

My first weekend, I made $29. I remember thinking at the time that if I could only make $500 a month from the site, it would be a huge success.

What I didn't realize at the time was that I was among the first wave of early adopters taking advantage of Google AdWords to drive cheap, targeted traffic to my websites. AdWords was wildly profitable back then, and easier, as well. No matter how bad your ads were, you could make money. That $29 turned into $200 by the end of the week. My first month's revenues totaled over $3,000. Small? Sure. But I'm still pretty proud of that growth curve. It was one heck of a first month. And it was entirely due to pay-per-click (PPC) advertising.

However, success cannot (and never does) go unnoticed. My competitors caught on quickly. As they increased the sophistication of their campaigns, the bar was set higher, and it became more difficult (and expensive) to generate traffic from the search engines.

Even though they were making it tough on me, however, I was able to steadily increase my websites' profits throughout this period. Why?

Because I had made it my business to study the search tactics each of my competitors was using. Every time they tried something new—whether it was a new keyword, better ad copy, or a specific bidding strategy—I tested it and applied what worked to my own campaign.

By 2005, the PC security industry had topped out, yet I continued to pull in good profits for several years while most of the competing websites quit advertising altogether.

This success wasn't due to some magic marketing bullet. It came from being just a little bit better than each of my competitors in many different areas. I guessed—correctly—that if I could discover their best tactics and apply them to my campaign, then, taken together as a whole, this would put me far ahead of the pack.

My secret for doing this was a software program I wrote that would actively hunt for my competitors' ads and tell me everything it could about them. By the end of my first year of business, this software allowed me to grow my sales sixfold, all while working less than ten hours a week.

It was when I cashed my first $100,000 check that I realized that this technology could probably help many other companies as well. We named the software AdGooroo (pronounced "Ad Guru") and quietly sold it by word of mouth only.

As time passed we acquired more customers. Today, AdGooroo has grown from a tiny software company to a global presence. Our software is used by more than two-thirds of the largest interactive agencies in the world, as well as thousands of other consultants, agencies, and in-house brand advertisers. Our quarterly reports on the state of the search engine industry are eagerly consumed and reported by the media.

As busy as AdGooroo keeps me, I still make time to run our PPC campaigns. I talk daily with other search marketers and attend several tradeshows every year. And perhaps most importantly, the AdGooroo database grants me insider access to the search marketing activity and rankings of virtually every advertiser in every imaginable type of business on the planet. I have the luxury of seeing what works and what doesn't.

It was from this vantage point that I wrote my first book, *Mastering Search Advertising: How the Top 3% of Search Advertisers Dominate Google AdWords*. In it, I revealed several little-known strategies that savvy search marketers were using at the time to gain an edge on the competition. I chose those strategies because each of them had the potential for big rewards and none of them required a lot of time or money to implement.

The book was more popular than I anticipated, and so with the help of Entrepreneur Press, I incorporated my reader's input and requests into a sorely needed guide to advanced paid search strategies. The book you are now holding is the second edition, which has been updated to reflect the new realities of paid search circa mid-2013.

If you attend one of the popular search engine marketing trade shows (such as SMX Advanced), you'll be lucky to learn one or two of these techniques. But this manual contains virtually every technique used by the best-paid search managers in the industry. All of the strategies covered in my previous works are included here. However, you'll find new insights and techniques we've gained from new research and developments (including sections on mobile search marketing, product listing ads, and more recent changes to the quality score algorithm). This edition also covers more about Bing, which has been growing in popularity and now represents approximately 30 percent of all U.S. search traffic.

While to the newcomer some of these topics may seem to be tangential to the business of PPC advertising, I will explain in due course why you simply cannot compete without being at least somewhat competent in these areas.

The book you are holding in your hands represents the current state of the art in search marketing. With it, you have the tools needed to propel your business into the top 1 percent of search advertisers.

Good luck,
Rich

AUTHOR NOTE

About AdGooroo

AdGooroo, a Kantar Media company, is a leading provider of digital marketing intelligence that drives competitive advantage for internet marketers. Founded in 2004, more than 4,000 advertisers and agencies use AdGooroo's on-demand tools to tap into the world's largest database of search and gain actionable intelligence on their top competitors' keywords, ad creative, campaign statistics, budgets, and more.

LEGAL NOTES

AdGooroo is not affiliated with Google, Yahoo!, or Microsoft. Our views and opinions do not reflect those of any search engine or any entity other than our own.

Nothing in the world can take the place of Persistence.

Talent will not; nothing is more common than unsuccessful men with talent.

Genius will not; unrewarded genius is almost a proverb.

Education will not; the world is full of educated derelicts.

Persistence and determination alone are omnipotent.

The slogan "Press On" has solved and always will solve

the problems of the human race.

—Calvin Coolidge

Chapter 1

99 Percent of Advertisers Are Failing at Paid Search

As a small advertiser starting out in 2003, I was drawn to Google AdWords because it allowed me to level the playing field with far larger competitors. With nothing more than a credit card and a little elbow grease, I could tap into a huge reservoir of highly motivated buyers that most other advertisers had overlooked.

This great democratization of advertising played no small part in catapulting Google to becoming a multibillion-dollar company. However, this is no longer the case.

AdGooroo conducted a study in late 2012 to determine just how evenly distributed advertising impressions were among search advertisers. We looked at a wide variety of industries and measured the advertiser concentration in each.

There's nothing inherently unfair about search engine advertising; everyone in the market has access to the same knowledge, the same training materials, the same experts, and so on. It would be reasonable to assume that advertising exposure is fairly well distributed among all participants in the marketplace.

We were shocked to learn that it just isn't so.

A FEW ADVERTISERS IN EVERY COUNTRY DOMINATE PAID SEARCH

In September 2012, we recorded 775,000 advertisers on Google in the United States. We estimate that there were approximately 844 million clicks on paid search ads. Of those clicks, 675 million were generated by just 8,332 advertisers.

In other words, less than 1.1 percent of all advertisers on Google generated over 80 percent of the clicks.

And if we look at it by total spend, we come up with a similar answer. Those 8,332 advertisers generated about 79 percent of total AdWords revenue during that same month.

We see a similar concentration of advertisers in other markets. Figure 1–1 shows the same figures for the UK and France.

Google US	United States	United Kingdom	France
Total paid search clicks	844 million	348 million	153 million
Total number of advertisers	775,000	211,000	104,000
Number of advertisers generating 80% of paid search clicks	8,663 (1.1%)	2,169 (1.0%)	1,248 (1.2%)
Percent of total paid search revenue generated by these advertisers	78.8%	79.4%	80.4%

FIGURE 1–1. Paid search concentration in three major markets.

We see similar results with other engines. On Bing US in September 2012, we estimate that 301,000 advertisers generated 209 million total clicks. Just 3,541 advertisers generated 80 percent of those clicks (and 82 percent of spend).

This presents us with an intriguing problem. Assuming two capable and equally motivated competitors, what could explain why one is successful while another is not?

But the facts paint a very different picture. The utopia of a "fair" advertising marketplace is nothing more than an illusion.

VIRTUALLY EVERY BUSINESS CATEGORY IS "OWNED" BY A FEW ADVERTISERS

What happens if we narrow our focus down to a specific business category?

Let's start with "apparel and fashion," an extremely high-traffic and competitive category on Google AdWords. Figure 1–2 depicts the number of impressions on the x-axis, the number of clicks on the y-axis. The size of each bubble corresponds to the advertiser's relative spend.

We see that the category is dominated by some well-known names: Victoria's Secret, Express, 6PM, and Designer Apparel. What is not so easy to tell from the chart is the sheer number of other advertisers—1,053 in all—who are fighting each other for the remaining share of impressions and clicks.

Despite the above figures, it may be surprising to hear that as far as competing in paid search goes, the apparel and fashion industry isn't so bad. It could be much worse.

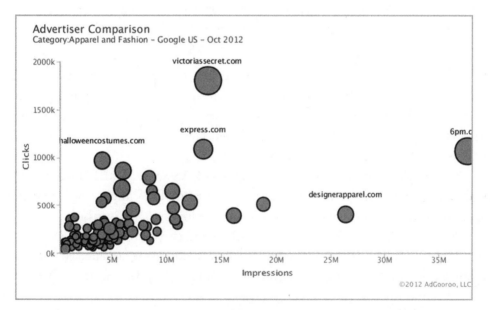

FIGURE 1–2. Apparel and fashion advertising activity, Google US, October 2012. (*Source*: AdGooroo Industry Insight)

Let's take a look at the car rental industry (Figure 1–3). Enterprise.com is soundly trouncing the competition in clicks. They are running a respectable second to RentalCars.com when it comes to impressions. Nobody else even comes close:

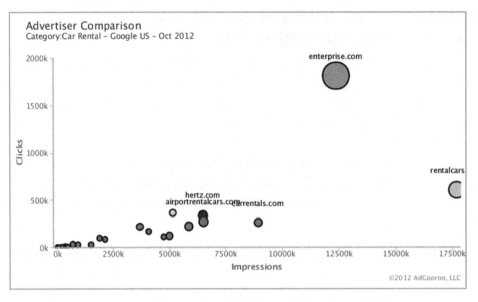

FIGURE 1–3. Car rental advertising activity, Google US, October 2012. (*Source*: AdGooroo Industry Insight)

Another way to compare these two industries is to compare their "share of voice," that is, the percentage of the available impressions each advertiser is capturing. Share of voice is particularly important to brand advertisers because there is evidence that even if a search engine user doesn't click the ad, the mere fact that they saw it predisposes them ever so slightly more toward a future purchase.

In the apparel and fashion category (Figure 1–4), we see that the 15 most dominant advertisers are capturing around 25 percent of the available impressions. This leaves approximately 75 percent of the traffic for the remaining 1,053 advertisers.

This isn't great news if you are in the fashion industry. But look on the bright side: It could be worse. Figure 1–5 shows that the 14 most dominant car rental companies are capturing over 90 percent of the available search impressions, leaving just 10 percent for the remaining advertisers.

In my 2007 book, *Mastering Search Advertising*, I showed data that proved 97 percent of advertisers were being shut out of most of the available search traffic. Virtually every data point we look at, regardless of search engine or country, shows that this is still the reality. In fact, more recent data suggests that today's figure is closer to 99 percent.

What this means is that if you want to succeed in paid search advertising, you need to be prepared to invest a significant amount of time and effort. Paid search is not something you can simply dabble in and expect to win. In the following chapters, you're going to learn exactly how it's done.

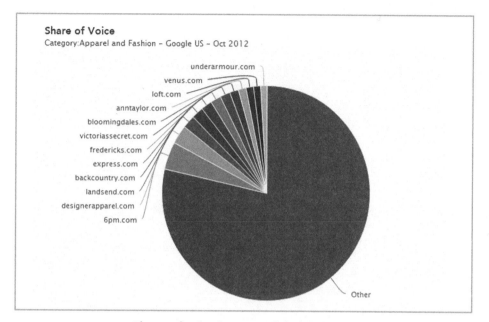

FIGURE 1–4. Share of voice in apparel and fashion, Google US, October 2012. (*Source*: AdGooroo Industry Insight)

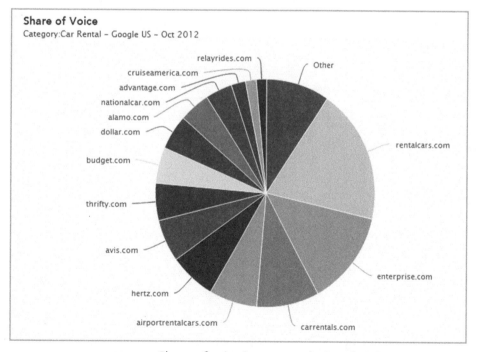

FIGURE 1–5. Share of voice in car rental, Google US, October 2012. (*Source*: AdGooroo Industry Insight)

Chapter 2

The Foundation of Successful Paid Search Campaigns

Before we dive into pay-per-click, we need to have a word about the proper order in which to tackle things.

When most advertisers go about starting their pay-per-click campaign, they begin by creating an advertising account (usually on Google), randomly choosing some keywords, creating an ad or two, and picking a starting-bid price out of thin air. The clicks start coming in, but more often than not, the profits fail to follow.

These undisciplined campaigns rarely pay for themselves. This is a real shame, because although pay-per-click is a cutthroat business, it's still as easy as shooting fish in a barrel if you do it right.

The reality that these advertisers fail to take into account is that no matter what business you're in, someone has probably been there before you. Blindly rushing in with a half-baked website is a guaranteed way to ensure that your competitors will outbid (and outsell) you.

Starting a campaign without having access to analytics is marketing suicide. You need tracking to know how much you can profitably spend for each of your ads. You'll also need it to learn to which pages on your site you should be sending visitors from the search engines.

And if you have tracking installed on your website but haven't optimized your website's ability to convert visitors into buyers, you probably won't be able to compete for the best possible placement for your ads. As a result, your ads will appear infrequently, buried deep within the search results pages. And more importantly, you'll be capturing only a small percentage of the sales you would have captured by identifying and eliminating sales bottlenecks.

Patience is vital. If you haven't spent the time on these preliminary steps, your website won't be able to keep up with the competition. Neophyte search marketers are all too quick to jump into a campaign without really knowing what they are doing. Consequently, their campaigns end up a mishmash of poorly aligned keywords, ad copy, and landing pages. Impressions are slowly choked off, and first-page bid prices rise until their ads are shut out of what could be the most profitable keywords in the campaign.

So I encourage you to take a disciplined three-step approach. Start by installing an analytics service on your website. Learn it inside and out, and then use it to optimize your landing pages. If you create a better converting offer than your competitors, it's far more likely that you will become the dominant advertiser in your industry.

I've honed this approach through years of creating pay-per-click campaigns. If you follow these steps in the order I've laid them out for you, you should be able to capture a majority of the available impressions and generate high clickthrough rates at a fraction of the price most of your competitors are paying.

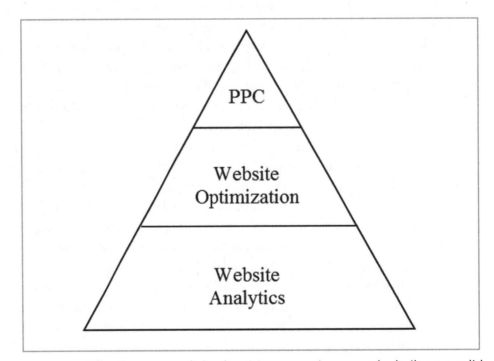

FIGURE 2–1. Effective pay-per-click advertising campaigns must be built on a solid foundation of analytics and website optimization.

Chapter 3

Your Marketing Will Fail without Tracking

Pretend for a moment that instead of promoting your business over the web, you were to take a more traditional approach, such as television advertising. You might be prepared to spend upwards of a quarter-million dollars just for production, to be followed by potentially millions of dollars of national media buys.

With so much at stake, it seems unlikely that you would simply write a check and forget about it. Not by a long shot. I bet that you'd be watching the sales figures like a hawk to see if your campaign was bringing customers in. And if it didn't perform, you'd cut your losses quickly (and probably fire your marketing manager).

Most of our businesses will never grow to the scale where we can afford big-ticket television buys. Fortunately, internet advertising now gives us a way to purchase smaller, more reasonably priced blocks of traffic.

The downside of this is that these less expensive campaigns tend to fall off the radar of most managers and entrepreneurs. There is a false sense of security that comes from spending "only" $500 a month or so on search. We tell ourselves, "Maybe it will come in, maybe it won't," or "Let's just start it and see what happens."

This is nothing more than a shortcut to failure, and I don't want you to fall into that trap. So please, take this firm, but friendly, piece of advice:

If you don't track your campaign . . . you will lose. Period.

If you blow off the numbers behind your business, your marketing will be mediocre because it will be built on opinion and guesswork.

Guesses and opinions are the enemy of good marketing. If you let the numbers tell you the truth, you'll make your website better. You'll make your advertising better. Your sales will end up 5, 10, even 100 times over where you started.

Marketing Sherpa reports that 90 percent of search marketers use some form of analytics. While I believe that this figure is optimistic (the majority of advertisers I talk to have no website tracking in place or never look at their reports), the fact remains that your serious competitors (the top 1 percent) will certainly be relying on some form of website tracking to improve their returns. You need to do the same if you want to level the playing field.

You must have tracking installed on your website. There are no ifs, ands, or buts about it.

WHAT WEBSITE ANALYTICS WILL TELL YOU

Website analytics is the study of online user behavior for the purpose of improving sales. By adding analytics capabilities to your website, you will be able to measure:

- Where visitors are coming from (e.g., search engines, type-in traffic, banner ads, etc.)
- What pages they are visiting the most
- How much and how often they convert (e.g., buy your products, sign up for your email newsletters, request more information, etc.)
- How long they stay on each page
- How quickly they leave
- How much every page on your site is worth to you

With this information, you can make your site better.

You'll have the insights you need to improve your site design, create a better user experience, and streamline your conversion pages.

CONVERSIONS

Sales, leads, signups, donations—whatever it is you're trying to get your visitors to do on your website—is what we mean when we're discussing "conversions."

The end result? Higher return on every advertising dollar you spend.

These insights will be contained in your website analytics reports, your new best friends.

LEARNING MORE ABOUT ANALYTICS

The first edition of this book contained detailed information on analytics reporting. However, in the past few years, analytics has become a big field, so much so that the subject can take up an entire book. So this edition focuses more on getting people to your site and not so much about what they do once they get there.

However, I strongly recommend that you purchase a good book on the subject, such as *Web Analytics 2.0: The Art of Online Accountability and Science of Customer Centricity* by Avinash Kaushik. Another excellent companion that will help you get more return from your paid search campaigns is *Landing Page Optimization* by Tim Ash, Maura Ginty, and Rich Page.

Chapter 4

The First Requirement for a Profitable Paid Search Campaign

ands down, the surest way for most marketers to improve their returns from paid search advertising is to improve the efficiency at which their website converts visitors into buyers.

Too many marketers hope that adding an AdWords campaign will redeem a low-performing website or product. If that doesn't fix their business, they compound their error by raising their bids. They make the same mistake that many dotcom companies made during the late '90s: they pour money into a losing business in a mistaken attempt to "grow to profitability."

To do it right, you have to accept PPC advertising for what it is: a way to multiply your existing business. If you add PPC to a bad business, you'll simply lose money faster.

On the other hand, if you add PPC to a good business, you will make more money . . . but *only* if you do it right.

WEBSITE OPTIMIZATION

A proven technique for improving the efficiency of your online business is through *website optimization,* which is the art and science of enhancing the user experience of a website with the goal of converting users into customers.

To see why this is important, you need to become familiar with the concept of cost-per-action (CPA). CPA is simply the average cost you incur for turning a visitor into a customer. To calculate it, you add up the entirety of your variable costs for a given time period (which for most websites consists largely of traffic acquisition costs) and divide by the total number of customers during that same time.

For instance, if in a given month your website generated 25 customers and you spent $1,000 on acquiring traffic, then your CPA is $40.

Your priority as a marketer is to minimize your CPA. It should be well below your average order size (ideally, around half). The difference between them tells you how much profit your website is generating.

If your average order size was $60 during a time when your average CPA was $40, then you made money to the tune of $20 per customer. If, on the other hand, your average order size was only $30, then you lost $10 per customer.

As you can see, CPA is a convenient way for general managers to measure the overall profitability of a website. However, as this example shows, it provides no guidance on how to actually go about improving your profitability. You need a better set of measures if you hope to succeed.

A BETTER WAY TO MEASURE WEBSITE PROFITABILITY

The inability of CPA to lead to any actionable strategies has led to the creation of two alternate measures by which you can assess the profitability of a website: cost-per-visitor (which in pay-per-click advertising translates to cost-per-click, or CPC) and $/Index (commonly referred to as the "Dollar Index").

The $/Index is calculated by dividing your total revenue by the total number of visitors. Unlike the CPA metric we discussed above, $/Index can be (and typically is) calculated for individual pages on your website. This makes it very useful as a tool for measuring the effectiveness of a page.

In other words, we can directly compare the $/Index to the average price you're paying for each visitor to tune our bid prices.

A short example to illustrate these points is shown in Figure 4–1 on page 15. Let's take a one-page website that purchased 1,000 clicks from Google AdWords for $1,950, and another 300 visitors from the Yahoo! Bing Network for $150. Through the process of converting visitors on this page, the website generated 25 customers at an average order size of $100, for a grand total of $2,500 in revenue.

We calculate the CPA by dividing our total traffic acquisition costs ($2,100) by the total number of customers (25) to arrive at $84 per customer. This is well below the $100 average order size, so you know we turned a profit. If you stopped here, though, you would be leaving quite a bit of money on the table.

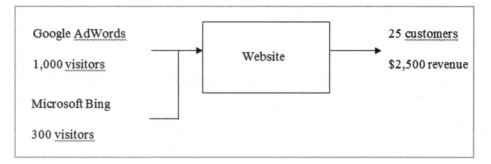

FIGURE 4–1. A simple single-page conversion example.

Next, we calculate the $/Index for the page by dividing our total revenue ($2,500) by the number of visitors to the page (1,300). This figure is equal to $1.92. This figure gives you a sense of how much a typical visitor to this page is worth to us.

Next, we compare that with the average cost-per-click (CPC) that we're paying each engine. The CPC for Google AdWords is $1.95 ($1,950 total cost divided by 1,000 visitors). The CPC for Microsoft Bing is $0.50 ($150 divided by 300 visitors).

This is actionable information. These figures tell us that we're actually losing a few cents per visitor from our Google AdWords traffic. However, we're making it up because we're paying a very attractive price for visitors from Bing. We could immediately improve profitability by lowering our average CPC for the Google AdWords traffic (we would get less traffic as a result). At the same time, we would raise our average bid price for Bing traffic to increase the amount of traffic from that source.

Later in this book are various strategies for improving profitability by adjusting your average CPC (either up or down). For now though, we want to consider another possible outcome of this exercise.

What if, instead of adjusting our bid prices on the search engines, we made this landing page better?

In our example above, the landing page converted visitors at the rate of 25 out of 1,300. Dividing these figures gives you a conversion rate of 1.92 percent.

By finding a way to improve this landing page so that it converted at a slightly higher rate—say 35 out of 1,300 customers (2.7 percent conversion rate)—our $/Index would increase to $2.69 ($3,500 total revenue divided by 1,300 visitors). This means we wouldn't have to lower our average CPC on Google; we could even possibly raise it and get even more traffic!

While this example is overly simplified, it is representative of the interplay between bid prices and landing page conversion rates that we frequently encounter in the real world. Website owners are usually in a big hurry to get their PPC campaigns rolling, but this is a huge mistake if they've never given a moment's attention to their landing page conversion rates.

SOMETIMES CONVERSION OPTIMIZATION ISN'T CRITICAL

One of the things you're going to hear a lot when starting out is that conversion optimization is the most important step you can take as a digital marketer. However, there are certain cases when it turns out to not be all that important.

Conversion optimization does best with single-step transaction models, such as lead generation, ecommerce, and most other types of B2C business models. However, it becomes much less important if any of the following are true:

- Your customers are sophisticated (e.g., scientists, engineers, and other professionals).
- You cater to a small niche market.
- You sell primarily to corporate buyers.
- You engage primarily in direct sales (e.g., you sell offline through salespeople).

In my experience, these are the types of scenarios in which conversion optimization is unlikely to be your best tactic for improving your marketing results. Mind you, there is no excuse for poor design. But having said that, you aren't going to get a big lift in these scenarios by using a different shade of blue in your logo.

Chapter 5

Is Pay-Per-Click Advertising Right for You?

Chances are you've heard about the amazing ROI that can be had with pay-per-click. A return of 300 percent or even higher is not at all unusual with this form of advertising. (Back in 2003, I was making more than $10 for every $1 I spent on Google AdWords.)

When it works, it works well. But what we don't usually hear are the stories of people who lost their entire ad spend. As with anything else in business, it's best to be realistic from the onset about your chances of success.

In this section, we'll talk about who usually wins with PPC and who often loses.

PPC WORKS FOR DIRECT-RESPONSE MARKETERS AND ONLINE RETAILERS

Direct-response marketing is a specific form of marketing that sends its messages directly to consumers, usually asking them to take a specific call-to-action (for instance, to call a free phone number or fill out a request for more information) or to purchase a product online.

Typical businesses that make use of direct marketing include software companies, newspapers and magazines, sellers of information products, and online retailers.

Traditional direct-response marketing relies heavily on having access to performance statistics, such as open and response rates. PPC provides many comparable statistics (such as clickthrough rate, conversion rate, coverage, and many more) so the performance-based marketer should feel right at home with this channel.

PPC WORKS FOR BRAND ADVERTISERS

On the other end of the spectrum lie brand advertisers. The goal of these advertisers is to build a psychological construct (the "brand image") in the minds of their target audience, typically for the purpose of influencing offline or later purchasing behavior. This image can be highly successful in convincing consumers to pay high prices for products that are extremely cheap to make. It is also quite successful in predisposing specific targeted consumer segments toward certain brands. Although it may seem abstract to some, the brand itself begins to accumulate significant—perhaps even staggering—value over time. And paid search is a powerful tool that can help to increase this value.

Brand advertisers depend less on the types of performance-based statistics mentioned above and more on statistics that attempt to measure both the exposure and perception of the brand in the mind of their target consumers. In the offline world, these statistics include brand awareness, brand recognition, and top-of-mind awareness.

While you cannot measure these metrics using paid search, you can measure share of voice (SOV), which offers the brand manager an easy way to determine if their ads are being seen more or less frequently than direct competitors. In addition, savvy brand managers make use of *engagement sites* that are intended to associate the brand with certain experiences. For instance, the popular baby formula brand, Enfamil, once advertised their online encyclopedia of baby names quite heavily. In Europe, Nestlé promotes an online gaming site targeted to young children to build brand awareness and preference.

Paid search also offers a few other incredible advantages to brand advertisers.

First, it is incredibly cheap in comparison to the seven- and eight-figure advertising budgets. I know of one advertiser who funded their entire paid search campaign for a year by pulling a single television commercial.

There's also a difference in user intent. Most advertising reaches users through an interrupt mechanism (for instance, a television or radio commercial). Search engine users, however, are actively searching for something either strongly or weakly associated with your brand. This may be information about your product ("Enfamil ingredients"), promotions ("Enfamil coupons"), or a deeper but less obvious association ("baby upset stomach"). In a sense, you can think of search engine users as being the leading edge of your larger audience. This little fact is exploited by a few savvy CPG (consumer packaged goods) brands who use paid search to assess the impact of different ad copy strategies without having to spend a fortune in focus groups and local market test runs.

Finally, PPC gives brand advertisers unprecedented control over their message, allowing them to vary their copy based on searcher intent, geography, culture, and so on.

WHY PPC MAY NOT WORK FOR YOU

Only a small percentage of companies using paid search can be considered brand advertisers. The vast majority falls into the direct-response marketing category. These advertisers tend to run into problems that prevent PPC from being a viable advertising medium.

There are six primary reasons why PPC campaigns fail. Three of these are fully under the control of the advertiser, while the remaining three are somewhat out of the control of the advertiser.

By far, the most common reason for failure is that the advertiser is unwilling or unable to manage their PPC campaigns properly. PPC campaigns cannot be ignored if you expect to turn a profit.

Another reason search advertising campaigns tend to fail is due to a lack of tracking. Without tracking, you'll be unable to figure out which keyword buys are working and which are not. You won't be able to tune your campaign and cut out the waste. Installing tracking is a low-cost, one-time effort. There's really no reason other than negligence or ignorance for this.

Finally, if your conversion rate and/or your average order size is too low, you'll be unable to afford even the most modest PPC buys. Your profit margin on successful transactions needs to absorb the cost of acquiring not only the customer, but also all of the other visitors who didn't buy from you. The reason most affiliate marketers have been priced out of Google AdWords is because they're earning only a small commission (5 to 15 percent) on every completed order.

There are three other cases when PPC campaigns might not be a good fit for your business. These are somewhat out of your control, but there can be workarounds.

The first situation arises if your target customers aren't looking on the search engines for the types of products you sell. In this case, you'll need to identify alternative advertising channels (see sidebar by Perry Marshall on page 20).

Another common problem is that your products or services require a high-touch sales process to sell successfully. If prospects buy from you only after they talk to a field rep, then you'll need to resort to a multistage sales process. You can work PPC into this process without being unduly reliant on it. For instance, you will likely have considerable success using Google AdWords to generate qualified leads, which sales reps can then call on. The key here is to recognize when you should sell directly to a customer versus taking a more personal, "high-touch" approach.

Finally, you may run into difficulties with PPC campaigns when bid prices are so high that you are priced out of the market (this is a common problem when selling high-cost consumer services such as auto insurance). Many advertisers simply give up on PPC at this point. However, we've discovered that even in these hypercompetitive markets, there is still plenty of inexpensive search traffic available to those advertisers who are willing to work hard on improving the campaign quality. You'll learn exactly how to do this using the techniques described throughout the following chapters.

WHEN GOOGLE ADWORDS IS THE LEAST EFFECTIVE WAY TO REACH YOUR TARGET CUSTOMER

Perry Marshall, co-author, *The Ultimate Guide to Google AdWords*, www.adwordsbook.com

Because I'm author of some of the most popular books on Google AdWords, my clients are surprised to hear me say that sometimes Google might be last on your list of best ways to sell your product. Let me give you some examples; all lend insight into Google's place in the world:

· Once I had a client who manufactures AC adapters: You know, those big black plugs that provide power for your CD player or charge your cell phone. We tried mightily to make Google AdWords work and couldn't. Why? Because this company sells custom lots of 500 units or more to manufacturers, but all the traffic for "AC Adapters" and related keywords consists of everyday consumers looking to buy one unit at a time. Our Google campaign was a total failure, despite valiant efforts to disqualify noncustomers. The ads would say "minimum lots of 500," but Joe Consumer would click on the ad anyway, then leave. A manufacturing directory is a much better way to reach other manufacturers than Google in that situation.

· Let's say you sell some kind of high-end equipment, software, or consulting to high-level executives, and lower-level people are a waste of time for you. (Very common scenario!) Is bidding on keywords a good way to target those executives? No, not really. Maybe only 1 percent of the people searching are executives; the rest just waste your clicks. Direct mail would be much, much better for that. A FedEx envelope on the executive's desk is a rifle shot.

WHEN GOOGLE ADWORDS IS THE LEAST EFFECTIVE WAY TO REACH YOUR TARGET CUSTOMER, CONTINUED

· Keyword-based advertising only works when people know they have a problem and can describe it to themselves and believe that somebody on the internet has a solution. But many people have severe problems they don't even realize they have. If that's the case, search engine marketing isn't a very good way to reach them. You need to interrupt them instead. So again, direct mail, ads in magazines they read, TV, radio—all of those media might be better. Search engine marketing only gets you people who are proactively looking to solve their problem right now.

Sometimes search traffic gets you, ironically, the lowest quality, least-interested, and least qualified prospects. People who regularly visit specific websites are much more interested and much more qualified. Here's an example: Let's say you are doing fundraising for environmental activism. You could bid on the keyword "environment," but what you'd probably get is high school kids doing homework assignments and writing papers about the environment.

Now, it may be nice to reach those kids with your message, but you ain't gonna get any money out of them. And if you think about it, people who are already active and interested in that probably are not typing "environment" into a search engine. They already have sites they like to go to. You get much better traffic, and more donations, advertising on those sites. (That's why, in some categories, AdSense gets you better traffic than Google searches.)

Every kind of advertising media slices the world in a different way. Bidding on keywords slices the world according to who's got an itch to scratch, right now. Direct mail slices the world according to what magazines people subscribe to, what mail-order products they've purchased, what charities they've donated money to. Compiled mailing lists slice the world according to where they live, what income level they're in, what positions they hold in their jobs, what kind of home they live in.

"Rock—Paper—Scissors"

Print advertising slices the world according to topics people are interested in; if you advertise in *Bass Fisherman* magazine, you get guys who are rabidly interested in bass fishing. If you advertise on the radio at 7:30 in the morning, you get people who are

WHEN GOOGLE ADWORDS IS THE LEAST EFFECTIVE WAY TO REACH YOUR TARGET CUSTOMER, CONTINUED

on their way to work. The pros and cons of every form of advertising are sort of like that game "Rock—Paper—Scissors" where each has its unique advantages and disadvantages.

I told an exec from an online industrial directory that he just needs to come out and say that yes, sometimes Google is hands down the easiest, cheapest way to get new customers. (His prospect will be rather surprised to hear him say that! Coming clean will boost his credibility.) But he can point out that also sometimes, as with those AC adapters, Google may also be one of the worst ways to get a new customer.

For most people, the truth is somewhere in the middle. For most people, Google is a great way to get a certain amount of high-quality leads, but there are only so many available. It's like an oil well that pumps out just so much every day, and no more. Plus you never want to have all your eggs in one basket; that makes you very vulnerable. So you need to explore other avenues.

Many of my customers who advertise on Google have also used any or all of the following ways to acquire new customers:

- · Buying space ads in e-zines

- · Endorsed email blasts from affiliates

- · Popunder and popup ads on other sites

- · Postcard mailings

- · Direct mail

- · Magalogs: catalogs that look like magazines

- · Spots in other peoples' catalogs

- · FedEx envelopes to highly targeted prospects from carefully selected mailing lists

- · Banner ads

- · Radio

WHEN GOOGLE ADWORDS IS THE LEAST EFFECTIVE WAY TO REACH YOUR TARGET CUSTOMER, CONTINUED

- TV
- Telemarketing
- Social media sites like Facebook and Twitter
- Issuing a press release
- Writing a book
- Being an "expert" on a talk show
- Exhibiting at trade shows
- Fliers distributed house-to-house or business-to-business
- Doing a custom teleseminar for another person's email list
- Ads in magazines
- Remnant space in local newspapers, purchased at deeply discounted rates
- Speaking at seminars
- Card decks, i.e., a packet of postcards shipped to targeted prospects
- Writing magazine articles and e-zine articles
- "Buyer advocate" sites like Thomas Register and Globalspec
- Flier inserts in newspapers, magazines, or mail-order shipments (that's called "insert media")
- "Lumpy mail": sending people interesting objects, like one guy I know who mailed out a six-foot canoe paddle

When all you have is a hammer, everything looks like a nail. So save this list for the next time you have one of those days when it seems impossible to find a new customer!

WHEN GOOGLE ADWORDS IS THE LEAST EFFECTIVE WAY TO REACH YOUR TARGET CUSTOMER, CONTINUED

Remember that every other advertiser out there has access to some customers, and many of them know they can make a little more money (and not lose any business) by giving you controlled access to their customers. And, many times, even though those other media may have a higher customer acquisition cost, the customers may be higher quality.

Chapter 6

What If You Already Have a Great SEO Campaign?

A common question many online companies have is: Why bother with a potentially expensive PPC campaign if they have an effective search engine optimization (SEO) campaign already in place?

PPC offers a number of compelling advantages over SEO that advertisers should be aware of.

PPC VISITORS COME FROM A DIFFERENT DEMOGRAPHIC

The visitors who arrive at your site from search ads and natural search results are very different. Prospects who arrive at your site as a result of clicking on a "sponsored" ad generally have a higher predisposition toward buying something. On the other hand, visitors who click on organic results tend to just be looking for information and are less likely to spend money. While this is not true for every business (I have run across a number of exceptions to the rule myself), most advertisers report that PPC campaigns convert at a higher rate than organic ones.

Another tendency I've noticed is that visitors who arrive via sponsored ads tend to skew more toward women and technically unsophisticated visitors. If you are selling products that cater to these demographics, you will likely see a big improvement in results with PPC.

PPC CAMPAIGNS GET FASTER RESULTS

Getting new content indexed by the search engines is a painful process that tends to take a long time. With PPC, it's a quick process to get visitors to your desired landing pages (usually taking less than 24 hours). And with the ad quality score that Google provides you, you now have a feedback mechanism by which you can improve your campaign, potentially resulting in more traffic at a lower cost per click. There is no equivalent in SEO.

PPC CAMPAIGNS OFFER YOU BETTER CONTROL

No matter how good your SEO campaign, you have very little input into where your links will show up. Your organic rankings vary by geographic region, language, device, even browser and personal preferences! If you want to be on the top of the search results pages with SEO, you have an uphill battle ahead of you. You can work for months (sometimes years) and still never capture the coveted top position.

On the other hand, PPC lets you decide what, when, and where ads are displayed.

You can choose to display your ads in the search results only or also on partner networks (such as Ask.com or AOL). You can pick and choose particular geographic regions to show your ads. You can also use targeting options to filter out unwanted impressions, such as visitors looking for "free" products and services only. And if you really want those top positions (and are willing to pay for it), you can directly influence your quality score and bid prices in order to get them.

PPC PROVIDES YOU WITH TRAFFIC DIVERSIFICATION

The PPC algorithms change from time to time but not nearly as often or as dramatically as the organic ranking algorithms. It's rather unusual for a good ad campaign to stop working suddenly and without warning. The same can't be said for SEO. Not a few companies have gone out of business when their SEO rankings vanished overnight with nary an explanation.

If your customers are finding you only through your organic listings, your business is on very shaky ground. PPC provides you with a good way to diversify your traffic sources.

If you're already running a successful SEO campaign, you've proven that the search engines can be a valuable source of traffic for your business. Adding a PPC campaign to your marketing bag of tricks will result in more visitors and provide a valuable safety net in the event that your organic rankings ever drop.

Chapter 7

The Water Is Always Rising in Search

The water is always rising in search. If you don't rise with it, your campaign will drown.

Why? As you'll read in a few chapters, the search engines prize relevant, high-quality ads. Good ads keep the visitors coming back. And the more visitors there are, the more money the search engines make from the ads.

Whether or not your campaign is deemed to be better than others' depends on a variety of factors:

- The clickthrough rate of your ads
- How well your ad copy mirrors the visitor's search phrase
- The relevance and user experience of your landing pages

And a wide variety of other minor factors which are constantly changing, including:

- Historical CTR of your campaign
- The subject matter of your website as a whole

Just as in your grade school class, Google grades on a curve. If your ads are deemed to be of higher quality than your competitors, they will appear higher and more often.

PARANOIA IS JUSTIFIED: YOUR COMPETITORS ARE REALLY OUT TO GET YOU

Chances are that you are going to spend a good amount of time working on your campaign while reading this book. You may improve your ad copy, your keyword selection, or your landing pages. These will all likely have a positive impact on your campaign.

Now let's say you get things running smoothly. Your campaign is garnering lots of impressions, plenty of clicks, and a reasonable clickthrough rate. You step away to focus on other important things such as running your business or vacationing in Mexico. Before you know it, a year has passed. You log in to AdWords and find that your campaign now looks something like Figure 7–1.

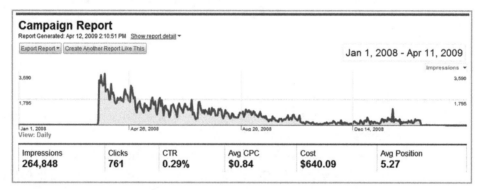

FIGURE 7–1. Actual results of an unmanaged Google AdWords campaign.

Wow? What happened?

The campaign initially received a high number of impressions, but these gradually dwindled down until January. At that point the ads stopped showing on Google's search result pages.

It would be wonderful if we could simply put our campaigns on autopilot and walk away. However, we can't, because our competitors are constantly taking steps to optimize their own quality scores.

Working together as a group, they are raising the bar on quality. As they do, the relative quality of your campaign is going down. In other words, your campaign is under constant assault from all sides, so you can't be complacent.

You simply must remain vigilant if you want to beat the competition.

Chapter 8

The $100 Bidding Myth

Many advertisers mistakenly believe that the cure for a bad campaign is a higher bid. And why not? If I'm willing to pay the search engine $100 for an ad, they make money and my ad runs. We're both happy, so why doesn't it work this way?

To see why, consider for a moment the following ad:

> **Free Puppies and Diamonds**
> Lottery winner wants to give away
> his fortune and pets. First 100 only!
> www.MillionaireGiveaway.com

Most of us won't be bothered to click on an ad like this these days, no matter how much we like free puppies and diamonds. At one time, however, these ads were fairly common, and they appeared for a variety of search terms, typically with a landing page that looked something like the one in Figure 8–1 on page 30.

Most people don't like these ads or the landing pages behind them because they are deceptive and people get burned out on them pretty quickly. The search engines realized long ago that it's not enough to serve just the needs of the advertisers. They had to serve the needs of the users or they would eventually stop coming back, as illustrated in Figure 8–2 on page 31.

FIGURE 8–1. Example of a spam landing page.

If the search engines hadn't cracked down on this a few years ago, search marketing would probably not have ballooned into the $30 billion industry that it is today.

Spam campaigns are generally low-quality and not all that believable. They only work when the spammer can acquire massive amounts of traffic at a very cheap rate. In 2008, Google implemented an automated solution for gauging the quality of the ad: **quality score**.

We'll get into the mechanics and history of quality score in a later chapter. For now, what you need to know is that Google looks at the content and performance of your ad and assigns it a "quality score" ranging from 1 to 10. This number represents how

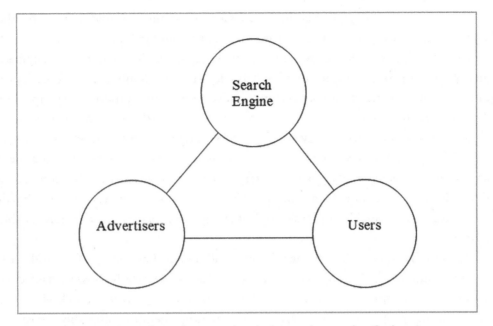

FIGURE 8–2. Search engines need to balance the needs of advertisers, users, and themselves.

Google perceives the quality of your ad and landing page. "Great" ads get a 10. And "poor" ads get a score between 1 and 3. Most ads fall somewhere in the middle, as shown in Figure 8–3.

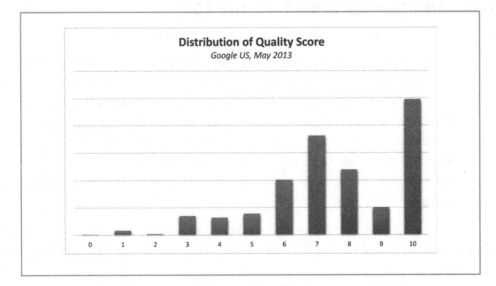

FIGURE 8–3. Distribution of quality score, May 2013.

Based on the outcome of this check, Google sets a minimum bidding price for the ads to appear. The higher your score, the lower your minimum bid.

Now, this isn't a foolproof system. Advertisers can, and do, try to reverse-engineer quality score in order to gain an edge. Google was continually changing the rules (much to the consternation of legitimate advertisers who couldn't keep up), but ultimately there was no way to keep spammers out of the system. So next they implemented a clever twist. They subjected new campaigns to the automated review and, if they passed, allowed them to run but only very slowly. Instead of giving these new advertisers equal access to the system, they are subjected to a benchmarking period during which time the ads are tested in every ad slot but receive only a small percentage of the available impressions—just enough to generate a statistically reliable sample.

The search engines will raise the minimum bids of ads that don't perform well with this small amount of test traffic. Legitimate advertisers—particularly those with effective landing pages—eventually prove their worth (although they may have to stick with it for a while) while spam sites will eventually drop out altogether due to steadily increasing costs and poor traffic.

This approach is superior in that it doesn't rely on an "unbeatable" algorithm, nor does it give new and untrusted advertisers the same access to search traffic as older, more established advertisers. If a spammer does get through, Google will grant them only a limited number of impressions before raising their minimum bids.

YOU CAN'T BUY YOUR WAY TO THE TOP

In general, this system works well. However, take note of these implications:

- It will typically take 30 days for a brand-new campaign to reach its traffic potential. Until that time, the campaign will receive a paltry number of clicks.
- The amount you are willing to pay for placement is only of secondary importance. The perceived quality of your ads and landing pages matters far more.
- If your campaign isn't deemed to be of high quality, you will have to pay more than other advertisers to have your ads shown in the same spot.
- And even then, you'll receive only a small portion of the available paid search (typically 1 to 5 percent).

In other words, even if you are willing to pay $100 for a click, you'll be charged a high opportunity cost (in the form of missed impressions) that you can't buy your way out of.

ALMOST EVERY ADWORDS ADVERTISER IS BEING THROTTLED

Chances are, you aren't a spammer. In that case, most of everything written above is of mere academic interest. However, this next bit is critical and should be the one thing you take away from this chapter: **Even if you pass the initial testing period, it is extremely likely that your campaign will have areas in which your ads are being throttled due to relevance issues. These ads will not appear for all searches and sometimes may be shut down altogether.**

This affects virtually every advertiser on AdWords.

That's right. It doesn't matter who you are, how large your budget is, or how great your campaign is. You are almost certainly missing out on a huge chunk of the available search traffic. We know this because we can measure it.

Chapter 9

The Little-Known Metric That Can Increase Your Search Traffic 400 Percent

What if I told you there was a metric that you could use to diagnose poor ad copy, quality score problems, and budget and billing issues and increase your search traffic by 400 percent or more?

Well, there is. I discovered this metric in 2004 and used it to quietly blow the doors off every search campaign I worked on. A freelance copywriter friend of mine had to stop advertising on Google within 48 hours of using this data because his phone was ringing off the hook. I personally used it to become the number-one affiliate marketer in the computer security industry in the space of a few short months.

This metric is called coverage.

Coverage is the percentage of the time that people see your ads when they search on your targeted terms. (Be careful not to confuse this with clickthrough rate, which is the percentage of visitors who click your ads after actually seeing them.) In other words, it is the percentage of the total possible impressions your ads received.

Most advertisers don't measure coverage. And most don't have any idea of how much traffic they are missing out on. As we saw in our opening chapter, 99 percent of advertisers are splitting just 20 percent of the available search traffic between them. If you're one of these advertisers, you could increase your traffic fivefold—or more—by maximizing your coverage.

In 2004, I started a company to disseminate this metric to the marketplace. You might think that, after all this time, advertisers would have caught on and diminished its importance as a key campaign statistic. Yet they haven't. Even today, in 2013, not one advertiser in 500 is making use of this data to build their competitive advantage (but those few who are, are making a killing).

Coverage is rarely discussed in any online forum, but it is one of the key differences that separate great campaigns from mediocre ones. In this chapter, we'll discuss this concept and teach you what may be the most important rule in search marketing: *Always maximize your coverage.*

LOW COVERAGE MEANS LOST OPPORTUNITIES

Take a look at Figure 9–1. On this graph, we've plotted coverage along the left axis and the average position on the bottom axis. At the upper right are a few advertisers who appear about 90 percent of the time when people search for the term *cheap iPhone 4s.* At

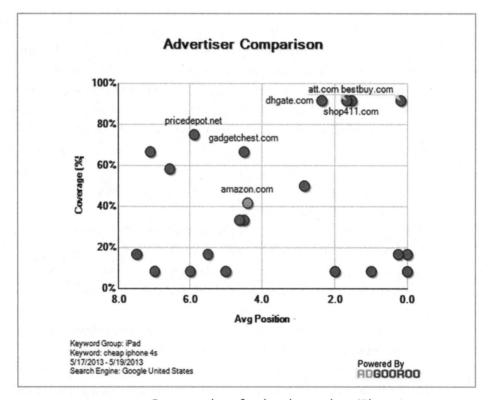

FIGURE 9–1. Coverage chart for the phrase *cheap iPhone 4s.*
(*Source*: AdGooroo SEM Insight)

the lower right are several advertisers who are bidding high enough to end up at the top of the search results, yet their ads appear for only a small percentage of searches.

These unlucky advertisers probably think that this is a low-traffic keyword, because they see few impressions on the campaign reports. Little do they know that they could increase their traffic by a whopping 1,200 percent if they fixed their coverage problem.

To put it a different way, there are approximately 21,000 searches on this term on Google US each month. The advertiser at the lower right is appearing on only 1,750 of them. By taking a few simple steps, they could tap into an additional 19,250 potential customers each month.

Many people think that increasing their bids will give them more traffic. There is some truth to this, because higher bids tend to increase your position on the search results pages. Higher positions in turn translate to higher clickthrough rates. You could typically increase your traffic by 20 percent, 50 percent, or even 100 percent by increasing your bids as a result of the improved clickthrough rate alone. That pales in comparison with the 400 percent gains I regularly see advertisers get from improving their coverage.

Bidding more for a term doesn't work as well because it doesn't guarantee you higher coverage. In fact, increasing your bid can actually reduce your coverage if several well-entrenched advertisers are already bidding for the top positions on the page! This is likely what happened to the unfortunate advertisers above. They may have gone from getting 60 percent coverage at the bottom of the page to getting only 8 percent of the coverage at the top. No increase in clickthrough rate is going to make up for the loss in ad impressions that comes from trying to compete with advertisers who have better campaigns than you.

At the end of this chapter, we'll talk about strategies for increasing your coverage. But for now, you just need to realize that impressions don't cost you anything, and they can actually build your brand awareness. So, ideally, you want to have 100 percent coverage.

Now let's look at the uglier side of the low-coverage problem.

LOW COVERAGE MEANS YOU ARE OVERPAYING FOR TRAFFIC

Figure 9–2 on page 38 is another example chart, this time for the phrase *keyword tool*. From this chart you can see that AdGooroo.com has a coverage of 100 percent. Referencing our campaign statistics, we learn that we're getting an average 1 percent clickthrough rate for this keyword. We pay $1.40 for each visitor (CPC) and get about 12 clicks per day, for an average daily total of $16.80.

The advertiser below us at position 2.0, whom we'll call ABC.com, is bidding roughly the same amount but is getting a coverage of only 10 percent. We could assume that if

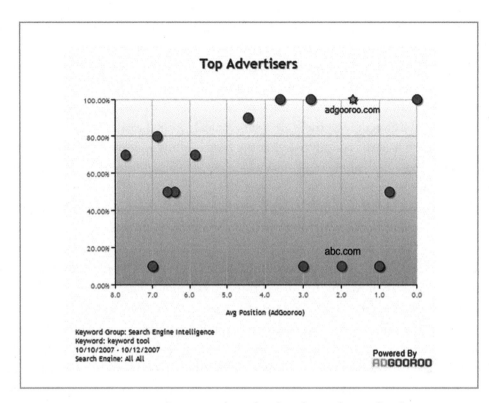

FIGURE 9–2. Coverage chart for the phrase *keyword tool*.
(*Source*: AdGooroo SEM Insight)

their ad performance is roughly the same as ours, they are getting 1.2 clicks per day for an average daily cost of $1.68.

The reason ABC.com is showing up only at 10 percent coverage is that it is facing a number of well-entrenched advertisers (including us) who can't be easily dislodged. One strategy the company could try is to reduce their bid for this keyword. Although this will drop their average position on the search results page, it often has the effect of increasing coverage.

Let's assume that this strategy works. ABC.com drops their bid to $.75. Their average position drops to 5.0, their coverage increases to 100 percent, and their clickthrough rate drops by 40 percent. Here's what their keyword performance looks like now:

Average position: 5.0

Average CPC: $0.75

Coverage: 100 percent

Impressions: 1,200

Clickthrough rate: 0.6 percent (40 percent lower at position 5.0)

Clicks: 7.2 (1200 × 0.6 percent)

Daily cost: $5.40 (7.2 × $0.75)

So what happened? ABC.com is now paying 45 percent less for each visitor, and they've increased their traffic by 600 percent.

If you had a dollar to spend, would you rather spend it all to get one visitor to your site? Or would you rather pay a quarter each for four visitors? Or perhaps a dime each for ten visitors?

This leads us to an important maxim in search marketing.

WIN THE BATTLE AT THE BOTTOM OF THE PAGE BEFORE YOU FIGHT FOR THE TOP

Generally speaking, the advertisers at the top of the search results page have one of two things over their competitors: bigger budgets and superior campaigns.

Bigger budgets don't automatically translate to more exposure the way they do in other advertising channels such as television or print. It will get you attention from digital agencies and ambitious search engine customer service reps. Sometimes these people know what they are doing. Most of the time, however, they have a small bag of tricks that they use to get results quick, and then things taper off. A big budget can give you an edge, but it doesn't make you unbeatable.

High placement and excellent coverage on the search results pages is for the most part determined by how relevant your ads are. The best ads end up on top. Why? Because good ads bring in more clicks from visitors. This brings in more advertising dollars. And that's good for the search engines.

If you think that you have any chance of beating that game, think again. You won't be able to merely outbid everyone else and get a decent percentage of the search traffic. The search engines will let you pay top dollar for placement, but they won't give you much of it. That's the approach that won Yahoo! the battle back in 2005 but lost them the war in 2008 (nobody likes seeing floral ads on every search).

Instead, to win in search, you need to take out the weak competitors at the bottom of the page. You know you've done that when your coverage is at least 90 percent. Then, and only then, should you think about bidding higher. But chances are, you won't have to. By beating those competitors, Google and the other search engines are likely to have given you a placement bonus, which means your ads automatically appear higher without you having to pay a single cent more.

The moral of the story is that before you think about increasing your bids to compete for more traffic, make sure that you've already maximized your coverage; otherwise, you're just wasting money.

COVERAGE PROBLEMS ALERT YOU TO CAMPAIGN PROBLEMS

If you find more than a few keywords in your account that are receiving a low percentage of the available impressions, it indicates that you have some serious structural issues with your campaign. You'll need to address these problems if you hope to outperform the competition, as they'll continue to drag down your campaign indefinitely.

What makes coverage truly interesting is that it is often the only way you can diagnose these issues. The vast majority of advertisers are not dominating pay-per-click because they fail to monitor this important metric.

TROUBLESHOOTING COVERAGE PROBLEMS

Once you identify a coverage problem, there are six possible causes.

Your Budget Is Capped

Make sure your budget cap is higher than the search engine's recommended daily amount. More on this in Chapter 25.

You're Trying to Muscle Your Way to the Top

Per the previous advice given about winning the battle at the bottom of the page first, you want to look at your average rank for the problem keyword. Is your ad appearing only a small percentage of the time but high up on the page?

If so, you need to start by dropping your bid until it hits the bottom half (position 5 is a good rule of thumb). It's so much easier to compete at the bottom that your coverage problem may go away by itself. And even if it doesn't, it makes the next troubleshooting step much easier.

Ineffective Ad Copy

Google grades ads on a curve. If your ad only has a 0.2 percent CTR (horrible in most business categories), but your close competitors are all getting 0.05 percent CTR, you're actually doing OK. Your ads will likely appear a pretty good percentage of the time, while theirs will appear less often.

Conversely, if you have a 2 percent CTR, but your top competitors have a 3 to 5 percent CTR, then your ad coverage will suffer. The only solution here is to craft an ad that's as good as or better than theirs.

Your coverage gives you a way to estimate how well your quality score compares to other competitors. If you are showing up less than 90 percent of the time for a particular keyword, the first thing you should consider is tweaking your ad copy (this concept is explained more fully in Chapters 20 and 21).

Advertising on Off-Target Keywords

Improving your ad copy works only if the keyword is a good fit for your business. For instance, *identity theft* offers a very tempting, high-traffic opportunity for Surf Secret, makers of personal privacy software. However, we find that searchers who enter this keyword are interested more in the identity theft programs than they are software solutions.

In order to compete with identity theft companies on this keyword, I would essentially have to copy their ads and completely misrepresent the business in order to get a comparable CTR.

If I'm not willing to go that far, then I should also be open to the fact that maybe this isn't the right keyword to be advertising on.

Poor Landing Page or Domain Alignment

Even if a company was willing to go so far as to use misleading ad copy in an effort to artificially boost their CTR, it still wouldn't work. The reason for this is that both Google and Bing factor in landing page and general website content into their quality scores. This system (more or less) succeeds at limiting attempts to spam the search engines with bogus ads. It's not perfect and advertisers often don't agree with it. But given all options, your easiest path to success is to experiment with different landing pages until you find something that gives you better results. You can objectively measure the impact of landing page changes using coverage.

Keyword-Matching Problems

Another possible way to fix low-coverage problems is to consider your match types. Many advertisers make the mistake of entering only broad match terms into their search accounts. This puts them at a disadvantage to advertisers who are using phrases or exact matches on the same keywords.

If you follow my advice on setting up your ad groups, you won't have this problem. However, you may have neglected to add the specific keyword to your account and have just been catching it with an umbrella term.

For instance, when I initially set up an account for a PC security software company, I was receiving low coverage for the search phrase *how to remove cookies*. When I looked at the search account, I realized that I had been targeting only the keyword phrase, *remove cookies*. After adding the phrase *how to remove cookies* (including the phrase and exact match variations), my coverage shot up to 100 percent.

Another way this can factor into your account is through Google's AutoMatch algorithm, which automatically targets synonyms and plurals of your targeted phrases. If you target *remove cookies* in your search campaign, your ads will also show up for *remove cookie*. However, you won't have as close of a match as if you had entered the singular version explicitly into your account.

As you can tell, there are some pretty subtle things you have to be watching out for. If you could predict all of these problems ahead of time, you would be a much better search marketer than I (you'd probably be the best search marketer on the planet, in fact). But you would also have an enormous, unwieldy, and difficult-to-manage campaign with a lot of hours sunk into it.

If instead you follow the steps in Chapter 16 through 22, you'll end up with a campaign that will get you partial coverage (at least) in all of the important keywords and their variations. Then you can use coverage to diagnose and fix the remaining problem areas.

It's a huge time saver.

HOW TO MONITOR COVERAGE

Although spotting problem keywords is easy to do using the coverage metric (just look for keywords with coverage below 90 percent or so), you'll need a third-party tool to collect this statistic for you.

I use AdGooroo's SEM Insight for this. I recommend that users log in to the tool once per week to quickly scan for any low-coverage keywords. If you spot any, you'll want to start working through the troubleshooting steps as soon as possible. They are often a sign of quality issues, and once Google decides that your website is a poor performer for a particular keyword, it can be difficult to get your ads activated again.

In SEM Insight, the Advertiser Detail report plots the coverage and rank of all keywords for your campaign (each circle represents a keyword). Using the chart in Figure 9–3, just look for keywords with a coverage of less than 90 percent. These are problem areas that should be diagnosed and corrected quickly before they turn into permanent penalties.

Impression Share

Impression share is a statistic that is closely related to coverage and can be thought of as the percentage of the available search impressions in which your ads appear. It differs from coverage in that it takes total search volume into account and is calculated across all of your keywords.

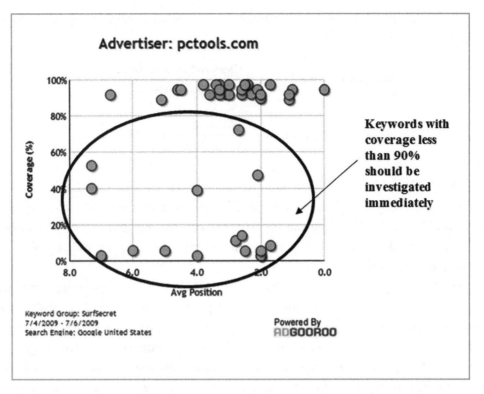

FIGURE 9-3. Use coverage charts to quickly identify problem keywords.

For instance, let's say that you are advertising on only two keywords, one of them a broad, high-traffic term, and the other a very specific, niche term (see Figure 9-4).

Keyword	Monthly Search Volume	Coverage	Captured Impressions
Rear-projection TV	1,000,000	50%	500,000
Kabuchi Model A751 DLP rear-projection TV	500	98%	490
Total	1,000,500		500,490
Impression Share			50.02%

FIGURE 9-4. Comparison of coverage.

The coverage numbers are shown for each of these keywords in the third column. By multiplying the coverage for each keyword by the monthly search volume, we can generate an estimate of how many impressions our pay-per-click campaign is capturing.

To find the impression share, you divide the number of captured impressions by the total search volume:

$$\text{Impression Share} = \frac{\text{Captured Impressions}}{\text{Total Search Volume}}$$

$$\text{Impression Share} = \frac{500,490}{1,000,500} = 50.02\%$$

The reason coverage is of more importance to search marketers is because it is more actionable. In this example, the coverage clearly showed that this advertiser needs to work on improving their exposure for the keyword "rear-projection TV." In contrast, the impression share figure told us that something was wrong, but it didn't give us any clues on how to fix it.

Furthermore, if there are a few high-traffic keywords in your campaign, they will dominate the impression share, making it difficult to measure the effect of the more profitable, but lower-traffic, niche keyword campaigns. The coverage statistic doesn't suffer from this problem because it doesn't take search volume into consideration.

Nevertheless, both statistics are useful. Impression share serves as a high-level indicator of the overall health of your campaign. Coverage serves as way to pinpoint problems down to the individual keyword.

Chapter 10

Clickthrough Rates Explained

Clickthrough rate lies at the very heart of the algorithms the search engines use to determine which ads get shown and which don't. While most search marketers typically have a vague understanding that clickthrough rate increases as an ad moves higher up on the search results page, the whole concept is shrouded in mystery.

In this chapter, we'll talk about the factors that we know improve clickthrough rates (and even a little about those factors we aren't so sure about).

WHY IS CLICKTHROUGH RATE SO IMPORTANT?

Outside of coverage (impression share), clickthrough rate is likely the most important metric you need to track in your campaigns. The formula to calculate is simple:

$$\text{Clickthrough Rate} = \frac{\text{Clicks}}{\text{Impressions}}$$

For example, if one of your ads received 1,500 impressions and generated 35 clicks, then your clickthrough rate is 2.33 percent. Pretty respectable!

As you can see, clickthrough rate measures the amount of traffic any particular ad (or your campaign as a whole) is driving to your website. It merits your attention for this reason alone.

Moreover, the clickthrough rate of your ads relative to your competitors is an important component of your quality score. Your quality score, in turn, determines the share of impressions that your ads receive. A high quality score can also result in your ads appearing higher on the search results page (at no additional cost), which in turn can further increase your clickthrough rates!

THE DIFFICULTY IN ESTIMATING CLICKTHROUGH RATE

Clickthrough rates are notoriously volatile and difficult to predict. Computer modeling may be the only way to tackle this problem. The reason is simply because clickthrough rates vary widely based on keyword, position, day of the week, and even time of day.

In Figure 10–1, you can see just how difficult it can be to predict clickthrough rates. At the bottom of the search engine results page (positions 4 to 11), it's fairly easy because there is so little variance. However, as position increases, so does the variability. In fact, in the premium positions we see clickthrough rates ranging all the way to 75 percent on AdWords!

We see a similar dynamic on Bing. Figure 10–2 on page 47 looks a bit different than the previous chart due to the fact that Bing reports average ad position in whole numbers only. However, the dynamics are similar. From position 1 to 10 (ads appearing

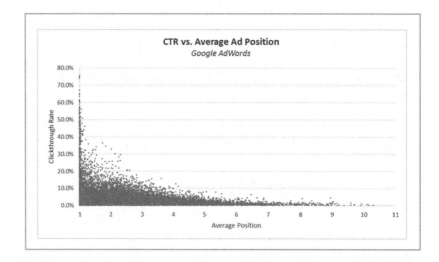

FIGURE 10–1. Predicting clickthrough rates is difficult because of the extreme variability in higher positions. (*Source*: AdGooroo)

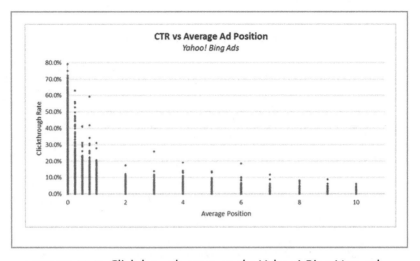

FIGURE 10–2. Clickthrough rates on the Yahoo! Bing Network.
(**Source**: AdGooroo)

to the *right* of the search results), we have relatively low variance in clickthrough rates. In the premium positions (those ads that appear *above* the search results), clickthrough rates can be as high as 80 percent.

The apparent volatility motivated us to study the underlying factors that drive clickthrough rate. After testing hundreds of different models, we uncovered some useful data for search marketers and wound up with a predictive model that explains more of the mysteries behind clickthrough rate than has ever been possible before.

The chart in Figure 10-3 shows how well our current model predicts actual clickthrough rates. Overall, about 70 percent of the variability we see in clickthrough rates can be explained by simple causes that we'll discuss in this chapter. That is more than enough to give us some useful guidance on how we can improve our search campaigns. Instead of spending months or years in trial or error, we can feed our ads into the model and get clues about what we might be doing right or wrong.

BRANDED AND NAVIGATIONAL TERMS

As we'll see in a later chapter, the queries run by search engine users tend to fall in a few broad categories. One of these categories consist largely of *branded* terms—such as *American Airlines* or *Netflix* —and *navigational* terms such as *aa.com* and *Netflix.com*.

Your relationship with the specific term will have a dramatic impact on your clickthrough rate. If the term refers to your site (either by brand or domain name), then you will likely receive a dramatic increase in clickthrough rate. On the other hand, if the term refers to a competitor's site, your clickthrough rate will suffer.

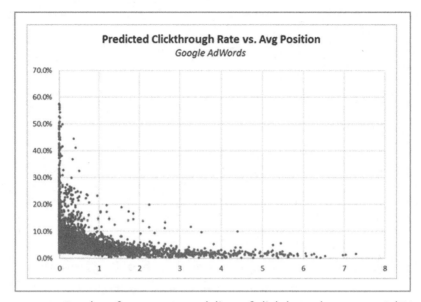

FIGURE 10–3. Results of computer modeling of clickthrough rates on AdWords. Compare to Figure 10–1. (*Source*: AdGooroo)

Much of the variance in the premium ad clickthrough rates can be explained by this phenomenon.

THE POSITION OF YOUR ADS

In conversion optimization, an important principle is that things that are seen immediately upon page load are more likely to catch the user's attention. In contrast, page elements that the user needs to scroll to see ("below the page fold") are far less likely to receive attention.

The same holds true on the search engine results page, and it explains why the position of your ads determines your clickthrough rate.

The higher an ad appears on the search results pages, the more clicks it will receive. This naturally increases your clickthrough rate. Check out these heat map comparisons of Google and Bing in Figure 10–4, page 49.

As you can see, users spend more time focused on ads at the top of the page. Fully 90 percent of searchers viewed premium ads as opposed to just between 28 and 21 percent who looked at the side ads. And furthermore, the users spent more time reading the top ads (0.9 to 0.7 seconds each versus 0.16 to 0.11 seconds on the right rail).

Our model is in agreement with this fundamental observation. The predicted clickthrough rate for a broad (single-word) phrase on Google AdWords is shown in

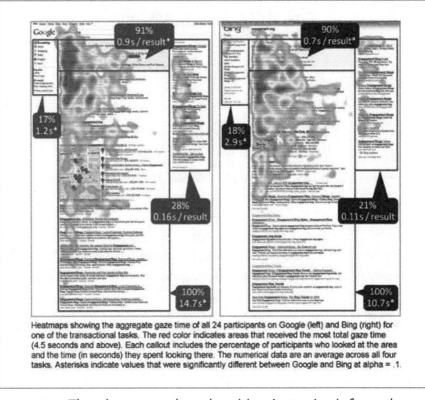

Heatmaps showing the aggregate gaze time of all 24 participants on Google (left) and Bing (right) for one of the transactional tasks. The red color indicates areas that received the most total gaze time (4.5 seconds and above). Each callout includes the percentage of participants who looked at the area and the time (in seconds) they spent looking there. The numerical data are an average across all four tasks. Asterisks indicate values that were significantly different between Google and Bing at alpha = .1.

FIGURE 10–4. These heat maps show that visitors' attention is focused on ads near the top of the page. (*Source*: "Eyes Linger Longer with Google Than Bing: User Centric Takes a Second Look," January 2011, User Centric Inc.)

Figure 10–5 on page 50. The model assumes that the ads haven't been optimized. As you can see, ads at the bottom of the page drive small amounts of traffic (typical clickthrough rate of 0.1 percent), while ads in the premium positions have typical clickthrough rates of up to 1.4 percent.

Obviously, as ad position increases, so does the clickthrough rate. Because of this relationship, more of the traffic driven from a broad keyword ends up going to advertisers in the top few positions. This in turn means that most of the advertising revenue the search engine makes from these keywords will come from the top advertisers, giving them a powerful incentive to display less bottom-of-page inventory.

If you've managed your own campaigns before, you'll probably have realized that the relationship between average position and clickthrough rate is never this consistent—it varies considerably from day to day. The following chart shows how a typical example of how actual clickthrough rate can vary for every day in a given month.

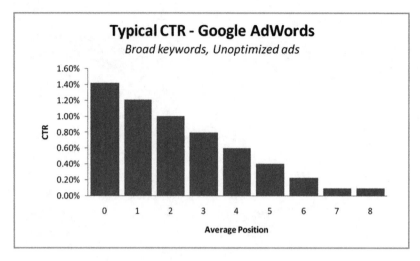

FIGURE 10–5. Typical clickthrough rates for broad keywords on AdWords (position 0 = premium ad placement, position 8 = bottom of page).

While it's not possible to predict the clickthrough rate on any particular day, there is clearly a relationship with the average position of the ad that holds over longer date

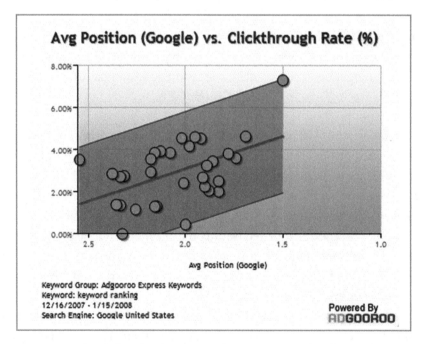

FIGURE 10–6. Chart showing how actual CTR can vary by day and position.

ranges. In our studies, we have found this to be universally true across hundreds of thousands of keywords.

SIMILARITY BETWEEN AD COPY AND KEYWORD PHRASE

While many search marketers know that the closer the similarity of your ad copy to the searcher's keyword phrase, the higher the clickthrough rate, few realize that ad copy plays an even more important role than the position or price of your ads!

The chart in Figure 10–7 depicts the effect that optimized ad copy can have on clickthrough rates. Again, this chart assumes that we are targeting a broad keyword phrase.

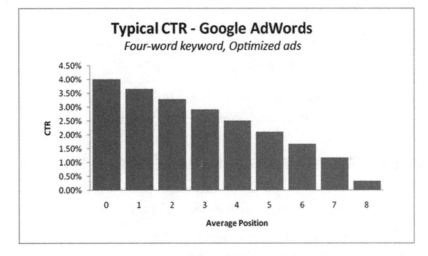

FIGURE 10–7. Chart showing typical clickthrough rates for a four-word keyword phrase with corresponding optimized ad copy.

The lift on clickthrough rate is profound. In the premium positions, the clickthrough rate increased from 1.4 percent to nearly 4.0 percent. This increase held for ads at the bottom of the search results pages as well. The typical clickthrough rate for those ads increased from 0.1 percent to 0.33 percent, more than three times higher.

Figure 10–8 on page 52 provides another illustration of just how powerful the effect of optimization can be. We've overlaid the predicted clickthrough rates for each ad on top of an example search results page. The optimized ad in the fifth position on the right of the page is expected to outperform the four ads appearing above it. This is due entirely to the effect of optimized ad copy.

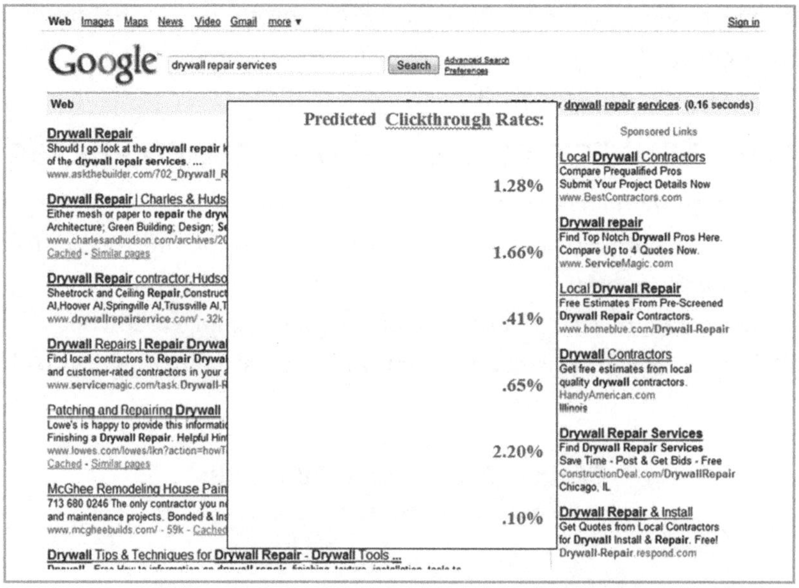

FIGURE 10–8. The optimized ad shown in position five is predicted to receive a higher clickthrough rate than the four ads above it.

OVERALL COMPETITIVENESS OF THE KEYWORD PHRASE

An underappreciated factor that affects clickthrough rate is the degree of competitive bidding for the search phrase. This can be measured in a number of ways, including:

- Actual number of advertisers bidding on the term
- The estimated CPC for the top ad position
- The competition level as reported by the search engines
- The number of words in the phrase

Figure 10–9 on page 53 shows how this plays out in practice.

In this case the clickthrough rate ranges from 0.30 percent to 3.90 percent. Compare this with a low-competition keyword phrase shown in Figure 10–10 on page 53.

The clickthrough rates for low-competition phrases ranges from 0.43 percent to 4.34 percent. This represents clickthrough rate improvements over high-competition terms of 11 percent and 43 percent, respectively.

Two important conclusions can be drawn from this data.

First, it is much better to target a larger number of specific search phrases in your campaigns than just a handful of broad terms. The level of competition will be much lower, and as a result, you'll get a much bigger bite of the apple.

Second, the benefits of niche keyword targeting are typically higher for advertisers appearing in low positions than for those advertisers who appear in high positions. So

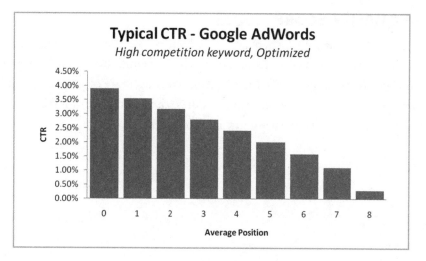

FIGURE 10–9. Typical clickthrough rates for an optimized ad targeted to a high-competition phrase.

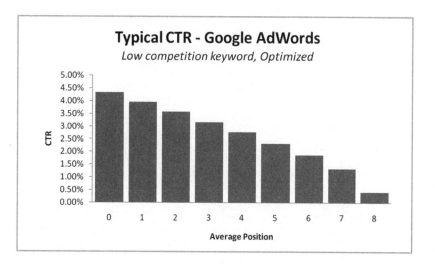

FIGURE 10–10. Typical clickthrough rates for an optimized ad targeted to a low-competition phrase.

if you can't afford to bid as much as your competitors, it's important that you find less competitive keywords to target.

This is why I advise you to spend so much time in the planning phase of your campaign finding longer, more specific keyword phrases. Most marketers fail to do this and instead add phrases in a piecemeal fashion over time. If you follow my advice, your campaign will drive a higher overall clickthrough rate right out of the gate, resulting in placement bonuses and lower average CPC prices.

OTHER QUALITY SCORE ISSUES

As we'll discuss in Chapter 12, there are other factors that the search engines take into account that aren't exactly easy to measure. These include how closely your landing page and keyword are aligned, the historical clickthrough rate of your ads, and various assessments of your landing page. In our studies, these unknown ingredients account for about 30 percent of the variation in clickthrough rates.

Chapter 11

The Ever-Changing CPC Formula

When you buy advertising placement on the search engines, you specify the maximum price that you are willing to pay when someone clicks your ads. This is known as your maximum bid.

This maximum bid is the price that you are willing to pay for a visitor to your site. It is not usually the actual price you pay per visitor, the cost-per-click (or CPC.)

The actual formulas used to calculate CPC are well-guarded secrets and change often. This makes it impossible to predict with a high degree of accuracy. Nevertheless, by studying the history of the PPC algorithms in conjunction with a bit of computer simulation, we can develop a reasonable idea of how it works and even some valuable insights that will help us gain an advantage over our competitors.

THE EVOLUTION OF PAY-PER-CLICK

In the late 1990s, the pay-per-click advertising model ran a distant second to the pay-per-impression (CPM) model that dominated at the time. Although a number of ad networks had been experimenting with pay-per-click since at least 1996, it was not widely accepted due to rampant click fraud.

The attractive thing about PPC was that advertisers paid only when people clicked on their ads. This greatly reduced waste and improved the ROI of internet advertising. For those who knew how to use the medium, the return on search engine advertising was far in excess of the traditional gold standard, email marketing (back then, you could buy traffic for a penny).

In the early Overture/Yahoo! days, the CPC you paid was pretty straightforward. You specified a price that you were willing to pay (with no minimums!) for a specific position, and that was that. Advertisers' ads would appear in the order of bids, much like an eBay auction.

Advertiser	Maximum Bid	Position
A	$25.00	1
B	$1.77	2
C	$1.35	3
D	$0.75	4
E	$0.01	5

FIGURE 11–1. Hypothetical example of several advertisers bidding for the same keyword.

The simple model shown in Figure 11-1 left a lot of risk on advertisers' plates. As you can see from the example above, the top advertiser was paying $25.00 per click, while the advertiser below was paying only $1.77. Obviously, the advertiser paying a higher price would exhaust their budget more quickly and receive a lower return on their spend (if they made a profit at those prices at all).

In response to this, both Google and Yahoo! tweaked their bidding algorithms so that advertisers would only pay a penny more than the nearest competitor below them ("penny plus"). Even if advertisers specified a maximum bid that was far too high, the system would automatically drop their bids to just one cent more than the next advertiser as shown by the "Actual CPC" in Figure 11-2.

Advertiser	Maximum Bid	Actual CPC	Position
A	$25.00	$1.78	1
B	$1.77	$1.36	2
C	$1.35	$0.76	3
D	$0.75	$0.10	4
E	$0.01	$0.01	5

FIGURE 11–2. Comparison of bids and CPCs using the "penny plus" algorithm.

Another important consequence of this auction-based model is that it led to the development of defensive and offensive tactics for interfering with competitors' campaigns. For instance, one of these tactics, bid jamming, consisted of bidding one penny below the top bidder. This forced them to pay their maximum bid. So if advertiser B was bid jamming, they could bid $24.99 and drain advertiser A's budget, illustrated in Figure 11–3.

Advertiser	Maximum Bid	Actual CPC	Position
A	$25.00	$25.00	1
B	$24.99	$1.36	2
C	$1.35	$0.76	3
D	$0.75	$0.02	4
E	$0.01	$0.01	5

FIGURE 11–3. Hypothetical illustration of "bid jamming." Note that Advertiser B has forced Advertiser A to pay an inflated price through the use of a high maximum bid.

This "pay-for-position" model was modestly successful and straightforward, but it led to a proliferation of low-quality ads. Search engine users tended to despise these ads due to their poor relevance, and clickthrough rates suffered. Had this trend toward untargeted ads gone unchecked, most people would have trained themselves to ignore the ads, and search engine marketing may have never matured into the billion-dollar industry it is today.

Yahoo! recognized this problem and attempted to clean up their listings through a manual review process. Advertisers would submit ads and then be forced to wait up to five days for a customer service representative to approve them. This improved the quality of the ads being shown and led to higher clickthrough rates, far in excess of those available from banner advertising.

However, the delays introduced by this cumbersome process prevented advertisers from reaching the maximum profit potential of their campaigns. It was difficult to split test ads, so advertisers took few steps to improve their clickthrough rates. And of course, this slow process made it difficult to add thousands of highly specific, niche keywords necessary to create a world-class pay-per-click campaign. (Yahoo!'s cumbersome user interface at the time didn't help things any either.)

It was primarily because of these obstacles that search engine advertising remained the realm of a few thousand savvy webmasters for so long. It wasn't until 2003, when Google launched their "do-it-yourself" advertising platform, that pay-per-click advertising finally caught on with advertisers.

THE PAY-FOR-POSITION BIDDING MODEL WAS BAD FOR SEARCH ENGINES, TOO

A fascinating consequence of the simple pay-for-position bidding model is that it failed to maximize the total revenue that Yahoo! could have made selling search ads. At best, this approach allowed them to earn only half of what they could have made from a model such as the one Google later introduced.

For more on the complex math behind ad auctions, see "AdWords and Generalized On-line Matching" by Mehta, Saberi, Vazirini, and Vazirini (www.eecs.berkeley.edu/~vazirani/pubs/adwords.pdf).

ADVERTISERS GO GAGA FOR GOOGLE

Google entered the online ad scene in 2000 with their AdWords Select program. (Google's fascinating history is in a convenient timeline at www.google.com/about/company/history.) At the time, it was only open to big budget advertisers, and ad buys were sold face to face by sales reps, in much the same manner as traditional ad buys. In 2003, they opened up the platform so that any advertiser could participate with nothing more than a website and a credit card.

Google added an important new twist to the Yahoo! model: Ads would be awarded placement not only by the maximum bid price advertisers were willing to pay but also by their clickthrough rate. This not only led to better quality ads (and higher clickthrough rates), it also allowed Google to get rid of the manual ad-approval process. As a result, advertisers could manage their campaigns far more easily than before, and Google quickly picked up small and medium customers that Yahoo! had missed.

However, this change removed much of the transparency of how ads were priced because popularity was now being factored into the pricing equation. Specifically, if one ad were twice as effective as another, the first ad would be ranked as if its maximum bid were double what the advertiser actually set. The advertiser would, however, pay only their original price.

Sound complicated? It was simple in comparison with what was yet to come. The algorithms were tweaked and even sometimes overhauled over the next few years to address a variety of issues ranging from quality control to deliberate attempts by spammers to bypass the checks and balances of the system.

Today's AdWords Pricing Algorithm

Fast-forward to 2013, where the CPC pricing model is far more complicated. Google now calculates a quality score for every ad on its system. We'll talk about how the quality score algorithm works later, but to understand this discussion, you simply need to know that the quality score ranges from 1 to 10, where a higher number indicates a better ad (at least in Google's opinion).

In any given keyword, the quality score is multiplied by the advertiser's maximum bid price to determine the ad rank, illustrated in Figure 11–4.

Advertiser	Maximum Bid	Quality Score	Ad Rank
A	$4.00	1	4
B	$3.00	3	9
C	$2.00	6	12
D	$1.00	8	8

FIGURE 11–4. Hypothetical illustration of the Ad Rank calculation.

The ads are then sorted in order by their ad rank to determine the order in which they appear. (See Figure 11–5.)

Advertiser	Maximum Bid	Quality Score	Ad Rank
C	$2.00	6	12
B	$3.00	3	9
D	$1.00	8	8
A	$4.00	1	4

FIGURE 11–5. Ads are displayed in descending order of their calculated Ad Rank.

To find out how much each advertiser actually has to pay for a click, Google calculates the minimum amount necessary to retain their position. They do this by comparing the prices and quality scores for each adjacent ad.

For example, to find the price for Advertiser C above, we compare it to Advertiser B using the following equation:

$$\text{Price}_c \times \text{Quality Score}_c = \text{Price}_b \times \text{Quality Score}_b$$

$$\text{Price}_c \times 6 = \$3.00 \times 3$$

$$\text{Price}_c = \frac{\$3.00 \times 3}{6}$$

$$\text{Price}_c = \$1.50$$

BUDGET AND AVERAGE CPC PRICES

Budget plays an important part in determining how many impressions your ads receive, but it doesn't appear to play a significant role in determining the average CPC of your ads. However, some advertisers who use the pre-payment option on Google AdWords report that if their account balance reaches zero, then their average CPC will increase for a period of time after they deposit additional funds in their account. Something to keep an eye on!

You then repeat this process for each of the remaining advertisers. The lowest ranked advertiser pays the minimum bid, which can be as little as just a few cents. See Figure 11–6.

Advertiser	Maximum Bid	Quality Score	Actual Price
C	$2.00	6	$1.50
B	$3.00	3	$2.67
D	$1.00	8	$0.50
A	$4.00	1	Minimum Bid

FIGURE 11–6. Calculation of the actual price (CPC) paid by each advertiser.

As you can see from this example, paying more does not guarantee you the top ad spot. Rather, the price you pay is determined by the quality of your ads in relation to the advertiser just below you. Mathematically, this is expressed as:

$$\text{Your Price} = \frac{\text{Competitors' Bid x Competitors' Quality Score}}{\text{Your Quality Score}}$$

This formula explains much of why the methods you are reading about in this book are so effective. Success in ad copy and landing page optimization increases your ad rank, resulting in higher placement for your ads.

SIMULATING CPC USING COMPUTER MODELS

Now that you have a pretty fair idea of how Google's pricing mechanism works, to understand how prices work in a real-world environment, let's again turn to computer modeling.

Quality score throws a serious monkey wrench into any attempt to understand the mechanics of CPC pricing. In order to estimate quality score, you have to look at the targeted keyword phrase, ad copy, and landing page for *every* advertiser appearing for a given term (not just your own). Given the number of back-end "tweaks," general unknowns about the specifics of the quality score algorithm, and not to mention the sheer number of keywords that need to be analyzed, this makes guesswork—even for those who have access to copious amounts of real-world data—virtually impossible.

Although Google and Bing provide us with average CPC prices paid by all advertisers through their APIs, even this valuable source of data isn't without its problems. As we'll see in the next section, Google sorts their terms according to average price into high-, medium-, and low-price buckets. The price they give for low-price terms tends to be quite accurate. The price for high- and medium-priced terms is decidedly less so. So keep in mind that inherent in any effort made to model CPCs, accuracy will be higher for cheaper terms and lower for more expensive ones.

Recent developments in machine learning have made it possible for us to correct for many of these problems. It turns out that you can develop a fairly good understanding of how CPCs work in the real world. In the rest of this chapter, I'll share with you the most important factors that impact bid prices.

Number of Advertisers

Perhaps as should be expected from an auction-based system, the overall price you will pay for your ads is determined by the number of advertisers bidding for those terms. Here are the *average* CPC prices for a few high-demand search terms on Google AdWords and the Yahoo! Bing Network in May 2013. Keep in mind that some advertisers are paying less while others may be paying substantially more.

Keyword	Google US	Bing US
Structured settlement	$293.39	$9.96
Mesothelioma lawyers	$243.91	$29.29
Back injury attorneys	$143.38	$14.81
Raid 5 data recovery	$135.64	$16.10
Donate car	$104.84	$12.18
Internet business training	$99.36	$0.71
Donate my car	$98.43	$6.53

FIGURE 11–7. Comparative CPC prices for high-value keywords on Google and Bing.

Notice how the same terms are radically cheaper on Bing because there are fewer advertisers on that platform. As more advertisers become aware of the cheaper source of high-quality traffic available to them through Bing, we will expect average CPC prices to increase.

The same dynamic holds true for different countries. For instance, "Raid 5 data recovery" has an average CPC of $135.64 in the U.S., but only $24.71 in the U.K. and about $8.28 in France (when translated to French, of course).

If the number of advertisers were the primary determinant of CPC prices, we would expect there to be a linear relationship, as shown in Figure 11–8.

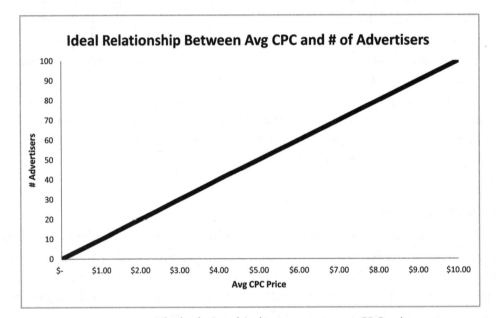

FIGURE 11–8. Ideal relationship between average CPC prices and number of advertisers.

However, the relationship we see in the real world is radically different. In the chart shown in Figure 11–9 on page 63, I've plotted the average CPC price for 10,000 keywords against the number of advertisers bidding for them on Google AdWords.

Clearly something else is at work here.

Return on Ad Spend/Average Customer Value

Not all keywords are created equal. Some terms are highly prized, and advertisers will pay an absurd amount of money for the top positions. Although there is a relatively small amount of traffic for legal-related terms (*structured settlement*), the revenue generated by these leads can be enormous in comparison to costs. On the other hand,

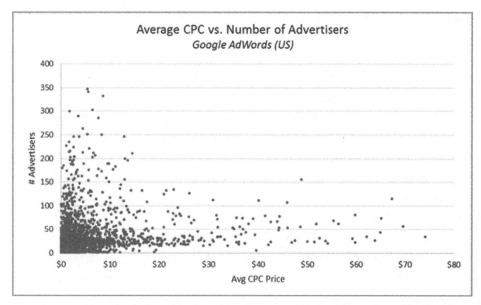

FIGURE 11-9. Actual relationship between average CPC and number of advertisers.
(*Source*: AdGooroo, August 2013)

product-related keywords (*Galaxy S3*) generate a much lower amount of revenue per customer.

This has a huge impact on CPC prices advertisers pay because no matter how many advertisers want ad placement, few are willing to lose money to get it. Figure 11-10

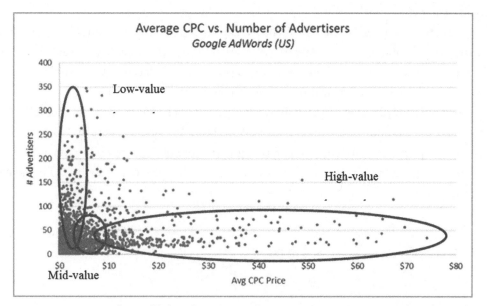

FIGURE 11-10. Number of advertisers versus average CPC price—Google AdWords.
(*Source*: AdGooroo, August 2013)

contains the same chart shown previously with several clusters of data points called out.

Many of these keywords are clustered in the lower-left corner of the chart. These keywords typically have between 25 and 75 advertisers and have a CPC of up to $10. These are known as "mid-value" keywords.

Notice the other two "legs" of points emanating from the bottom-left corner of this chart. The first leg is nearly horizontal and shows how the average CPC price rapidly increases even with relatively few advertisers. These are known as "high-value" keywords.

The other leg is almost vertical and shows a different group of keywords in which the average CPC remains relatively steady regardless of how many advertisers bid for them. These are "low-value" keywords.

With mid-value keywords, advertisers can compete on either CPC or quality, but usually the latter approach will prove more successful. Advertisers on low-value keywords will be faced with relatively low CPC caps, so more relative effort will be required to improve ad quality and coverage. Finally, in order for advertisers to secure placement on high-value keywords, they need to be willing to place high bids (at the time of this writing, the average CPC for the term "auto insurance" was $71.78!).

Gladiator Bidding

There is a third factor that we've been able to identify through computer simulation. Some marketers irrationally attempt to buy the top spots at any cost and without regard to ad quality.

Sometimes the advertiser succeeds at capturing the top-side ad placement and pushes other, higher-quality advertisers further down the page. However, their low quality score fails to secure them the coveted premium ad placement (above the organic results), and it ensures they will pay a price close to their maximum bid.

An overly simplified example is shown in Figure 11–11. Our gladiator bidder is BigCo, who buys the top spot with a massive $25.00 bid but a low quality score of 3. Below them is a better-optimized competitor who has a quality score of 7 and is willing to pay $10.

We can plug these values in the formulas above to see what price BigCo is paying for the top spot.

$$\text{Price}_{BigCo} \times \text{Quality Score}_{BigCo} = \text{Price}_{LittleCo} \times \text{Quality Score}_{LittleCo}$$

$$\text{Price}_{BigCo} \times 3 = \$10.00 \times 7$$

$$\text{Price}_{BigCo} = \frac{\$10.00 \times 7}{3}$$

$$\text{Price}_{BigCo} = \$23.33$$

Figure 11–11 shows the same information in tabular format.

Advertiser	Maximum Bid	Quality Score	Actual Price
BigCo	$25.00	3	$23.33
LittleCo	$10.00	7	Minimum Bid

FIGURE 11–11. Illustration of a low-quality advertiser attempting to purchase high ad placement ("Gladiator Bidding").

As you can see, this is somewhat reminiscent of the old bid-jamming days, except instead of making competitors pay for the top spots with high bids, it's done with moderate bids and high quality scores (and usually the damage is self-inflicted).

It is vitally important that you avoid having this happen to you. To do so, look across your campaigns for keywords in which you are appearing consistently in the first ad position on the right rail *and* where there are also premium advertisers appearing above you. If your coverage is below 90 percent, then you almost certainly have an unresolved quality problem on that particular keyword. At that point, you'll need to work on your ad copy and landing page to improve your relevance. Once your coverage starts increasing and/or your ad begins to appear in the premium positions, you've solved the problem. (You'll need third-party software to use this technique. Not only is the Google AdWords quality score indicator notoriously unreliable, Google does not provide a way to view the actual position of your ads.)

Position

Surprisingly, average position and CPC are only weakly related. The chart in Figure 11–12 on page 66 shows the relationship between CPC and average position (normalized to the top-most ad) for several hundred diverse keywords on AdWords. Across all keywords, the

KEY CONCEPT: AVOID GLADIATOR BIDDING

If your ads are consistently appearing in the top-right position AND there are advertisers appearing above you in the premium positions AND your coverage is below 90 percent, then you are throwing money away. Temporarily back your bids down to lower your average position and work on improving your clickthrough rate through ad copy optimization.

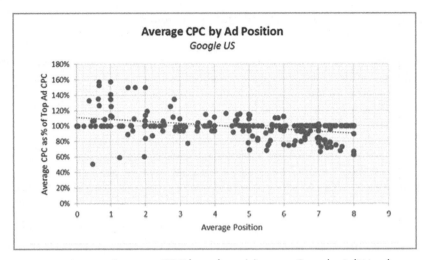

FIGURE 11–12. Average CPC by ad position on Google AdWords.

CPC curve is slightly positive, but it is a tenuous relationship at best. However, there are some interesting dynamics. At position 1 (top right rail) as well as in the lower premium positions, we frequently see a large increase in average CPC due to gladiator bidding. We also note a similar dip in CPC in the lower positions.

If you've followed along with everything written above, it shouldn't surprise you to see that there is a positive slope for keywords on Bing. This is due largely due to a lower number of advertisers (lower demand). You would expect to pay a much lower CPC price for ads on the bottom of the results pages than you would on the top. At the time of this writing, there is still a lot of variance in quality score on Bing, so gladiator bidding tends to play a larger role here as well.

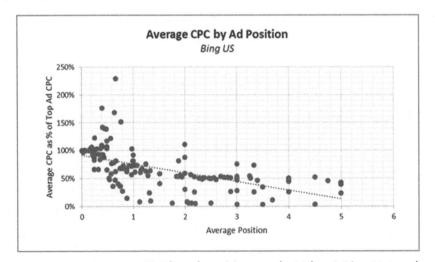

FIGURE 11–13. Average CPC by ad position on the Yahoo! Bing Network.

However, these are just general rules. When we dig deeper into the data, some new patterns emerge. It turns out that the exact behavior of the CPC curve can vary by keyword. Here is an example keyword (*ipad 3*) from November 2013. Note how clicks are concentrated in the top position and CPCs gradually *decrease* beginning with position 6 (shown in the top line).

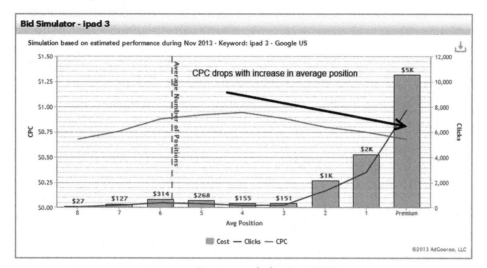

FIGURE 11–14. Downward-sloping CPC curve.

In contrast, here is the same chart for the keyword *ipad features*. Clicks are more evenly distributed throughout the top positions, and the average CPC increases with higher placements.

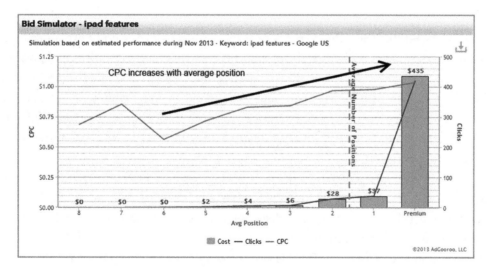

FIGURE 11–15. Upward-sloping CPC curve.

LIMITATIONS OF THE ADWORDS BID SIMULATOR

The data and charts shown in these figures were generated using the AdGooroo Bid Simulator tool. This tool is based on data taken from all advertisers appearing on a particular keyword.

Google also offers a tool called the AdWords Bid Simulator. This tool is intended to show you the impact of changing your bid and is based solely on your past campaign performance. This limitation means that it cannot show you what results you can expect as a result of improving your quality scores.

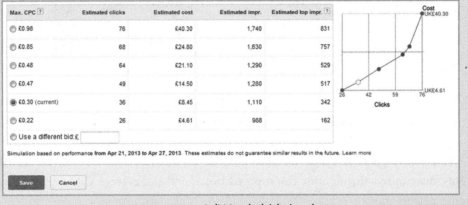

Max. CPC ?	Estimated clicks	Estimated cost	Estimated impr.	Estimated top impr. ?
£0.98	76	£40.30	1,740	831
£0.85	68	£24.80	1,630	757
£0.48	64	£21.10	1,290	529
£0.47	49	£14.50	1,280	517
£0.30 (current)	36	£8.45	1,110	342
£0.22	26	£4.61	988	162
Use a different bid: £				

Simulation based on performance from Apr 21, 2013 to Apr 27, 2013. These estimates do not guarantee similar results in the future. Learn more

Save   Cancel

FIGURE 11–16. AdWords bid simulator

It turns out that the differences in these keywords can once again be explained by ad quality. In the case of a downward-sloping CPC curve (CPCs get cheaper as ad position improves), we usually find that there is a large discrepancy in quality score between the advertisers who appear at the top of the page and the ones who appear lower. The lower positions get very little relative traffic, and even if those advertisers are willing to bid higher, it's unlikely to help. Higher quality scores are the only way to improve one's placement.

In the more traditional case of the upward-sloping CPC curve (CPCs get more expensive with improved ad position), we find much less disparity in ad quality between advertisers. Clicks are more evenly distributed between the premium and right rail positions (although the premium spots always get more). Both improved quality scores as well as higher CPCs can be effective at improving one's average position.

SUMMARY

Most advertisers believe that average position and quality score alone determine the price you pay for each click. While these two factors are important, the reality is that your competitors' actions are just as critical. Every keyword is different: Some keywords will be more costly near the top of page while others will be less expensive than they are on the bottom. This is known as the CPC Curve. Your approach to managing each keyword will differ depending on the slope of the CPC Curve. We'll talk extensively about this in Chapter 20.

Chapter 12

How Quality Score Works in 2014

April 2007 brought with it a major change to AdWords that effectively shut down many advertisers' campaigns overnight. This change, also known by some as the Google Slap, was intended to get rid of low-value affiliate and one-page sales letter sites from the paid listings, but there was plenty of collateral damage. Many high-quality sites (including some affiliates) were shut out of the paid search listings, while many not-so-high-quality sites (including some affiliates) posing as high-quality retail or review sites were awarded rankings and coverage bonuses.

Like many others, I had sites that were affected by this change. The minimum required bid for keywords where I had been advertising profitably for years increased to $10.00 because of Google's insistence that my sites were no longer relevant.

I don't believe it was Google's intent to shut down legitimate sites that provide value for search engine visitors. Rather, they instituted this new algorithm to encourage advertisers to raise their own ad quality. Where Google went wrong was in providing little guidance to advertisers as to exactly what constituted quality. Furthermore, the algorithm has continued to evolve over time, making it a moving target that advertisers constantly have to chase.

As we saw in Chapters 10 and 11, managing your quality score is a critical step in effectively managing a paid search campaign. Quality score affects your average position, coverage, clickthrough rate, and your cost-per-click. So this information contained in this section should prove invaluable.

WHAT ARE QUALITY SCORES?

For every keyword in your AdWords campaign, Google will assign you a quality score between 1 and 10 A low score indicates a low-quality ad while a high score indicates a high-quality ad.

WHY IS QUALITY SCORE IMPORTANT?

Quality score is one of the components used to calculate your ad rank. Higher quality scores help to both push your ads higher up on the page and also increase the difference between your maximum bid and the average CPC. In other words, high-quality ads cost less and gain exposure to more search traffic (impression share).

Another benefit of having a high quality score is that it will lower the estimated bid to reach the first page of the search results. This metric, also called the first page bid estimate, approximates the CPC needed to reach the first page of the Google search results when your ad is triggered by an exact match. A high-quality ad may cost as little as $0.03 to be shown on the first page, while a low-quality ad can cost as much as $100.00, so it's easy to see why you must be cognizant of your quality scores.

HISTORY OF THE QUALITY SCORE ALGORITHM

In the early days of paid search (2000), there was no quality score. Google sold placements in the traditional manner (through ad reps) to larger advertisers on a CPM basis. CPM—cost-per-*mille* (thousand)—meant that advertisers paid for every thousand impressions their ads received.

In 2002, Google opened up its advertising platform to anyone with a credit card under the name, "AdWords Select." A key innovation of this platform was the incorporation of clickthrough rate into the pricing formula. Unlike the Overture (Yahoo!) straight-auction model in which the highest bidder always received top placements, advertisers who received a higher CTR on their ads would pay less for their placements.

While effective, the platform was still rife with unwanted ads. Thus, the quality score algorithm was introduced by Google in August 2005 and underwent frequent iterations over the following years. The original version was not exposed to advertisers until 2007, when Google added the quality score designations, "Poor," "OK," and "Great." At the time, Google also added a feature that lowered the minimum bids for high-quality ads and raised the minimum bid for low-quality ones.

Quality score worked by searching for telltale signs of spam within the ad copy (Does it have multiple exclamation points? Does it use the word "free"? Does it match the targeted keyword phrase?) as well as the landing page (Is it a brand-new domain? Who's linking to the site? Does it take a long time to load?). There were also various metrics that played into the original quality score algorithm as well (keyword density, backlinks, page load time, and more). As advertisers became more aware of how quality score was being computed, Google continued to evolve the rules.

2008 brought several changes, including the incorporation of landing page load time, real-time calculation, and an adjustment to account for the impact of average position on clickthrough rate (quality score normalization). There were potentially many other minor inputs as well (Google filed patent applications in 2007 for 44 different quality score factors). However, any automated criteria can be gamed exactly the same way that spammers have been gaming the search engines for years, and this is exactly what happened after each of these changes. Through the use of clever tricks such as keyword stuffing, crash-and-burn domains, doorway pages, and so forth, spammers could find ways to get around some of these automated checks.

In response, we began to see an increase in the number of manual reviews that were designed to complement the automated checks and give advertisers a means to appeal the automated system. However, this approach did little to deter spammers (who would just close out their old account and start a new one) and turned out to be incredibly frustrating for many advertisers who were running legitimate campaigns. Imagine how it feels to wait two or three days for your ads to start running and then have someone tell you that your landing pages aren't "high quality" enough. Moreover, there were extreme lapses of judgment and abuses of the system, one of which eventually cost Google $500 million in fines (see "Drugstore Cowboy" by Jake Pearson, www.wired.com/threatlevel/2013/05/google-pharma-whitaker-sting/all/).

Another troubling aspect of the algorithm was that the minimum bid that Google calculated for all advertisers affected ads shown anywhere on the search network or partner sites. The "all or none" philosophy behind this approach angered advertisers and also resulted in a large drop in ad coverage ("AdGooroo Search Engine Advertiser Update—Q308," www.adgooroo.com/adgooroo_q308_search_marketing.php). This may have negatively impacted Google's revenues (management even said as much during their second-quarter 2008 shareholders meeting), and the algorithm was changed from a static, all-or-nothing approach to a dynamic one in September 2008.

The new approach calculated quality scores on the fly. This means that ads would be awarded higher quality scores for different keywords, in certain regions, and on different partner sites. While this newly added flexibility addressed the "all-or-nothing" problem, it was yet one more change that made the quality score algorithm even more complicated than before.

In the previous edition of this book, I expressed hope that Google would perhaps one day dial down the complexity and make things easier on us. Well, in 2011, chatter among search marketers suggested another change was taking place, and we independently discovered that some of the traditional quality score factors were being downplayed. We decided to test this with our own models and found that approximately 70 percent of the variance in quality score could be explained by a single factor: clickthrough rate.

THE OFFICIAL EXPLANATION OF THE ADWORDS QUALITY SCORE

A good place to start in our understanding of the quality score calculation is to read what Google has to say about it.

How We Calculate Quality Score

Every time someone does a search that triggers your ad, we calculate a Quality Score. To calculate this Quality Score, we look at a number of different things related to your account. By improving the following factors you can help improve your Quality Score:

- *Your keyword's past clickthrough rate (CTR)*: How often that keyword led to clicks on your ad.
- *Your display URL's past CTR*: How often you received clicks with your display URL.
- *Your account history*: The overall CTR of all the ads and keywords in your account.
- *The quality of your landing page*: How relevant, transparent, and easy-to-navigate your page is.
- *Your keyword/ad relevance*: How relevant your keyword is to your ads.
- *Your keyword/search relevance*: How relevant your keyword is to what a customer searches for.
- *Geographic performance*: How successful your account has been in the regions you're targeting.
- *Your ad's performance on a site*: How well your ad's been doing on this and similar sites (if you're targeting the Display Network).
- *Your targeted devices*: How well your ads have been performing on different types of devices, like desktops/laptops, mobile devices, and tablets—you get different Quality Scores for different types of devices.

These are nice definitions but how are they weighted?

1. *The most important component of your quality score is your keywords' historical CTR.* This is Google's bread-and-butter and hasn't changed for many years. However, it does seem to have increased importance more recently.

   It is not only the CTR you earn on a particular keyword that is important but also the CTR you earn on a particular landing page. Incorporating this as a factor prevents spammers from continually creating new AdWords accounts to show their ads once they've been banned. (They have to create unique landing pages as well.) This also means you should avoid using important URLs in your AdWords campaigns unless you are prepared to live with the consequences; your past performance history can stay with you for a long time.

2. *Next up in importance is your entire account's historical CTR.* This is a grossly overlooked point. Google strictly penalizes advertisers who target thousands or hundreds of thousands of keywords with no regard to their relevance. The same goes for advertisers who fail to remove or improve keywords with mediocre click-through rates. (If I can't achieve a CTR of at least 0.5 percent with a keyword after several attempts to optimize it, I delete it from my account.)

3. *Next up we have several relevance factors:*

   ■ *Keyword/ad relevance,* which attempts to determine how close of a match there is between your ads and the search query that triggered the ad. Years ago, most advertisers caught on to the fact that including the search query within the text of an ad tended to improve its quality score. One might wonder if Google caught on to this practice and somehow addressed it. Our models indicate that this factor now appears to have relatively little weight, so this may indeed be the case.

LANDING PAGE CTR

Google now factors in the CTR of each unique landing page into your quality score. If you are using the same landing page for every keyword in your campaign, it's likely that your lower CTR keywords could be adversely affecting the rest of your campaign. For this reason, it pays to have a variety of landing pages in your campaign.

■ *Keyword/search relevance* refers to the commercial intent of a particular search phrase. For instance, the search query *South Park* used to trigger a large number of ads. In 2012, this term stopped showing ads altogether. This was presumably because searchers weren't clicking on the paid search ads. Generally speaking, this is not a factor that is in your control (it is more likely determined by the combined performance of all advertisers).

4. *Geographic performance means that Google will calculate your quality score separately for each of the regions (even down to the city level) that you are targeting.*

5. *Your ad's performance on a site only affects display advertising.*

6. *Your targeted devices.* Just as with geographic territories, Google will calculate quality score separately on each type of device you are targeting (desktop, mobile, and tablets).

DO LANDING PAGE QUALITY SCORE FACTORS MATTER ANYMORE?

In the previous edition of this book, I shared the results from controlled experiments in which we attempted to identify the more important on-page factors that affected quality score. These factors included:

■ Site genre
■ Site age
■ Linking neighborhood
■ Presence of popups and popunders
■ Load time and page size
■ Trust signals (e.g., privacy policy, business address)
■ Number of pages and scope of site
■ Keyword density

Paid search marketers have endlessly debated the importance of these various factors for years. When the previous edition of this book was written, the above list was essential. Today, it appears that the on-page quality factors have been reduced in importance considerably (with the exception of potential policy violations, such as the use of popups and popunders, illegal or prohibited items such as pharmaceuticals, and the presence of malware).

What we have discovered instead is that the second most important factor in determining quality score is *average visit duration*, or the average amount of time a visitor stayed on your site after clicking your ad.

When a large number of searchers click an ad and then stay on the landing page or site for a long time, it strongly suggests a highly relevant advertiser. So combining average visit duration along with the CTR factors mentioned above makes intuitive sense. It is also a simple and elegant solution for both the search engines and advertisers, as it can be easily measured through the use of redirect or wrapper URLs inserted into each paid search ad (Google now wraps all landing page URLs in their own redirect URL beginning with "http://www.google.com/aclk? . . ."). Should a searcher click the back button, the length of the visit can be easily calculated. And what's more, this solution works even if the user opens the ad in a different browser window (for instance, by CTRL-clicking).

In fact, this metric was even added in mid-2012 to AdWords for users with linked Google Analytics accounts. To include it, navigate to the "Campaigns" area of your AdWords account, and click "Customize Columns." If you have a linked Google Analytics account, you should be able to add the "Average Visit Duration" column to your AdWords reports. (Note that it is unlikely that this is the exact figure that Google uses as they are measuring bounce-backs for all advertisers using the redirect URL shown above.)

```
Customize columns

  Select metrics

  Attributes            »                              Add all columns
  Performance           »     Bounce rate                        Add
  Conversions           »
  Call details          »     Pages / visit                      Add
  Competitive metrics   »     Avg. visit duration (seconds)      Add
  Google Analytics      »     % new visits                       Add
  Search Funnels        »
```

FIGURE 12–1. Adding "average visit duration" to your AdWords reports.

HOW TO CHECK YOUR QUALITY SCORES

In the Google AdWords interface, select the "Keywords" tab. Clicking the small balloon icon in the status column will reveal your quality score.

BEST PRACTICE: MANAGING QUALITY SCORES

It's important to understand the various mechanical factors that may impact quality score, but at the end of the day remember that it boils down to two key tasks:

- Getting a higher CTR than your competitors

- Maximizing your average visit duration

LIMITATIONS OF ADWORDS QUALITY SCORE REPORTING

Two main problems continue to linger on with the AdWords quality score report shown in Figure 12–2. The first is that it is inconsistent and hardly trustworthy. While Google has added a bit more transparency by providing ratings for "Expected clickthrough rate," "Ad relevance," and "Landing page experience," these ratings often do not correlate with the overall quality score assigned to the ad.

As an illustration of this, note that in Figure 12–2 our quality score is reported as 7, while all three of the contributing factors are shown as "average." Compare this to Figure 12–3 on page 79.

Here you can see that two of our contributing factors are shown as "above average," but now our quality score is only 4. Shouldn't it be higher?

Keyword: **key word advertising**

Showing ads right now?

No > • The keyword phrase doesn't currently trigger any of your ads. What can I do?

Quality score Learn more

7/10 > Expected clickthrough rate: Average
Ad relevance: Average
Landing page experience: Average

Ad Preview and Diagnosis

FIGURE 12–2. You can check your quality score directly within the AdWords interface.

```
Keyword: ad guru

Showing ads right now?
┌──────────┐
│   No     ⟩   • The keyword phrase doesn't currently trigger
└──────────┘     any of your ads. What can I do?

Quality score Learn more
┌──────────┐
│   4/10   ⟩   Expected clickthrough rate: Above average
└──────────┘   Ad relevance: Above average
               Landing page experience: Average

Ad Preview and Diagnosis
```

FIGURE 12–3. Quality score as reported for another keyword in
the same campaign.

The other problem is a bit more insidious. Before 2009, you could stay somewhat aware of holes in your campaign by simply looking at your AdWords reports. Back then, when Google said you had a low quality score, they meant it. Your ad wasn't being shown.

These days when you see a low quality score, you may still have ads appearing for the keyword in certain regions or on partner sites. If Google tells you that your ad isn't showing, another one of your ads, possibly an unrelated one, could very well be showing up in its place. Conversely, having a high quality score does not guarantee that your ad is being displayed, even if the tool says that it is. It may be showing up only on partner sites (such as AOL or Ask.com), in certain geographical regions, on certain devices such as tablets or phones, or on unrelated keyword phrases. There's no easy way to tell.

BEST PRACTICE: MONITOR FOR MISSING KEYWORDS

We recommend that advertisers utilize a third-party monitoring service to ensure that their ads are appearing for their selected keywords within each of their targeted engines and countries. There is currently no way to protect against this using the standard search engine reports.

QUALITY SCORE ON THE YAHOO! BING NETWORK

Contributed by Ping Jen, Bing Ads Product Manager

The goal of Bing Ads Quality Score is to help advertisers optimize the quality of their campaigns. It's designed to identify campaign optimization opportunities instead of measuring campaign optimization results. This approach enables Bing Ads be more transparent in providing insight to advertisers through its Quality Score.

In order to provide broader and deeper insights, in addition to tracking the performance of keywords during the auction, Bing Ads also:

- Factors in marketplace competition while generating a Quality Score by comparing potential clickthrough rate (CTR) of your keywords to potential CTR of other keywords targeting the same traffic.

- Generates Quality Scores for each individual match type because different match types exposes keywords, ads, and landing pages to different audiences and different competitors.

- Provides ad group and campaign-level Quality Score by aggregating (impression weighted) associated keyword Quality Scores.

Bing Quality Score Components

Advertisers can access the quality score from within the Bing Ads reporting interface (see Figure 12–4).

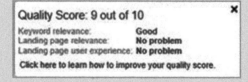

FIGURE 12–4. Bing ads Quality Score

To help advertisers better optimize their landing pages, Bing Ads provides specific feedback on landing page relevance and landing page user experience from search users' perspectives. In general, search users take two immediate actions after arriving in your landing pages.

QUALITY SCORE ON THE YAHOO! BING NETWORK, CONTINUED

Components	Definition	Possible Values
Quality Score	How competitive the keyword is in the marketplace.	1 to 10
Keyword Relevance	How well the keyword competes against others bidding on the same traffic.	Poor, No Problem, Good
Landing Page Relevance	How relevant the ad and landing page is to the search query.	Poor, No Problem
Landing Page User Experience	Whether the site meets Bing Ads' Relevance and Quality Guidelines	Poor, No Problem

- Locate information: Searchers want to consume the information right away.
- Judge information: Once located, searchers will assess whether the information addresses their intent.

For example, when people search for "golf vacation packages," they likely want to access the information immediately and will assess whether the information will enable them to proceed with their purchase journey of a golf vacation. Over the years, I have often noticed that some advertisers address only one of these two activities and lose out on opportunities to grow their business. Using the same example, some landing pages ask searchers to enter a phone number or email address before showing general golf vacation information, which generates a poor user experience. Some landing pages show a long list of various vacation packages unrelated to golfing, resulting in poor relevance

How Bing Ads Brings It Together to Calculate Quality Score

Having a "Poor" in one of the subscores makes the ad less eligible to be served and could lower its Quality Score to below a 6.

Not having a "Poor" in any of the subscores makes the keyword/ad fully eligible to be served and earns a Quality Score of 6 or higher.

QUALITY SCORE ON THE YAHOO! BING NETWORK, CONTINUED

Having a "Good" Keyword Relevance subscore indicates the ad has a higher CTR than most of other keywords/ads targeting the same traffic and can drives its Quality Score higher than 6.

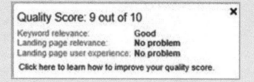

FIGURE 12–5. Bing Quality Score flowchart.

Score	Meaning
7–10	This keyword is very competitive in the marketplace. The ads will be eligible to be served in response to search queries with this keyword.
6	The keyword has average performance in the marketplace. The ads will be eligible to be served in response to search queries with this keyword.
1–5	This keyword is underperforming in the marketplace. The ads will have limited eligibility to be served in response to search queries with this keyword.
–	Insufficient data to calculate score.

Recommendations for Managing Quality Score on Bing

1. *Bing Ads updates Quality Score daily*. Use ad group and campaign level-Quality Score to prioritize optimization efforts, and use keyword-level Quality Score to identify specific improvement opportunities.

   Keyword Relevance reflects whether ad copy effectively present selling point and call for actions. Use it to track the performance of your ad copies.

   Landing Page Relevance reflects whether the content of the website could effectively address a searcher's intent. Use it to identify opportunities of improving content relevancy or tightening search traffic with negative keywords or broad match modifiers.

QUALITY SCORE ON THE YAHOO! BING NETWORK, CONTINUED

Landing Page User Experience reflects whether the website design allows searchers to consume content with ease. Use it to assess whether you are on track to convert each visitor into a customer.

2. Bing Ads provides historic Quality Scores at keyword, ad group, and campaign level. Use it to monitor campaign performance and marketplace dynamics.

3. *Use Quality Impact analysis, available in the Keyword Performance Report within Bing Ads,* to access the impressions lost due to a poor Quality Score to determine potential upside for improving Quality Score.

SUMMARY

This chapter talked about some of the factors that are used to determine your ads' Quality Score. However, it is important to realize that for most purposes, the absolute value of your Quality Score is not as important as your *Quality Score relative to your competitors' ads appearing at about the same average position as your ads.* We'll talk more about this in Chapter 20.

Chapter 13

How Do Shoppers Shop?

Way back in the Bronze Age of paid search (2007), selling online was much simpler than it is today. Consumers would go to a search engine as their first choice (usually), click a few ads, and buy from one of those advertisers; price may have played a part, as did the landing page. Comparison shopping engines played a smaller role, and to a much lesser extent, display advertising did, as well.

Nowadays the landscape is much busier. Buyers can learn about your business through a variety of channels, including:

- Paid search
- Retail sites
- Brand sites
- Mobile
- Social
- Local
- Television
- Print media
- Friends and family
- Brick-and-mortar stores

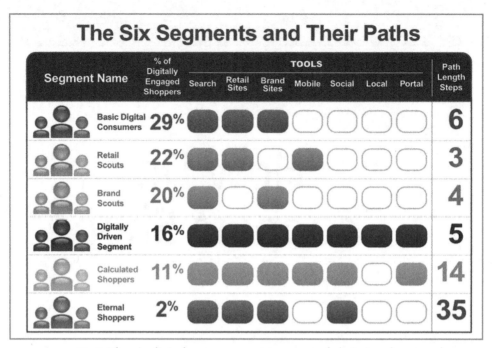

FIGURE 13–1. The six digital consumer segments and their purchase paths.
(*Courtesy*: GroupM Next)

This is further complicated due to the fact that there are no linear paths between these different channels. Consumers may—and do—choose between these options almost randomly.

Or so it would seem.

In May 2013, digital think tank, GroupM Next, released a study that made sense out of the chaos. In this research, they examined over 168,000 purchases of consumer electronics, with the goal of finding out where digital buyers go online and why.

They discovered that there were elegant patterns contained in the data. Six distinct segments of online buyers emerged. These six segments took six different pathways, relied on some channels more than others, and took varying number of steps prior to making their purchases.

THE SIX TYPES OF ONLINE BUYERS

Nearly one-third (29 percent) of online buyers fall in the group, "**Basic Digital Consumers.**" This group is comfortable making purchases online. They utilize search, retail sites, and brand sites. They aren't highly mobile or social. They buy in much the same way that most consumers did back in the "good old days."

The second group is called "**Retail Scouts**" and makes up 22 percent of buyers. This group makes fast purchase decisions (averaging only three steps per purchase). They prefer search and retail sites (such as Amazon and Walmart) to brand sites, and they are likely to use mobile and tablet devices, even from within the home. They are the most receptive group to digital coupons.

The next segment, "**Brand Scouts**," are similar in size to the preceding segment (20 percent). They make fast decisions as well and similarly place great reliance on paid search, but prefer specific brand sites to retail sites (and thus are more loyal as a whole). They are less likely to base their decisions on price and depend more on features and perks such as free shipping and money-back guarantees—a fact you should consider in your paid search campaign.

The fourth category (which makes up 16 percent of consumers in the study) is the "**Digitally Driven Segment**." This group is highly mobile and social. They value convenience and will go to great lengths to avoid going to a store. They are also more receptive to advertising: Buyers in this group are 30 percent more likely to find ads valuable than other groups (especially paid search ads).

The fifth group, "**Calculated Shoppers**," takes a long time to make a purchase (14 steps on average). They are in no hurry and will carefully consider all of their options in getting the best deal. Buyers in this group are likely to be "showroomers" and will use their mobile device to price compare when they are close to a purchase. This group is highly likely to use search and are responsive to advertising that offers discounts and specials.

The final group covered in the GroupM Next study was "**Eternal Shoppers**." This is a small group, made up only 2 percent of the purchasers, but they stand out in the extremely long path to purchase (35 steps!). They will research their purchases on virtually every online channel but typically use paid search to navigate between them.

What These Groups Have in Common

Did you notice the common thread shared by these six categories of digital consumers? That's right: Every one of them relies heavily on paid search at some point of the purchase lifecycle. This finding was further corroborated by a separate 2012 study by Google and Shopper Sciences in which they found that search was utilized by 50 percent of shoppers when making purchase decisions (*source*: Google/Shopper Sciences, Zero Moment of Truth Macro Study, April, 2011).

No other channel—not social, not mobile, not even retail sites—is utilized to the same extent as paid search. In fact, search scored about the same as "talking with friends and family about the product" in the Google study. **This means that advertisers who fail to run effective paid search programs will be at a severe competitive disadvantage to those that do (and especially the top 1 percent).**

Takeaways for Paid Search Marketers

The GroupM Next study provided advertisers a number of valuable insights regarding other channels such as brand sites, Amazon, mobile, and social. However, relative to our focus on paid search, Figure 13–2 contains a brief recap of what their study teaches us about reaching each of the six buyer segments.

Consumer Segment	Ideal Paid Search Tactics
Basic digital consumers	Promotions and coupons
Retail scouts	Use retail sites as landing pages; promotions and coupons; ensure you have best price on product-based keywords
Brand scouts	Perks such as free shipping and money-back guarantees; features and capabilities; product comparisons
Digitally driven segment	Target mobile and tablet; convenience-based advertising
Calculated shoppers	Promotions and coupons; loyalty programs and email capture
Eternal shoppers	Loyalty programs and email capture

FIGURE 13–2. Ideal paid search tactics for each buyer segment.

As you proceed through the remaining chapters of this book (particularly Chapters 16 and 21), keep these recommendations in mind.

Chapter 14

How Do Searchers Search?

Before you create your first campaign, choose your keywords, or write a single ad, you should understand the basic mechanisms behind how people search.

The psychology of search is a deep subject, but fortunately for us we have two easy-to-understand and surprisingly practical frameworks that can help us when designing our search campaigns.

The first model is called the "Visitor Intention Model" and can be used by virtually anyone selling anything online. The second model, called the "Brand Ladder," is primarily intended for companies with well-recognized brand names that typically don't sell online (many consumer package goods companies fall in this latter category).

These models form the foundation for keyword selection, ad copy, and even bidding strategies. They take only a few minutes to learn, and the payoff is well worth it.

THE VISITOR INTENTION MODEL

This model of search behavior postulates that there is a correlation between the phrases that people type into search engines and their *purchase intent*. In other words, you can predict how likely it is that someone will buy something from you based on their search phrase.

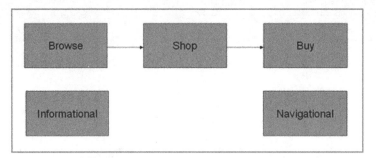

FIGURE 14–1. The visitor intention model.

Under this model, search engine users tend to fall within one of three primary categories or two secondary categories.

***Browsers* are in information-gathering mode.** The search phrases they enter tend to be short and not very specific (e.g., *Las Vegas, coupons, spyware,* etc.). While traffic

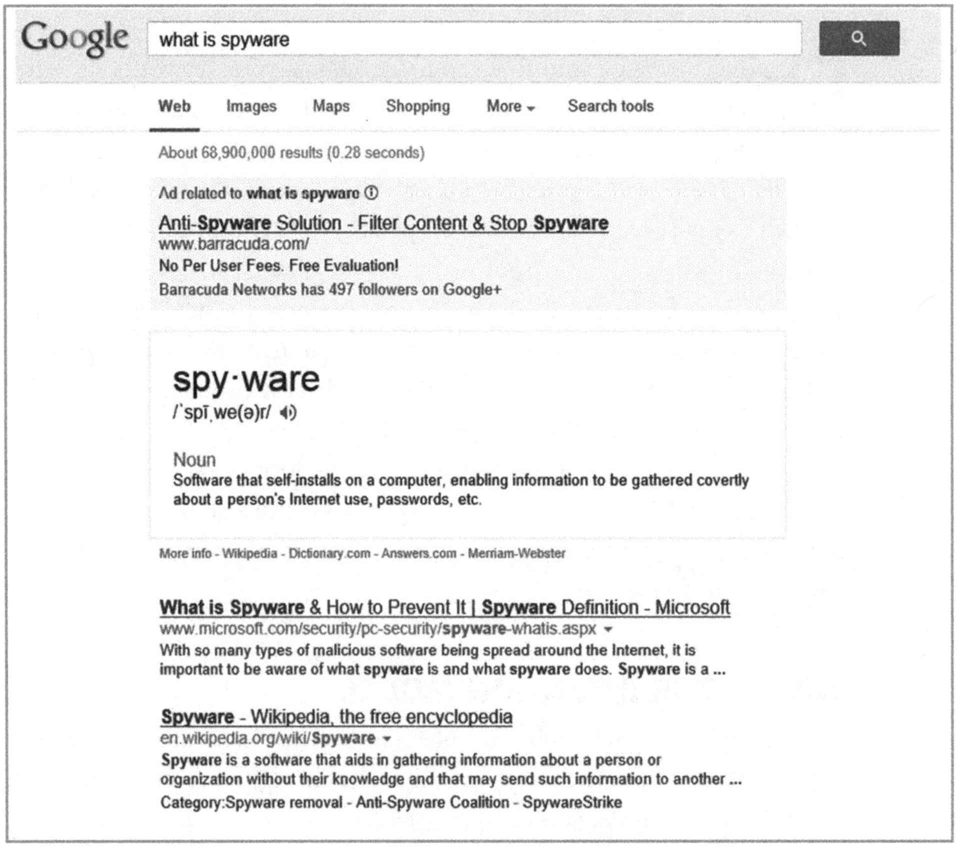

FIGURE 14–2. A typical result page returned for a browse query.

tends to be high for this group of terms, searchers are unlikely to make an immediate purchase, so paid search ads targeting these phrases tend to have a very low return.

Browsers are generally looking for information rather than products, and so they tend to click on natural results more often than ads. When they do click on ads, they will often click more than one as they gather as much information as possible. They usually start at the top of the page and work their way down (becoming more selective as they go along). Both search engines and advertisers respond to this low effectiveness, and as a result we often see few ads (or even none) for popular browse queries (see Figure 14–2).

The browse group is closely related to the *informational* group. The difference is that the former are potentially buyers, whereas people in the informational group are highly unlikely to buy at all. A good example is searchers who type in the phrase *South Park*. It is very difficult to sell anything to those who search on this term. In fact, the search engines stopped serving ads for this term in late 2011. As shown in Figure 14–3. These days, both Google and Bing serve supplementary information where the ads normally appear.

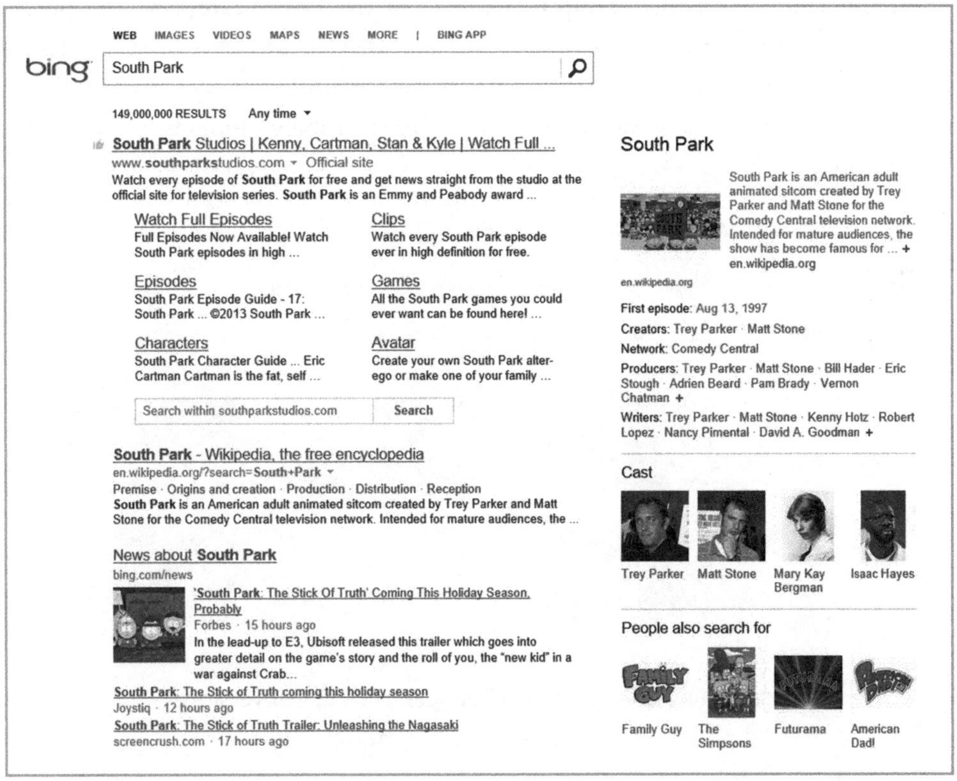

FIGURE 14–3. A typical result page served for an informational query.

Most people using search engines fall within one of these two groups, but you're far more likely to make a sale to a *shopper*. These people have an identified need and are considering their options. They are often using a search engine to compare different products or services.

You can almost think of shoppers as tire kickers. They might be seriously interested in buying now or later, but the immediate need is to assess their options. By appealing to that information-gathering need, you can often convert them to buyers (or at least capture their information for when they are ready to buy). Keywords in the shop per category tend to have both decent traffic and conversion rates.

***Buyers,* on the other hand, are ready to buy now.** They might be looking for a specific product, or just the first product that seems to meet their needs. Their information gathering is largely done, and they spend less time on the search engine and more time on vendors' websites.

Aggressive emotional or impulsive appeals often work with these visitors because the logical part of their brain has already been satisfied through prior research. Often, they need just the slightest push to buy from you. You want to tempt with promotional offers, and you should cater to instant gratification: fast shipping, high quality, low price, and so forth.

Finally, the *navigational* group is a subset of the buyer category. The purpose of their queries is to reach a particular website that they already have in mind, typically because they've visited it in the past or because they assume that such a site exists. For instance, someone who searches for *greyhound bus* is probably looking to visit http://www.greyhound.com.

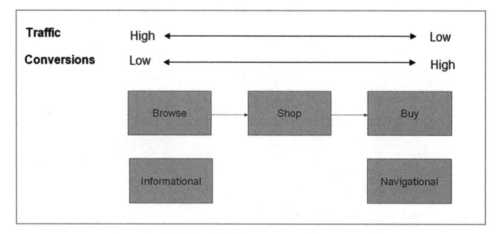

FIGURE 14–4. Relationship between traffic, conversions, and visitor intention model.

Visitors in the navigation group are quite hard to convert. Unlike other types of searchers, they usually have only one "right" result. They know the site they want to visit, and only that site will do. Although making a sale to these visitors isn't impossible, it's certainly an uphill battle—one that will tie up an inordinate amount of your time and money.

IDENTIFYING YOUR VISITORS' PURCHASE INTENTION

The information above is critical for any marketer to know. In the offline world, companies pay dearly for this type of market research. Fortunately, you don't have to.

You can guess which group a visitor falls within simply by the length and specificity of their keyword phrase.

- Short, one-word keyword phrases that generate a lot of traffic are dominated with browsers.
- Two- and three-word phrases that contain comparison words such as *best, cheap*, or *review* are shoppers' terms.
- Phrases with four or more words or phrases that refer to specific products, SKUs, or model numbers are used by buyers to find what they want quickly.
- Specific URLs, companies, or brand names identify navigational searchers.

Figure 14–5 on page 94 gives some examples of visitor group "tells" to get your wheels turning. In the coming chapters, we'll show you how to use this insight to transform your search advertising radically.

SOME KEYWORDS ARE HARD TO CLASSIFY

It is often difficult to distinguish between "shop" and "buy" keywords. Eventually you get a knack for it. One rule of thumb that I follow when dealing with products is verbs are often "shop" terms and nouns are often "buy" terms. For instance, "internet files clean" is likely a "shop" phrase, while "internet files cleaner" is most likely a "buy" phrase. Write different ads for each and even be willing to pay a little more for the latter phrase.

Browse	Shop	Buy	Navigate
Television	HDTV HDTV reviews	Panasonic 43" Plasma TV HVD3002 best price	Panasonic
Las Vegas	Las Vegas airfare	cheap Las Vegas	Expedia
Spyware	Best antispyware software	Spyware doctor 4.0	Pctools.com

FIGURE 14–5. Examples of different keyword types.

THE BRAND LADDER

The Visitor Intention model works well for most advertisers. But what if you are advertising a good or service that isn't typically purchased online? There are many types of businesses that fall within this category, including many B2B services, quick-service restaurants (fast food), and consumer package goods (CPG). In many cases, these products or services are commoditized so the most successful businesses have turned to branding as a means to differentiate themselves. However, this strategy has limited application in paid search because branded terms will typically drive a miniscule amount of paid search traffic (and this is exactly what the visitor intention model would predict). So what's a brand advertiser to do?

For these advertisers, the solution lies in branching out beyond brand names into higher-traffic terms that are directly related to their offering. The brand ladder model illustrated in Figure 14–6 on page 95 can help paid search marketers explore the spectrum of possible keywords choices, from most specific (but lowest traffic) to most general (but highest potential traffic).

Let's consider some examples. In the "owned" category are the small set of keywords that reflect a brand name. An example from the online education category might be "University of Phoenix." Searchers who enter this particular phrase are generally looking for a very specific website, and it will be difficult for competitors to successfully target this phrase (although not impossible). It's not uncommon to see "official" ads such as the following when searching on these terms. This helps searchers quickly determine who the brand owner is and can be an effective tactic to increase clickthrough rates.

Next are "product" keywords. These phrases target visitors who are looking for a category of products but not any one in particular. This is a particularly critical moment for marketers as it's often the point immediately before a buying decision is made. Figure 14–8 on page 95 shows an example of an ad that appeared for the product term "criminal justice degrees."

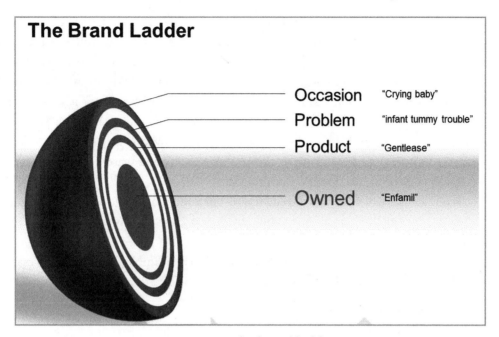

FIGURE 14–6. The brand ladder.

FIGURE 14–7. "Official" is often used within ad copy to help searchers quickly determine the true brand owner.

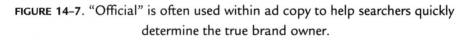

FIGURE 14–8. Product keywords target visitors looking for a category of product as opposed to a specific one.

In many cases, product keywords represent a readily-available source of traffic as opposed to owned keywords, which typically exhibit very low traffic unless supported by branded marketing efforts in other channels (such as offline or display advertising).

Next are "problem" keywords, such as "lose weight fast." Like "browse" keywords (from the Visitor Intention model), these phrases tend to be somewhat generic and generate a large amount of traffic. Unlike those keywords, however, these keywords tend to reflect an urgent pain on the part of the searcher. By targeting these pain-loaded phrases, you have the opportunity to connect with motivated searchers and tap into a potentially enormous amount of search traffic.

"Problem" keywords are an excellent way for sellers of branded products to get the word out. But be forewarned: Many advertisers have already figured this out so competition will be stiff.

Let's recap what we've learned so far with a different example from the world of diet shakes. After all, what could possibly be more commoditized than weight-loss products?

Brand keyword: *Slim-Fast*
Product keyword: *diet shakes*
Problem keyword: *Lose weight fast*

Here's an ad in Figure 14–9 that recently appeared for this problem keyword. Note how the copy addresses a specific urgent need ("Get The Sexy Look You Really Want, Fast.")

Slim-**Fast**® Diet Plan - slim-**fast**.com
www.slim-fast.com/
Try Slim-**Fast**® & Get The Sexy Look You Really Want, **Fast**. Visit Us!

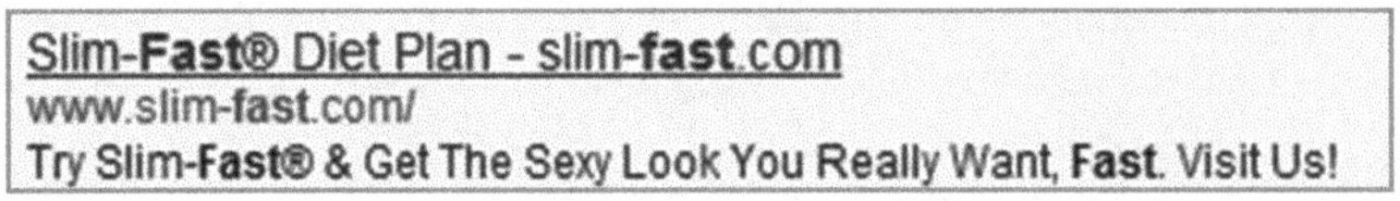

FIGURE 14–9. An example of an ad served for a "problem" keyword.

Finally, we have the "occasion" category. Not every business has a hallmark life event that they can connect with, but many do. And if you can find one, you can tap into a significant source of low-competition search traffic that many other advertisers overlook.

To succeed with these terms, you'll need to give a lot of thought to how you will engage with searchers at the instant at which they recognize they have a problem but have not yet discovered a solution. This is a tremendously powerful—and brief—moment during which the brand advertiser has the opportunity to make a lasting impression in the searcher's mind.

You may not be the only one. Most of the time in paid search, you are competing heavily with many other advertisers, and with occasion terms, this is can sometimes be the case as well. However, you might be surprised to see just how poorly most advertisers execute here.

What does an "occasion" look like for weight loss? This category may have more than any other, but one of the most powerful is: "lose weight for wedding."

As you can see from the screenshot in Figure 14–10, there is no shortage of advertisers on this term. However, only one, Nutrisystem, served an ad that actually connected to the searcher. There are two big giveaways that they've done so. First, their ads are appearing in the premium position (as discussed in previous chapters, the most relevant ads find their way to the top). Second, their ad is well aligned with the organic search results.

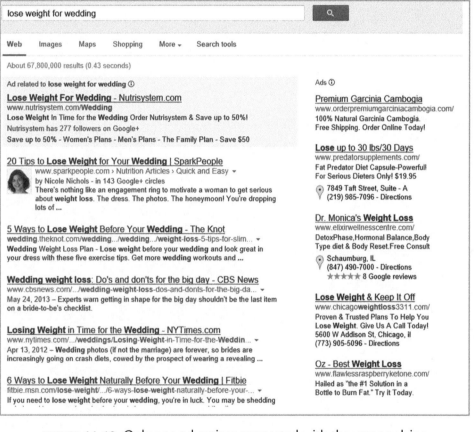

FIGURE 14–10. Only one advertiser connected with the urgency lying behind this search phrase.

We'll talk more about ad copy in Chapter 21, but for now you should start thinking about the problems and occasions your brand might target.

Chapter 15

Increase Your Clickthrough Rate by Nearly 50 Percent with Search Refinements

When one considers the high number of "touches" many online shoppers make before eventually settling on a purchase, it should come as no surprise that single phrases are rarely typed into a search engine in isolation. It is far more common for searchers to enter multiple phrases in rapid succession, building on each preceding one. The subsequent phrases are known as "**search refinements**."

Search refinement occurs much more frequently than many marketers suspect. According to data provided by Compete (Figure 15–1), when users visit a search engine, they conduct multiple searches nearly 65 percent of the time. Three or more searches were conducted in nearly half of all sessions, and 12 percent of sessions included a whopping 10 or more searches.

MULTIPLE IMPRESSIONS LEAD TO HIGHER CLICKTHROUGH RATE

There is no doubt that that many of these searches are related. Are users more likely to click an advertiser who appears on each subsequent search? There is a surprising lack of research available on this subject. To this end, I analyzed estimated clickthrough rates for 268 advertisers who consistently appeared on subsequent search refinements (for instance, "oven reviews" and "convection oven reviews").

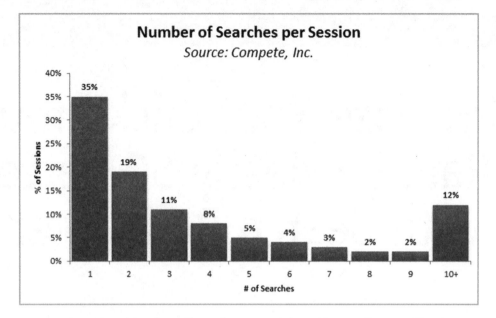

FIGURE 15–1. Number of searches per session. (*Source*: Compete Inc.)

My study showed that users were more likely to click on advertisers who appeared more often in the same session. More specifically, my data showed that an advertiser who appears at least 10 percent of the time for both the initial query, as well as the follow-up query, received an average lift of 47 percent of their initial clickthrough rate on the subsequent search. As an example, take an advertiser who received a clickthrough rate of 1.0 percent on the term *Venetian Hotel*. That same advertiser appearing on the search refinement, *Venetian Hotel Vegas*, would be expected to experience a CTR "bonus" of .47 percent relative to other advertisers because they appeared on both terms.

Years of experience have taught me that repeated impressions from the same advertiser—even within the space of a minute or two—can have a significant impact on clickthrough rate. And now we have some data to support it.

It is, of course, not merely the impact of repeated impressions that results in this effect. It is also partly due to the fact that those advertisers who are more thorough in targeting search refinements also tend to be more rigorous in their approach to ad copy and landing page design. The best advertisers go to great lengths to ensure that their campaigns are responsive to searchers' intent and thus deliver a more harmonious experience.

A Real-World Example

To illustrate this, I recently looked over a friend's shoulder while he shopped for a used Mercedes Benz ML350. I recorded his initial search phrase ("Mercedes") and his subsequent refinements as he attempted, using Google, to locate some local cars for sale. I asked him to pause in between each refinement to provide me with his feedback on what he was seeing.

Search Phrase	Ads Shown	Buyer Response
1. Mercedes	Official Mercedes-Benz site Ad from local dealer #1 Generic auto-trading site	"This doesn't look specific enough."
2. Mercedes Benz	Official Mercedes-Benz site Ad from local dealer #2 advertising a Mercedes C250 Volvo ad	"I'm not interested in a C250. Why is a Volvo ad showing up? This still isn't what I'm looking for."
3. Mercedes Benz M-class	Official Mercedes-Benz site (unchanged from previous searches) Local dealer #1 ad with a link to their new M-class inventory Local dealer #2 ad with monthly lease price for an M-class Several ads for used Mercedes M-class from internet auto sites.	"I want used, not new. I'm not leasing. I want to go see it so I'm only interested in local options."
4. Mercedes Benz M-class used	Official Mercedes-Benz site—now changed to reflect "Certified Pre-Owned" stock Local dealer #1 ad offering over "one hundred pre-owned Mercedes models to choose from" Local Toyota dealer #2 used Mercedes-Benz in stock, Prices starting at $23,628"	"That's a great price." He clicks the Toyota ad to find that both Mercedes are the wrong models (C-class and E-class) and are a few years too old. "I want the latest model. It has to be a 2012 or 2013." Clicks the back button, and returns to the search results.

FIGURE 15–2. Example of an actual search session for a used Mercedes.

Search Phrase	Ads Shown	Buyer Response
5. 2012 Mercedes Benz M-class used	Local dealer #1 ad (same as previous) Official Mercedes-Benz site Local Acura dealer Kelly Blue Book ad Land Rover ad Lexus ad DealerClearingLots.com ad Carmax ad	User finally clicks local dealer #1's ad to land on a complicated inventory search page, which includes nine search fields and requires their personal contact information (Figure 15–3). "There's no way I'm providing them with my phone number just to see what they have in stock." Ends search, and goes to eBay Motors.

FIGURE 15–2. Example of an actual search session for a used Mercedes, continued.

Ultimately, this search engine session failed. My friend was a highly motivated shopper (he ended up purchasing a $63,000 vehicle just a few weeks later) who entered five increasingly specific searches. But he never found what he was looking for. He eventually gave up and went to a different site (but not before clicking on two ineffective ads).

His first two queries were too generic. However, both local dealers managed to squeeze an impression in. Although these two impressions didn't directly lead to a click, they made my friend aware of these two local dealerships, and they didn't cost a dime!

On the second refinement (the third search), both dealers layered their ads by successfully targeting the phrase *Mercedes Benz M-class*. The first dealer's ad offered up new models while the second dealer's ad highlighted the lease price. Neither quite got it right, but that was still a successful impression.

On the next search, local dealer #2 didn't show up. By missing that single impression, they may have missed out on my friend's five-figure sale. Local dealer #1 did show up but missed out on the click because a competitor happened to show a much better ad that included a great price (and they weren't even a Mercedes dealer).

On the fifth and final search, local dealer #1 finally got the click but blew it with the landing page in Figure 15–3 on page 103.

My friend became so frustrated at this point that he abandoned his search. I wonder what might have happened had the other local dealer not missed that critical final search. I took the opportunity to go visit local dealer #2's landing page (the one

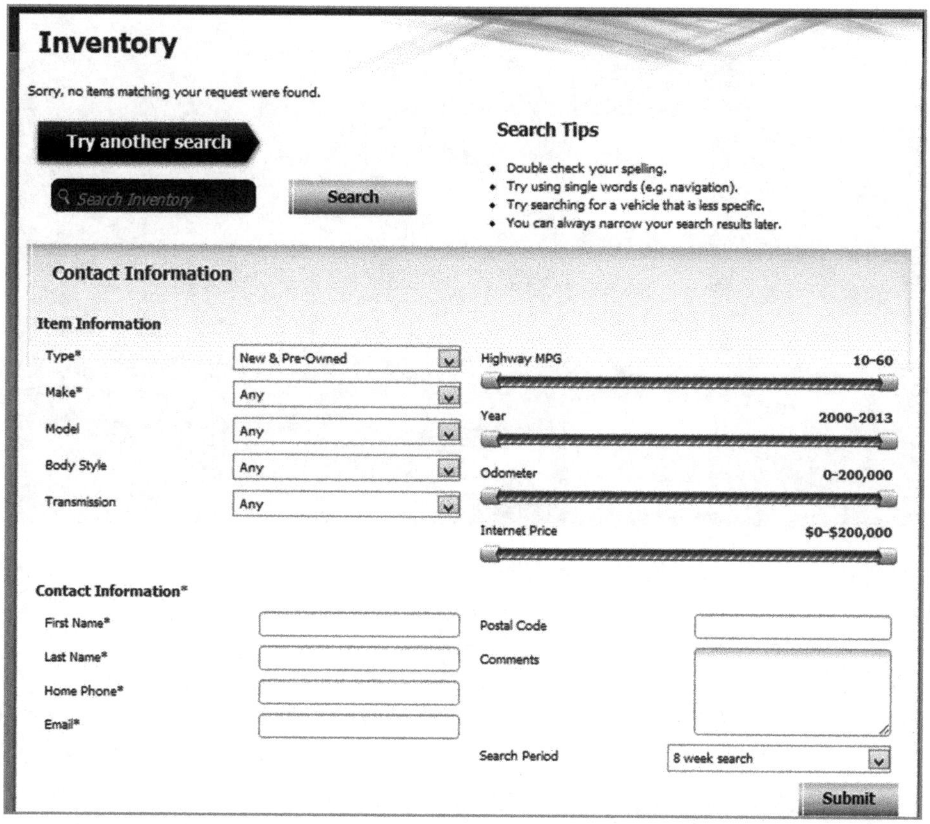

FIGURE 15–3. This complicated landing page doesn't lead to a positive user experience.

we might have seen, had his ad appeared on the prior search), and it was pretty good (see Figure 15-4 on page 104).

This landing page offered everything that my car-hungry friend was looking for. But the dealer missed out on a potential sale because of the seemingly innocuous mistake of not including the word "used" in his keyword lists.

Search refinements are incredibly under appreciated. While many advertisers focus heavily on initial keyword expansion and ad copy optimization, relatively few think about the impact that their ads might have when seen in rapid succession.

FIGURE 15–4. This landing page delivers a much better experience by providing exactly what was promised in the ad.

THINK ABOUT SEARCH REFINEMENTS WHEN CREATING YOUR CAMPAIGN

Leading search marketers consider not only the keywords they are targeting but also the *sequence* in which those keywords may be entered as users refine their initial searches.

By ensuring they have high coverage and relevant ads across the entire chain of search refinements, they increase their clickthrough rate not only on the initial search phrase but on longer, more specific phrases as well. Few things in paid search are more tragic than spending considerable time and money optimizing high-traffic terms only to lose your prospects just before the sale.

Chapter 16

Building
Your Keyword List

In both organic and paid search marketing, keywords are the bait that lures prospective customers to your website. So it's important you get it right.

People will find your site based on the keywords where your ads appear. For this reason alone, it's important to expand your campaign with as many relevant terms as possible. Yet, according to Marketing Sherpa's "Search Marketing Benchmark Guide 2007," the average B2B (business-to-business) advertiser bids on only 50 terms. This is not a recipe for success!

Keyword selection may not be the most important success factor for paid search, but it's certainly in the top five. The time you spend perfecting your keyword list will dramatically improve the potential results of your pay-per-click advertising campaign.

THE FOUR MOST COMMON KEYWORD RESEARCH MISTAKES

Let's start out by discussing the four most common mistakes search advertisers make when establishing their campaigns.

Mistake 1: Not Using Enough Keywords

As stated earlier, the average B2B business has only 50 keywords in their paid search campaign. This is a huge mistake. No matter what your business is, you should be able to come up with thousands of niche terms that are relevant to potential customers. Aim to have no less than 5,000 keywords, but preferably 25,000 or more. You may end up deleting many of these keywords later on, but it's better to err on the side of having too many rather than too few.

Mistake 2: Relying Solely on Brainstorming

As crazy as it sounds, many small businesses casually type in a few dozen keywords off the top of their heads into their AdWords account and expect to start seeing results. This fails because brainstorming usually results in a limited set of keywords.

These keywords tend to be the obvious "browse" keywords and generate lots of traffic (and costs) but have much lower conversion rates than "buy" and "shop" phrases.

These keywords often reflect your own thoughts and conceptions about your business rather than your searchers' true intentions. The closer you are to your business, the less reliably you'll be able to think like a potential customer.

Mistake 3: Relying Solely on Popular or Free Tools

There are a number of inexpensive or even free keyword-research tools available. Some of them return good results. The major problem with them is that they are widely used, which means the keywords they return are more competitive. The other problem is that the algorithms behind them are based on total search traffic, which means these keywords will tend to drive more traffic but convert at a much lower rate than more specific niche keywords.

Mistake 4: Never Updating Your Keyword Lists

After you complete these next few chapters, you're going to have a great set of keywords. But don't forget to revisit your list from time to time. New buzzwords and niche areas will pop up from time to time, and if you never update your list, you'll miss out on new potential traffic sources.

QUANTITY IS IMPORTANT—TO A POINT

Given what we just said about these four common mistakes, it seems reasonable that we could play it safe, dump every possible keyword into our campaigns, and let the search engines worry about it.

Unfortunately, this doesn't work very well in practice.

The argument for using generic keywords is that you can reach more visitors with less work, and furthermore, the search engines will take care of showing your ads for closely related niche phrases. On the other hand, niche keywords that reflect your business will attract more qualified (but fewer) prospects who convert at a higher rate. Also, a targeted campaign consisting of fewer keywords is less likely to suffer from quality score problems, and you can potentially outcompete well-funded mega advertisers due to your laserlike focus on relevancy.

So which is it: a few, high-volume keywords, or thousands of niche terms?

The answer is that you'll need both. Start out with a core set of keywords that reflects your business. But over time, build that list into hundreds or thousands of niche keyword phrases that reflect both what visitors are searching for and what your business sells.

Blending both approaches in a holistic manner has many advantages.

Although generic keywords such as *plasma TV* are searched on by lots of people, these searchers are less likely to make a purchase, so you end up spending a considerable amount of your campaign budget on visitors in the early stages of their purchase cycle. Remember from Chapter 13 that 78 percent of online shoppers make five or more "touches" before making a purchase. Targeted keywords like "cheapest 43″ plasma TV" are generally much less expensive to bid on and have far better conversion rates because these searchers tend to be further along in their buying process.

On the other hand, if you completely ignore the broader, high-traffic terms, you miss out on the opportunity to engage with potential shoppers early. Some of these shoppers may flitter off to other channels (social media, retailer, and brand sites for instance) never to be seen again on the search engine (at least for the same purchase). The relatively high cost you may incur for these search terms can be partially recouped through email capture or indirectly in the form of brand awareness. And don't forget that when your ads consistently appear for a broad term, your ads appearing on longer variations of that same term will tend to earn a "clickthrough rate bonus" (Chapter 15).

Despite their advantages, it is more difficult to secure high quality scores on broad terms. Because these terms are more generic, writing highly targeted ads is a challenge. This is not a problem with more specific keyword phrases. To the extent that you can write better ads than your competitors, you'll earn placement and coverage bonuses relative to your competitors. Just keep in mind that you may need to do it thousands of times, so go slow.

Note that the above applies only if you have a sufficient budget, as you'll expect your campaign to start off fast and become more efficient over time. If you're operating under a limited budget, or your value proposition hasn't been well-tested, it is typically better

START WITH BROAD KEYWORDS, THEN EXPAND INTO NICHE TERMS

Start off your campaign with broad, high-volume keywords. Over time, expand your efforts to target more specific, niche search phrases. Although these phrases generate less traffic, a portfolio of them can dramatically outperform campaigns relying solely on a few generic terms. However, if your budget is limited, focus initially on niche terms.

to focus on niche terms in the beginning. You'll follow the same steps outlined later in the chapter; you just won't target those high-volume keywords in the beginning.

TO COME UP WITH KEYWORDS, THINK LIKE YOUR CUSTOMERS

As marketers, we all know how important it is to focus on putting the customer's needs ahead of our own. But before the internet and other highly measurable media forced us marketers to be accountable, many of us got away with focusing on the features of our products rather than emphasizing benefits.

Nowadays, if you're out there flexing your muscles, talking about how great you are, and trying to impress prospects, you're probably not going to get very far. Companies that succeed in today's cluttered marketplace start by doing the market research on what problems their prospects have.

They are desperate to understand the pains, fears, and hopes of their customers. They know how to empathize with their prospects. Once they have their market research, savvy marketers then know how to position themselves. They know how to say, "I feel your pain," and how to present a solution to ease that pain.

When people enter keywords into a search box, they have a pain. They have a need. They have a question that they want answered. They want to be served the solution in the form of information as to how they can resolve their problem.

Your job as a marketer is to put yourself in their shoes. You must ask yourself: What keywords are my ideal prospects going to type into Google or Bing?

That is the question all marketers should have been asking themselves all along, but if you don't know the right keywords that your prospects are asking, then your PPC campaigns aren't going to send you much qualified traffic.

This is where the visitor intention model comes into play (Chapter 14). To create effective PPC campaigns, you should always be asking yourself:

- What behavioral category does this keyword fall in (browse, shop, or buy)?
- Can I refine a browse keyword into one or more shop keywords?
- Can I refine a shop keyword into one or more buy keywords?

As you come up with each keyword, you will want to categorize it into one of the three categories. This step will come in handy while you are structuring your campaigns, writing your ads, and setting your initial bids.

A STEP-BY-STEP GUIDE TO KEYWORD GENERATION

Keeping in mind the three common mistakes we started this chapter with, we're now going to show you the steps to building a keyword list rich with high-converting terms.

As you start building your keyword list, you're going to be doing little more than guessing. By using the right analytical tools and performing the right analysis, you will expand your keywords and hone the list down by improving or eliminating under-performing keywords.

Step 1: Brainstorming

The logical place to start is by brainstorming about the kinds of keywords that are relevant to your customers and jotting them down on a pad of paper or in an electronic document.

As in any brainstorming, it is best to begin blue-sky thinking at first. In other words, don't edit yourself. Later, you will see that the actual results of your campaign will edit you by telling you which keywords work and which don't.

Err on the side of having more keywords rather than less.

Try to go beyond just one- or two-word keywords. These keywords are important but you want to own niches, so think in terms of key *phrases* so that you can dominate when a searcher looks for something specific that is relevant to what you have to sell.

The more keywords you have, the merrier. The exception to this is that you should make sure that your keywords are relevant to your business. If you are selling vacations to Mexico, the keyword "Mexico" probably isn't a good choice—it's just too untargeted, broad, and competitive. These general keywords tend not to show any ads, and even if they do, they will probably be exorbitantly priced. "Mexico vacations" is about as generic as you'll want to go.

Terms such as "Puerto Vallarta vacations" are even better. Don't be worried about taking it too far. You might later find that the keyword "Puerto Vallarta bed and breakfast" doesn't get much traffic, but for now, don't assume anything. You'll test it later.

Let's start with a little brainstorming session for a hypothetical identity protection company. Here are a few of the starting keywords that I came up with off the top of my head:

- Identity theft
- Identity theft protection
- Online identity
- Prevent identity theft
- Identity theft software

Step 2: Scour Your Marketing Collateral

If you have an established business, you'll want to sort through pamphlets, brochures, websites, retail boxes, and any other marketing copy you have available. You can also use your competitors' websites as well. Paid search landing pages are particularly good for this, as these pages have often been optimized for the most profitable keywords.

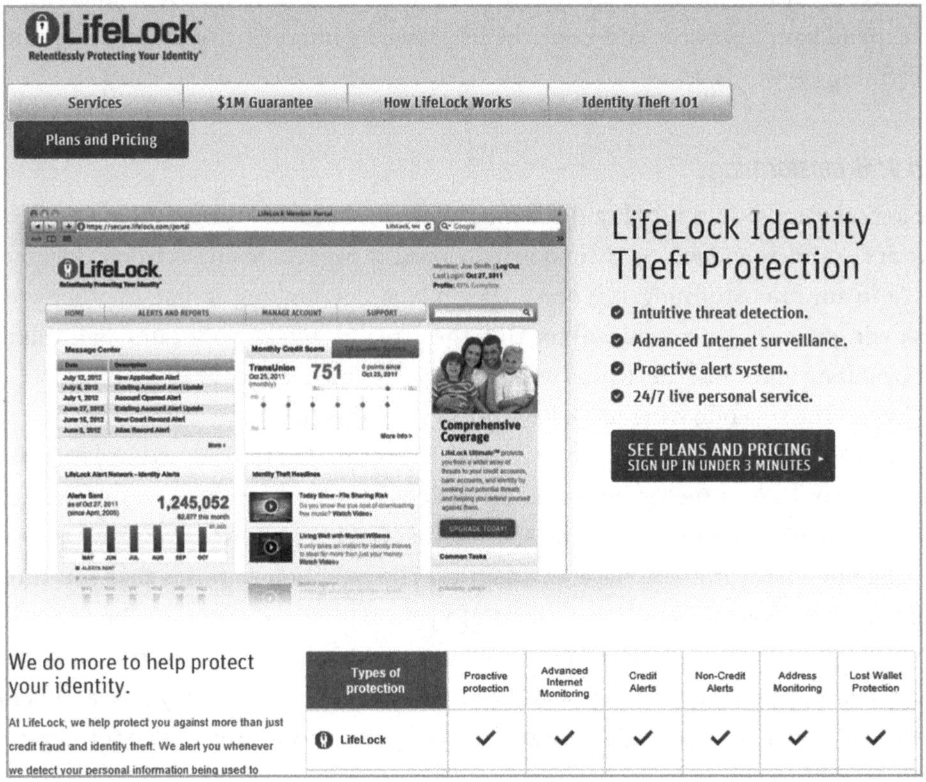

FIGURE 16–1. Website product pages are a good source of keyword ideas.

A quick scan of a few well-known identity theft websites resulted in 44 additional keywords, such as *credit fraud*, *id fraud*, *protect your identity*, *protect personal information*, and *identity theft protection tools*.

Step 3: Horizontal and Vertical Expansion Using Third-Party Tools

Your next step is to augment your brainstorming results with third-party keyword suggestion tools. Both Bing and Google provide these tools, which will generate related terms for any keyword you type in. I find that the current versions have different strengths, and both should be used.

So why do the search engines provide these tools? It's an important point to consider. They provide these tools because it is in their best interest. They want you to expand your keyword lists because that means that you are likely to spend more money with them. And even if your ads don't show up, the auction-style nature of paid search means that your bids will force other advertisers to pay higher prices.

What this means to you is that while you should use these tools to help seed your lists, don't take them as gospel. The data points they provide can be incomplete, misleading, or even downright incorrect.

For this reason, I recommend that you use multiple tools. As you'll see, no keyword-research tool is perfect. The worst of them return obvious keywords that can be easily guessed at and are highly competitive. The better ones return hundreds or even thousands of niche keywords that only a few savvy competitors are targeting. However, none are, or ever could be, complete because the universe of potential keywords is very large. Play it safe, and consult multiple sources. Don't skimp here—this is one of the most important steps in planning your campaigns.

Google AdWords Keyword Planner

The first tool you should use is the Google Keyword Planner (see Figure 16–2 on page 112). You'll find it under the "Tools and Analysis" menu within your AdWords account. This tool can be very helpful for your keyword list's horizontal expansion into various topics. However, it generates results largely based on potential search traffic so the keywords it returns tend to be more in the search engines' best interest rather than yours. Another disadvantage of the traffic-based approach is that the keyword lists tend to be rather shallow. Nevertheless, it's excellent at returning broad topics that are somewhat related to your entered terms, which makes it a good complement to brainstorming.

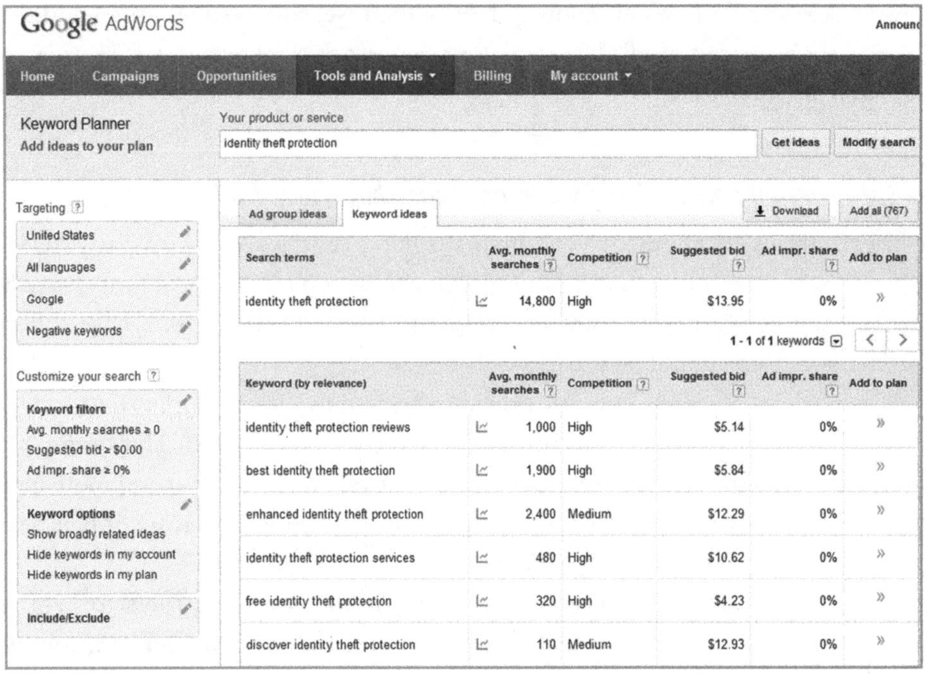

FIGURE 16–2. Google AdWords Keyword Planner.

Bing Keyword Research Tool

The second free tool I recommend is the Bing Keyword Research tool. To use this tool, you'll need to go to the Bing Webmaster Tools site (www.bing.com/toolbox/webmaster) and verify your site (see Figure 16–3 on page 113). Once you do this, you'll have access to a suite of useful tools including the Bing Keyword Research tool (found in the left navigation menu under "Diagnostics and Tools"/"Keyword Research").

The Bing Keyword Research tool feels a little less polished than the Google equivalent, but I find that it produces a better variety of candidate keyword ideas. Unlike Google, Bing doesn't filter the results, and the resulting output is far more useful for keyword research, especially when it comes to vertical expansion (e.g., generating more specific variants of the input keyword phrases).

AdGooroo Industry Insight

A paid option for keyword expansion is AdGooroo Industry Insight. AdGooroo monitors search engine advertising in 50 countries around the world and generates lengthy keyword lists for either individual advertisers or entire industries (over 160 standard business categories are included).

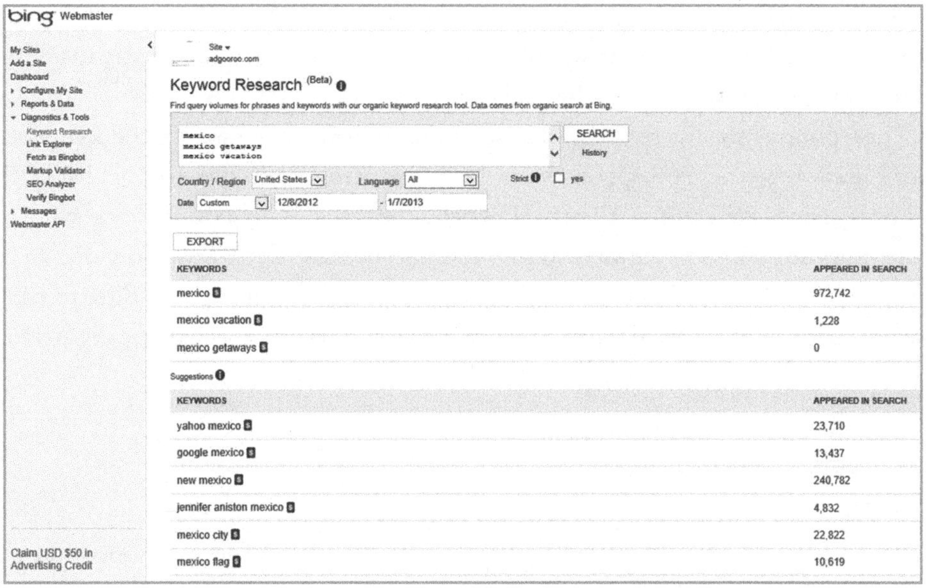

FIGURE 16–3. Bing Webmaster Tools includes an excellent keyword research tool.

One of the differences between the AdGooroo keyword reports and the other tools described here lies in the way that keywords are prioritized. Google and Bing prioritize keywords by search volume. Other tools use proprietary metrics. In contrast, the AdGooroo Keyword Research tool computes estimated paid search spend, CTR, CPC, and click volume for every keyword. This is a huge time saver when determining which keywords to attack first. While these estimates are not perfect (no model is), it provides you with real-world estimates that you can use to prioritize your efforts. Most important, the results you'll get from this tool are specific to paid search and take into account the presence of advertising, which means no more wasted time spent trying to optimize keywords with little or no advertising potential. Finally, you can generate keyword lists either for standard business categories or using the combination of specific advertisers that *you* select. If you have a few close competitors, this is a tremendously powerful shortcut that will eliminate keywords that they have found (usually through expensive trial-and-error) to be ineffective.

Continuing on with the example, I will show you how I use AdGooroo Industry Insight and SEM Insight (another AdGooroo product) to generate fully expanded keyword lists packed with relevant terms (and few irrelevant ones) in just a few minutes. Note that you can use either product by itself to generate keyword lists. However, combining them is an advanced technique that gets you a nearly perfect list in a fraction of the time.

I started by logging into my SEM Insight account and creating a new keyword group called "Identity Theft." I added 79 of the common terms from the keyword list I've compiled using brainstorming, competitors' landing pages, and free tools. If you know of a specific competitor, you can also just pull their keywords from Industry Insight and create a starting keyword group directly from this list.

These phrases are my "seed list" that will be used to identify a set of close competitors. Once I know who these competitors are, I can then create a fully expanded list of their keywords using the built-in filters. However, the trick is in figuring out who your competitors are. This isn't always so easy to do, especially if it's a category or a market that you don't know well. So to do this, I'll use my keyword group as a filter to narrow down the entire AdGooroo database to just the keywords I've selected (see Figure 16–4):

- Log in to Industry Insight.
- Select the "Industry Overview" report.
- Select the "All" category.
- Click the "Filter" button on the top toolbar.
- In the advanced filters area that appear at the top of the page, select the filter "Keywords in SEM Insight Keyword Group," and then select the group you've previously created.
- Finally, press "Apply Filter."

In a few seconds, you'll see the entire list of advertisers who appeared on those terms, sorted by spend (the screenshot in Figure 16–5 on page 115 shows only 10, but there are over 230 who appear in the full list). This is also an excellent technique for producing spend estimates for specific product categories. If you've ever wanted to know how much Amazon spends just on printer ink, now you can find out.

Note that you don't need to go to any great pains to narrow down your keyword list at this point. My list contained terms that were slightly off target for my purposes, such as "identity theft stories." As a result, there were companies on the list that we probably

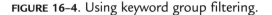

FIGURE 16–4. Using keyword group filtering.

Top Advertisers
Category:All - Google US - May 2013
Keyword Group:SurfSecret

Advertiser	Spend	Clicks	CTR	CPC	Impressions
identityprotection.com	$8,619	1,480	5.61%	$5.82	26,367
lifelock.com	$7,939	1,367	5.06%	$5.81	27,021
consumercompare.nextadvisor.com	$6,780	1,162	4.34%	$5.83	26,764
identityguard.com	$5,794	994	4.16%	$5.83	23,925
identitytheftlabs.com	$4,951	847	3.19%	$5.84	26,571
equifax.com	$4,340	744	2.88%	$5.83	25,870
experian.com	$4,272	732	3.75%	$5.84	19,492
free-pc-cleaner.sparktrust.com	$3,947	2,478	3.23%	$1.59	76,803
softwareindustryreport.com	$2,957	1,701	2.24%	$1.74	76,037
clean.myfasterpc.com	$2,685	3,057	6.28%	$0.88	48,673

FIGURE 16–5. Resulting list of advertisers appearing on the list of seed terms.

don't care about (avg.com, creditscore.com, geosurf.com, and many others). Just ignore these companies for the next step.

Now you'll narrow down your list of competitors to just a few close matches. If you can use direct competitors, then your final keyword list will need virtually no manual checks. On the other hand, if your competitors are active in multiple categories, you may end up pulling keywords that are a bit off. If this happens, you'll weed them out of your list later.

I chose a few well-known companies for my competitor set: lifelock.com, identityprotection.com, identityguard.com, and several others shown in Figure 16–6 on page 116. On each advertiser's dedicated page within Industry Insight there is a button that reads "Add to/Edit Launchpad," shown in Figure 16–7 on page 116. Click this button to bring up a dialog that allows you to save the advertiser to a shortcut area called the "Launchpad." You'll see this when you log in. It allows you to quickly navigate to these advertisers' reports.

Apart from the convenience of being able to quickly return to these advertisers in the future, adding them to the Launchpad enables you to filter the entire AdGooroo database down to just these chosen advertisers. That, in turn, will give you access to their combined set of keywords.

Again, you'll access the advanced filters section precisely as you did above, except this time you'll choose the "Advertiser is on Client Launchpad" filter, as shown in Figure 16–8 on page 117.

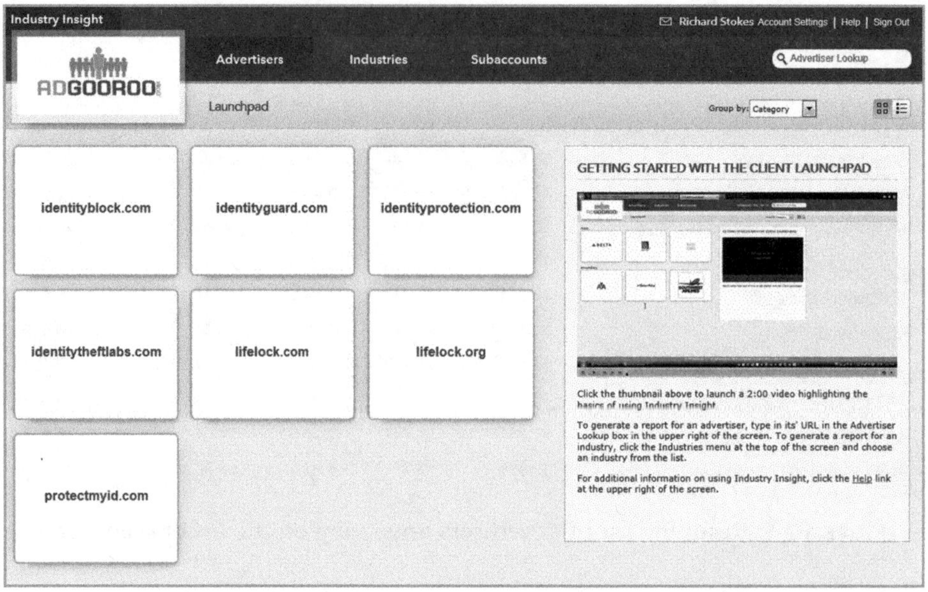

FIGURE 16–6. The Launchpad contains your list of handpicked advertisers.

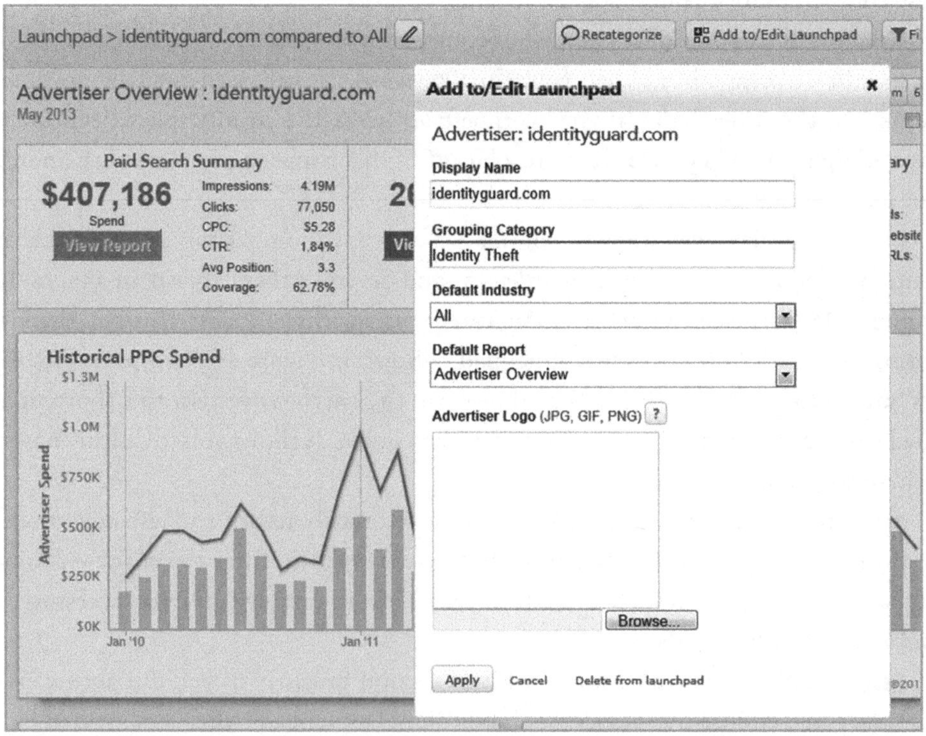

FIGURE 16–7. Adding an advertiser to the Launchpad.

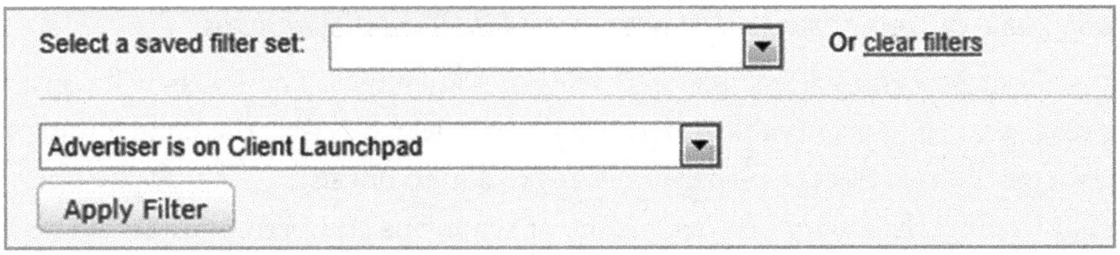

FIGURE 16–8. Filtering the entire database down to your chosen set of advertisers.

The final step in the process is to generate a list of keywords mined from these competitors. With this filter activated, navigate to the "Industry Keywords" report. This will produce a report that has the desired list shown in Figure 16–9.

Show 50 entries

	Keyword	Spend	Impressions	Clicks	CTR	CPC	Highest Coverage Seen
	credit report	$474,480	2,997,099	54,695	1.82%	$8.67	81.58%
	credit score	$249,154	2,559,740	32,783	1.28%	$7.60	81.76%
	identity theft	$246,267	4,524,622	77,235	1.71%	$3.19	84.80%
	credit reports	$58,535	323,717	6,652	2.05%	$8.80	81.62%
	credit scores	$51,616	350,431	5,909	1.69%	$8.74	81.32%
	identity theft protection	$46,550	216,657	8,487	3.92%	$5.49	84.25%
	credit check	$45,783	446,358	7,011	1.57%	$6.53	88.10%
	annual credit report	$26,877	823,358	30,473	3.70%	$0.88	68.58%
	credit protection	$17,696	107,433	2,884	2.68%	$6.13	92.31%
	identity thief	$13,130	466,940	21,341	4.57%	$0.62	46.63%
	social security	$12,757	359,481	7,046	1.96%	$1.81	3.54%
	credit reporting agencies	$11,130	78,289	2,634	3.36%	$4.22	84.01%
	credit score range	$10,854	115,106	2,231	1.94%	$4.86	73.44%
	credit monitoring services	$10,410	29,098	1,032	3.55%	$10.08	97.04%
	lifelock	$10,139	290,495	24,732	8.51%	$0.41	89.01%

Showing 1 to 50 of 1,821 entries   First Previous 1 2 3 4 5 Next Last

FIGURE 16–9. The expanded keyword list.

At this point, my working list has over 1,700 keywords. Although not shown in this example, I also filtered the list to exclude terms with less than $1 in combined spend. This eliminated about 150 oddball terms that I wouldn't want to spend time on. The list includes both high-traffic broad phrases in addition to many niche "shop" and "buy" phrases. These latter phrases will likely receive no more than a few clicks a month, but they will probably produce an abnormally high percentage of sales. And I now have hundreds of them on my list. But we're not done yet . . .

Step 4: Multiply Your Keyword List with Permutations and Synonyms

Next we'll inspect those keywords to develop synonym lists. These lists will consist of phrases that are interchangeable (even if they don't mean precisely the same thing). We'll then merge them to create new permutations to add to our list.

For instance, let's say we have two lists of synonyms and permutations such as are shown in Figure 16-10.

List 1	List 2
Protect	Identity
Guard	Id
Monitor	Credit
Protection	Fraud
Prevent	Fraudulent
Prevention	Theft
Report	Thief
Shield	Internet identity
Steal	Privacy
Monitoring	Scams
Stolen	Identity Theft
Security	

FIGURE 16–10. A starting list of keyword synonyms.

We'd like to combine them to end up with a master list of permutations as shown in Figure 16-11. Note that I've reversed some of these phrases to make the example clearer.

Permutations
Protect Identity
Guard Identity
Monitor Identity
Identity Protection
Prevent Identity Theft
Report Identity Theft
Identity Shield
Guard Fraud
Identity Monitoring

FIGURE 16–11. Some example permutations resulting from the synonym list created above.

You can do this by hand, but a much easier way is to use Excel. Open up a spreadsheet, and paste your lists in the first two columns.

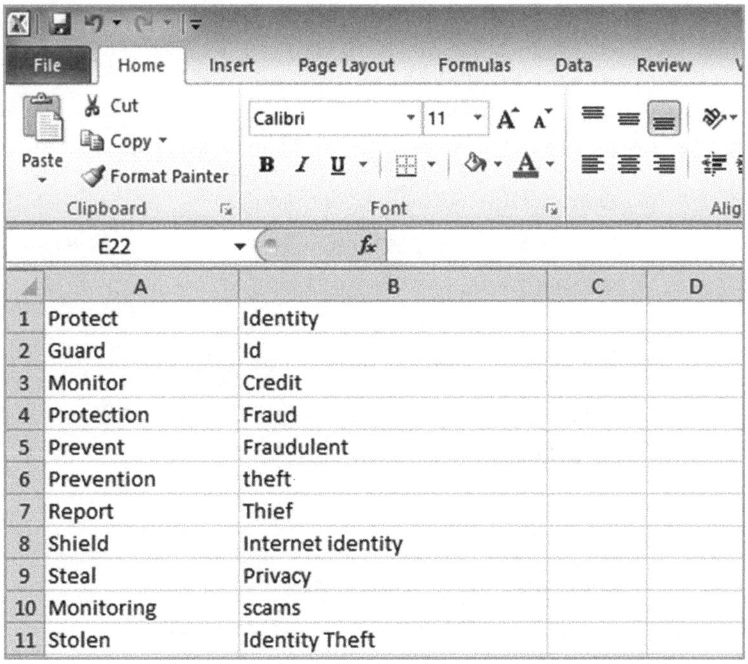

FIGURE 16–12. Paste your synonym lists into an Excel spreadsheet.

Next, you'll create a macro to do all of the work for you. Select the "Developer" menu item and click "Visual Basic." If the Developer tab is not shown, you can enable it. Click the "File" tab. Click "Options" and then "Customize Ribbon." In the "Customize Ribbon" category, in the "Main Tabs" list, select the "Developer" check box and then click "OK." A blank screen should appear. Copy the code in Figure 16–13 on page 120 into this window. If there is already some code in the window, scroll down and paste the code at the end.

When you're done, save the spreadsheet so you don't have to type the code in again.

Finally, run the macro by selecting "Macros" (on the Developer toolbar), then clicking "Run." Note that if you want to save your worksheet, later versions of Excel require you to choose the "Excel Macro-Enabled Workbook" option from the "Save As" dialog. Your new keyword list will appear in the fourth column of the spreadsheet (see Figure 16–14 on page 121).

This step netted me over 260 additional keyword phrases.

```
Sub CreateKeywordPermutations()
  Dim rngL1 As Range
  Dim rngL2 As Range
  Dim rngA As Range
Dim rngB As Range
  Dim rngOutA As Range
  Dim rngOutB As Range
  Set rngL1 = Range("A1", Range("A1").End(xlDown))
  Set rngL2 = Range("B1", Range("B1").End(xlDown))

  Set rngOutA = Range("D1")
  Set rngOutB = Range("D" & (rngL1.Rows.Count *
rngL2.Rows.Count * 2))

  For Each rngA In rngL1.Cells
    For Each rngB In rngL2.Cells
      rngOutA = rngA.Value & " " & rngB.Value
      rngOutB = rngB.Value & " " & rngA.Value
      Set rngOutA = rngOutA.Offset(1, 0)
      Set rngOutB = rngOutB.Offset(-1, 0)
    Next
  Next
End Sub
```

FIGURE 16–13. Type the above code into the Excel macro window.

Step 5: Remove Duplicates

While you have Excel open, you can perform the final step of removing duplicate keywords from your list. Paste your combined keyword list into the first column of a fresh spreadsheet, select the "Data" menu item, and click the "Remove Duplicates" option in the "Data Tools" section.

Excel removed 107 duplicate keywords, leaving a lengthy list of over 1,800 keywords (many of them "shop" and "buy" keywords).

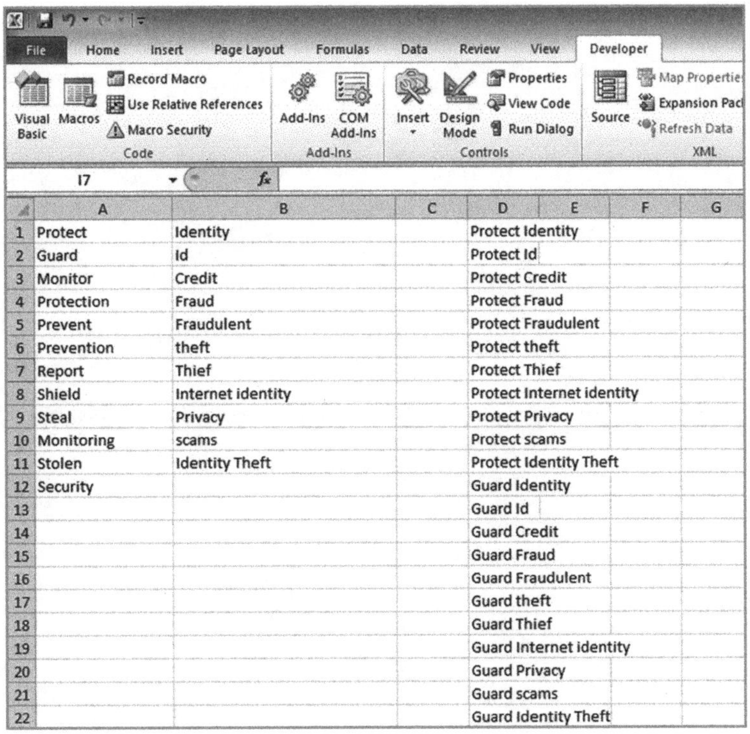

	A	B	C	D	E	F	G
1	Protect	Identity		Protect Identity			
2	Guard	Id		Protect Id			
3	Monitor	Credit		Protect Credit			
4	Protection	Fraud		Protect Fraud			
5	Prevent	Fraudulent		Protect Fraudulent			
6	Prevention	theft		Protect theft			
7	Report	Thief		Protect Thief			
8	Shield	Internet identity		Protect Internet identity			
9	Steal	Privacy		Protect Privacy			
10	Monitoring	scams		Protect scams			
11	Stolen	Identity Theft		Protect Identity Theft			
12	Security			Guard Identity			
13				Guard Id			
14				Guard Credit			
15				Guard Fraud			
16				Guard Fraudulent			
17				Guard theft			
18				Guard Thief			
19				Guard Internet identity			
20				Guard Privacy			
21				Guard scams			
22				Guard Identity Theft			

FIGURE 16–14. Our Excel spreadsheet will automatically calculate all of the keyword combinations for us.

Step 6: Remove Keywords That Are a Poor Match for Your Website

Finally, I recommend at this point that you manually work through the list and remove any keywords that you suspect won't be relevant for your campaign. This will help reduce the amount of work you'll perform later on while organizing your keywords.

In my list, I removed keywords such as "report privacy," "monitor scams," and "stolen thief." If you aren't sure about a phrase, it may help to paste it into a search engine and see what kind of organic search results come up. If they still don't appear relevant to your campaign, the delete the keyword phrase from your list.

SUMMARY

Choosing the keywords you're going to target is probably the most important part of running your search marketing. You should strive to develop a long list of highly specific "shop" and "buy" keywords. The best way to do this is by using a combination of elbow grease and third-party tools.

Chapter 17

How to Plan a Paid Search Campaign

M ake no mistake, the way you structure your campaigns will in no small part influence the amount of traffic you'll be able to drive to your website from paid search.

Several years ago I revamped a PPC campaign for a client using the technique described in this chapter. The client's traffic increased by over 1,000 percent. Eight months later, the client reported traffic had dropped 60 percent but offered no explanation why. I quickly found that they had substituted my carefully constructed campaign with one that had a simpler structure and was "easier to manage."

The client didn't realize that the campaign was created in a particular way to ensure that every important keyword was assigned its own optimized ad. The new campaign architecture didn't make as much allowance for targeting, and the clickthrough rate plummeted as a result. After a few months, the campaign stopped delivering visitors because it had been deemed no longer as relevant as competing campaigns.

Unfortunately, there's a tradeoff between convenience and performance, so you'll need to decide which is more important to you (I hope you will opt for "performance"). However, if you set up your campaign using an organizational scheme such as the one we discuss next, you'll find that you can minimize additional work while maximizing your campaign's traffic-generating potential.

TWO COMMON CAMPAIGN SETUP MISTAKES

There are two primary mistakes people make when setting up new campaigns.

The first of these is using too few ad groups. Ads perform best when they are targeted at a specific keyword phrase or perhaps a small group of closely related keyword phrases. Lumping all of your keywords in too few ad groups means that you'll have too few ads. This makes it virtually impossible to optimize the ad copy beyond a nominal clickthrough rate.

Ad copy optimization is one of the primary efforts you can undertake to beat your competitors, so your campaign should be set up in a way that allows you to tweak ads all the way down to the individual keyword level, if necessary.

The second mistake is failing to group closely related keywords together. This is the opposite end of the spectrum of the first mistake we just mentioned. Sometimes first-time marketers get overzealous and assign every keyword to its own ad group. A typical campaign should have over 1,000 keywords, so this ends up in over 1,000 ad groups. Although this affords a high degree of precision in tuning ads, managing your campaign becomes too cumbersome. In addition, when you fail to group synonymous phrases together, you risk having the search engine serve unwanted ads in place of your carefully chosen ones.

The solution lies somewhere in the middle: Group-related keywords together into a reasonable number of ad groups. Later on, keywords that drive the most traffic or sales can then be broken out into their own separate groups for fine-tuning. For most campaigns, between 20 and 30 ad groups are sufficient.

START BY CATEGORIZING YOUR KEYWORDS

Avoid the temptation of planning a new campaign directly from within the AdWords or Bing interface, because these interfaces are just too cumbersome, and you'll be prone to making mistakes. Instead, plot your campaign structure from within Excel. In this spreadsheet, create the following columns:

- Category
- Keyword
- Estimated traffic
- Browse
- Shop
- Buy
- Landing page idea

Start by using the tools mentioned in the previous chapter ("Step 3: Horizontal and Vertical Expansion Using Third-Party Tools") to build an extensive keyword list. Don't worry about categorizing them or assigning them to behavioral buckets yet. Just capture them in the keyword column.

After collecting an exhaustive list (aim for a minimum of 1,000 keywords), group the related keyword phrases together. Despite repeated attempts by software companies to automate the process, there's no exact science to this. Just group the keywords together into whatever reasonable categories you can think of. Twenty is a nice round number to start with. If you go higher than 50, you'll probably end up spending a lot of time managing groups that may not bring in much traffic.

Next, assign each keyword to one of the three primary behavioral buckets (browse, shop, or buy), and if you've used the brand ladder, include those categories as well (brand, product, problem, and occasion). You may also opt to add the navigational bucket for keywords such as competitors' company names or URLs, but we generally don't recommend advertising on these terms (use your discretion).

Assigning each keyword to one of these categories is a very important step. We are going to use these buckets to split our categories into more targeted ad groups. This will substantially reduce the time needed to make our campaign profitable.

Pay close attention to any keyword in the "browse" bucket. Consider the keyword carefully. Do you really need/want to advertise on this term? The traffic (and costs) will be high, but the conversions and clickthrough rates will be low. However, if you have the budget and a well-developed set of more-specific "shop" and "buy" terms, advertising on these keywords can result in clickthrough rate bonuses on your entire campaign. If you're not sure, then I suggest setting them aside in your initial campaign. You can always add them later.

Finally, if any landing page ideas jump out at you, you should jot them down in the last column (you'll make use of these notes later).

Figure 17–1 on page 126 shows how my spreadsheet looks for my identity theft protection company.

THE ADVANTAGES OF PLANNING AHEAD

Although it may seem like additional work, following this process as described will save you countless hours of effort later on.

If you were to manage each of your keywords individually, you could spend months just getting started, and you would be virtually certain to make many unintentional mistakes and omissions as your campaign evolves over time.

	A	B	C	D	E	F	G
1	Category	Keyword	Est Traffic	Browse	Shop	Buy	Landing Page Idea
2	identity theft	identity theft		x			
3	identity theft solutions	identity theft protection			x		
4	identity theft	online identity		x			
5	identity theft protection	prevent identity theft		x			
6	identity theft solutions	identity theft software			x		
7	identity theft protection	Protect Identity		x			
8	identity theft solutions	Identity theft protection software			x		
9	specific products	lifelock review			x	x	10% coupon page
10	specific products	lifelock coupon				x	10% coupon page
11	specific products	lifelock deal				x	10% coupon page
12	specific products	lifelock special				x	10% coupon page
13	identity theft	Protect Id		x			
14	identity theft	Protect Credit		x			
15	identity theft	Protect Fraud		x			
16	identity theft	Protect Fraudulent		x			
17	theft protection	Protect theft		x			
18	theft protection	Protect Thief		x			
19	identity theft protection	Protect Internet identity			x		
20	privacy protection	Protect Privacy					
21	identity theft protection	Protect scams			x		
22	identity theft protection	Protect Identity Theft		x			
23	identity theft	Guard Identity		x			
24	identity theft	Guard Id		x			
25	identity theft	Guard Credit		x			
26	identity theft	Guard Fraud		x			
27	identity theft	Guard Fraudulent		x			
28	identity theft	Guard theft		x			
29	identity theft	Guard Thief		x			

FIGURE 17–1. This spreadsheet becomes the blueprint for your entire campaign.

On the other hand, if you put all of your terms into a single ad group (a mistake many novice search marketers make), it would be easy to manage, but your ads and landing pages wouldn't be well targeted. Poor targeting results in high CPC prices, and in all likelihood your campaign would soon wind up with low impression share (or worse, killed off entirely by the search engine).

Instead, we work with our keywords in Excel in order to group them into a finite number of targeted categories. These will later manifest as ad groups in your paid search campaign. In my case, I ended up with just 13 initial categories, each consisting of many related keywords. Three of these categories had two keyword types, so I broke them apart and ended up with 16.

You should do the same. After coming up with your initial categories, it's important to subdivide them by browse/shop/buy in order to take advantage of the different dynamics of each keyword type:

- *Browse keywords* are terms that will attract visitors earlier in the sales process. They are likely to generate higher traffic and costs, but the lack of specificity means that we're going to have lower clickthrough and conversion rates. *Identity theft* is a phrase that falls in this category. If we do decide to keep these terms, we don't want to bid very high for them.

- *Shop keywords* are terms that will generate a decent amount of traffic as well, but a good percentage of these people are probably looking for how-to information, reviews, and comparisons. Nevertheless, a good portion of them can be convinced to buy. We'd be willing to pay a little more for these terms and write special ads targeting them. We may even want to experiment with special landing pages. *Identity theft protection* is a good example of this type of keyword.

- *Buy keywords* are the phrases that people enter when they are looking for specific products (*lifelock coupon* and *identity theft protection software* are two examples). While there tends to be lower traffic on these terms, they strongly suggest a near-term purchase. We should be willing to pay a premium for these visitors. We're also willing to write highly targeted ads and even create custom landing pages for individual keywords.

As you can see, we want to spend the most time on the buy keywords, but we don't want to ignore the browse or shop keywords completely. By having a smaller number of groups, it becomes much easier to organize and prioritize our efforts.

What if we tried to get by with just *three* ad groups (one for each keyword type)? In a pinch, we probably could. But some of these terms have different implications. Your landing page and ad copy will probably be completely different for the shop phrases *monitor credit* and *identity theft protection*, even though these terms mean roughly the same thing for many people. As we'll see later, the ads we serve for these phrases will do much better if we tailor them a bit. This is much easier to accomplish if they are in different ad groups.

You now know the secret behind planning a campaign that will scale over time and require a minimum of management overhead. More importantly, the campaigns you

DON'T CREATE ARBITRARY AD GROUPS

How you assign the keywords you choose to ad groups determines your campaign's long-term health. The vast majority of advertisers dump their keywords into arbitrary ad groups, and as a result, their campaigns are quickly throttled into obscurity. Don't be one of them. Instead, organize your keywords within Excel according to category and behavioral bucket. This blueprint will serve as the foundation for your campaign and will allow you to outperform the vast majority of competitors from the very start.

plan using this technique will be far less likely to be throttled into oblivion by the search engines.

Here's a recap of the entire process:

- Create a master list of all keyword candidates in Excel.
- Group related keywords together into named categories.
- Tag each of these phrases with the appropriate keyword type (browse, shop, or buy).

If a category has multiple keyword types, break it out into two or three subcategories so that each contains only a single keyword type.

Cut Campaign Waste with Keyword Matching

Most advertising campaigns contain an enormous amount of waste. With other channels you have to live with unwanted slippage, but not so in search marketing, because of a technique called *keyword matching*.

Keyword matching is an important method of cost control that allows you to refine your ad targeting and improve your returns. It works by eliminating unprofitable traffic from your ads showing up for searches not closely related to your offering.

Mastering this technique offers you some of the best return on time spent. You can audit a typical campaign in under an hour, and you shouldn't need to do it more than once every few months (if that). We've audited our campaigns twice in the past, cutting 70 percent of our spend after the first round and over 60 percent in the second. That's an 88 percent reduction in spend with no loss in sales. Excited yet?

GOOGLE AND BING MATCH TYPES

Broad Match

This is the default match setting. When you enter a keyword phrase in AdWords or Bing Ads without any additional punctuation, your ads will be served for all searches that contain the keywords in your phrase (in any order), as well as any closely related synonyms or plurals.

For instance, if you use broad match on the keyword phrase *plasma television*, your ad will appear when people search for *plasma TV, plasma display, television plasma, plasma televisions*, or even *buy 42-inch plasma televisions*.

We use broad match for most keywords in our campaign. However, it can sometimes generate unwanted clicks, driving up your total cost.

Broad Match Modifier

One issue with broad match is that it will trigger your ads on keywords that are closely related to your targeted terms. If you are targeting "plasma television" and your ad triggers on "plasma tv," this may not be a problem. On the other hand, let's say you targeted the phrase, "Maui hotels." It could be problematic if your ad is inadvertently triggered for the related phrase, "Maui rentals" (this could refer to jet skis or vacation rental homes).

You can fine-tune broad match targeting using a "broad match modifier." This option allows you to suppress certain words from broad matching while still allowing you to take advantage of it for the rest of the phrase. In our example above, we could make sure that our ads won't be triggered for "Maui rentals" by targeting the phrase "Maui +hotels". With this modifier in place, the word "hotels" must be in the query in order for your ads to be eligible to be served.

Phrase Match

A useful technique for refining your targeting is to incorporate *phrase match*. Do this by surrounding your keyword phrase in quotes.

Your ads will then appear for searches that contain your target keyword. Additional keywords may appear before or after, but your exact phrase must appear in the search query.

For instance, if you use phrase match on "plasma television" (with quotes), your ads will appear for *buy plasma television* but not for *plasma 42" television*.

Phrase matching results in less traffic than broad matching, but the clickthrough (and sometimes conversion) rate is usually higher.

Exact Match

Another important match type is exact match. To enable exact matching for a keyword, enclose it in square brackets, e.g., [*plasma television*].

Your ads will then appear only when people type your exact phrase. Plurals, synonyms, or additional words will not trigger your ads.

The volume with this match type will be the lowest, but the clickthrough rates can be absolutely astounding (15 percent is not unusual). If you utilize exact matching with a "superconverter" keyword (see Chapter 20) and some highly tuned ad copy, the result can often drive the majority of your search revenues.

Negative Match

This match type is used when you have a specific word you know you want to filter out. For instance, we broad match the phrase "keyword" in our advertising. This ensures that we show up when people search on phrases such as "keywords for dentists."

However, it turns out that that this phrase drives the majority of its traffic from programmers looking for lists of reserved keywords—definitely not our target market. We found that we could filter out most of this traffic by negative matching the term *java* (a programming language).

To do this, you simply need to precede the unwanted term with a negative sign and add it to your campaign or ad group. In our case, it looks like this: "-java" (without quotes).

Virtually every campaign can see a dramatic improvement in results by using this technique.

ADVANCED NEGATIVE MATCHING

by Matt Van Wagner of Find Me Faster (www.FindMeFaster.com)

Boxing In, Boxing Out

In the NBA, great centers know that boxing out and boxing in under the boards are key to winning games. One of my favorite tactics in PPC tactics is to use negative keywords both to box out ad impressions and unwanted clicks and to box in clicks so that the right ads get shown.

Boxing Out

Much has already been written about using negatives to keep your ads from showing for keywords that are not related to your searches. By reducing ad impressions, you keep your CTRs up, which improves your quality score and which keeps your ad spend under control by reducing unproductive clicks.

ADVANCED NEGATIVE MATCHING, CONTINUED

Boxing In

A second, less used application for negative keywords is boxing in clicks to make sure that only the right keyword matches to a specific search query.

It is very common that an AdWords account has closely related keywords across multiple ad groups, all of which could qualify for the ad auction for a single search query. When that happens, these keywords compete against each other for placement in Ad Rank auction, and unless you use negative keywords to prevent a match, the search engines can pick the keyword they like best, which could simply be the one with the highest bid and not necessarily the one you'd prefer to present on that search query.

In this case, you can use negative keywords to box in the choice of keywords to the one you want.

Let's say you have three ad groups, each with one broad match keyword, shown in Figure 18–1.

Ad Group	Keyword
Stone	Stone siding
Rock	Rock siding
Faux stone	Faux stone siding

FIGURE 18–1. Example ad groups.

On the user query, "fake stone siding," any of these three keywords may trigger ads. By adding in negatives, you can force the logic so that only one match can be made.

Ad Group	Keyword
Stone	Stone siding
	–faux
	–fake
Rock	Rock siding
	–stone
Faux stone	Faux stone siding

FIGURE 18–2.

ADVANCED NEGATIVE MATCHING, CONTINUED

Instead of three possible matches, Google now only has one, which is the one we forced. Boxing in like this lets you control the ad, and thereby tailor your bids, ad copy, and landing pages to your best advantage, and augments your broad, phrase, and exact match tactics.

Negative Exact Match

Years ago, I discovered a technique that even my Google AdWords rep didn't know about—the negative exact match.

We discovered that over 99 percent of the conversions from the term *keyword* came only when there was another word in the search phrase. We wanted to see what would happen if we stopped advertising on the phrase *keyword* but continued advertising on longer search phrases containing that word.

We found that we were able to do this by adding the term -[*keyword*] to our campaign. The minus sign indicates a negative match while the square brackets indicate exact matching. Combining the two prevents our ads from showing up when people search on the exact phrase, "keyword."

The next day, our ad spend dropped by 50 percent while sales stayed strong. This is a powerful technique I advise everyone to explore.

WHICH MATCH TYPES SHOULD YOU USE?

As you progress through the match types from least to most restrictive (e.g., broad, to phrase, to exact), an interesting thing happens. Although you'll receive less traffic, your clickthrough rate will increase dramatically (your conversion rates may also increase if you are using a well-targeted landing page).

This can lead to confusion, and newcomers to search marketing sometimes try to guess which of the match types they should be using. Fortunately, there's no need to choose. Not only can you use all three, you should.

So instead of just entering *Las Vegas vacations* into your PPC campaign, you'll enter the same keyword three times:

- Las Vegas vacations (broad)
- "Las Vegas vacations" (phrase)
- [Las Vegas vacations] (exact)

When you specify all three match types, the search engines will automatically choose the best one. This will allow you to maximize both your search volume and your clickthrough rates.

A Simple Refinement to Your Spreadsheet That Will Save You Hours of Work

In the previous chapter, we created a spreadsheet with seven columns. We'll now add two more columns to automatically add the brackets and quotes around your base keywords. This will save you the time of manually retyping each keyword three times.

Here's what you need to do:

- Insert two new columns to the right of the "Keyword" column
- Name the first of these columns, "Phrase Match." Enter the following formula into cell C2 (Note that the four quotation marks in a row are intentional):
- =CONCATENATE("""",B2,"""")
- Name the second of these columns "Exact Match." Enter the following formula into cell D2:
- =CONCATENATE("[",B2,"]")
- Select the cells C2 and D2 and copy them down to the end of your spreadsheet. The easiest way to do this is to double-click the tiny black square at the lower right of your selection. Another way to do it is to press CTRL-C to copy the selection, select the remaining cells in the columns, and then pressing CTRL-V to paste them.

My keyword spreadsheet now looks like Figure 18–3.

	A	B	C	D	E	F	G	H	I
1	Category	Keyword (Broad Match)	Phrase Match	Exact Match	Est Traffic	Browse	Shop	Buy	Landing Page Idea
2	identity monitoring	Monitor Identity	"Monitor Identity"	[Monitor Identity]			x		
3	identity monitoring	Monitor Id	"Monitor Id"	[Monitor Id]			x		
4	identity monitoring	Monitor Credit	"Monitor Credit"	[Monitor Credit]			x		
5	identity monitoring	Monitor Fraud	"Monitor Fraud"	[Monitor Fraud]			x		
6	identity monitoring	Monitor Fraudulent	"Monitor Fraudulent"	[Monitor Fraudulent]			x		
7	identity monitoring	Monitor theft	"Monitor theft"	[Monitor theft]			x		
8	identity monitoring	Monitor Thief	"Monitor Thief"	[Monitor Thief]			x		
9	identity theft	identity theft	"identity theft"	[identity theft]		x			
10	identity theft	online identity	"online identity"	[online identity]		x			
11	identity theft	Protect Id	"Protect Id"	[Protect Id]		x			
12	identity theft	Protect Credit	"Protect Credit"	[Protect Credit]		x			
13	identity theft	Protect Fraud	"Protect Fraud"	[Protect Fraud]		x			
14	identity theft	Protect Fraudulent	"Protect Fraudulent"	[Protect Fraudulent]		x			
15	identity theft	Guard Identity	"Guard Identity"	[Guard Identity]		x			
16	identity theft	Guard Id	"Guard Id"	[Guard Id]		x			
17	identity theft	Guard Credit	"Guard Credit"	[Guard Credit]		x			
18	identity theft	Guard Fraud	"Guard Fraud"	[Guard Fraud]		x			
19	identity theft	Guard Fraudulent	"Guard Fraudulent"	[Guard Fraudulent]		x			
20	identity theft	Guard theft	"Guard theft"	[Guard theft]		x			
21	identity theft	Guard Thief	"Guard Thief"	[Guard Thief]		x			

FIGURE 18–3. The keyword worksheet now contains two additional columns with the phrase and exact match keywords.

Keyword matching is a powerful technique you can use to eliminate unwanted impressions and clicks and thus reduce your costs. Utilize all of the matching options at your disposal to eliminate bad traffic and maximize those clicks that have the highest chance of converting to a sale.

Chapter 19

Create Your Ad Groups

You're finally ready to set up your campaign! Create your ad groups within the Google AdWords or Bing Ads interface (or better yet, use the desktop editors that both engines have made available; see the sidebar, "Use a Desktop Editor to Manage Your Campaigns"). Create one group for each unique combination of category and browse/shop/buy bucket. If you decide to skip the browse keywords for now, that's one-third less work you'll need to do.

Figure 19-1 shows some ad groups I created for the identity protection campaign. Note that I've appended the keyword type (browse/shop/buy) to the name of each group. While you don't *have* to do this, I find that it makes it easier to later recall my original thought process while managing my campaign later on.

Identity Monitoring—Shop
Identity Theft—Browse
Identity Theft Protection—Browse
Identity Theft Protection—Shop
Identity Theft Solutions—Buy
Privacy Protection—Browse

FIGURE 19-1. Your completed spreadsheet becomes the basis for your ad groups.

WHAT ABOUT AD COPY?

If you're using the AdWords or Bing Ads reporting interface to enter your ad groups, it will ask you to enter ad copy. For now, just enter some placeholder ad copy so you can complete the process and get your campaign set up.

If you are in a hurry to get your campaign started, you can begin with some generic ad copy. However, I strongly recommend first reading over the later chapters on writing targeted ads and at least starting off with reasonably targeted ad copy. The first two weeks of your campaign are very important because it's during this time that your campaign will be benchmarked against the competition. Achieving decent clickthrough rates early on will result in higher quality scores later. This in turn will translate to more traffic at a cheaper average cost-per-click.

Your Campaign Will Continue to Evolve Over Time

Realize from the beginning that your work doesn't stop here. By starting with a blueprint, you've cut months of work from your learning curve (and have likely saved yourself the extra work of having to later start your campaign over from scratch as it continues to grow).

However, over the next several months you'll likely discover new keywords, better ad copy, and breakthrough landing pages. You'll need to make extensive changes to your campaign structure to accommodate these new discoveries.

The most common situation you'll face is that your initial guesses on how to properly group related keywords together into ad groups were way off. You'll handle this with a technique called "peel 'n' stick."

USE A DESKTOP EDITOR TO MANAGE YOUR CAMPAIGNS

Setting up new campaigns in the Google AdWords or Bing Ads interface is a slow, tedious process. I prefer to use the desk editors provided by these engines to manage my campaigns (both are free). Not only are these tools faster, you don't have to specify ad copy when creating your groups.

At the time of this writing, these tools can be found at:

Google AdWords Editor: http://www.google.com/intl/en/adwordseditor/

Bing Ads Editor: http://advertise.bingads.microsoft.com/en-us/bingads-editor

The "Peel 'n' Stick" Technique Explained

Bryan Todd, Co-author, *Ultimate Guide to Google AdWords*
www.adwordsbook.com

Learn more about Bryan's consulting services at
www.PerryMarshall.com/Bryan

Peel 'n' stick is the magic fundamental key to everything Google and, to be frank, all things internet. It's as basic to AdWords as dribbling and shooting are to basketball, as "buy low, sell high" is to trading, as middle C is to playing the piano. It's a trusted friend, a familiar way of life to anyone, anywhere, who makes any living at all with pay-per-click.

Peel 'n' stick is, very simply, peeling an important keyword out of an ad group and sticking it into another (or a new) ad group with a pair of ads better matched for it.

It's what you do when you want a higher clickthrough rate and lower costs.

It's how you keep your message laser-targeted to every person who sees your ad and every person who comes through your sales funnel.

Peel 'n' stick is first about ads and keywords. But it can also be about ads and domains. Or about keywords and landing pages. More on that soon.

Some weeks ago I went online looking for cycling jerseys. On summer evenings I practically live on my bicycle, and I prefer riding the hour or two around dusk. So I needed a jersey that was brightly colored to make me visible to evening traffic. And the style had to fit my taste.

So I went searching on Google, hoping to find a series of sites that gave me a nice array I could choose from. My keyword? *Cycling jerseys.* Clear and simple.

I was shocked at what I found—or rather, didn't find. One ad announced "sporting gear." Another, "cycling shoes." Still another, "athletic jerseys." And another, "cycling gear." (Promising though it seemed at first, that one took me to a page about helmets, gloves, shorts, and shoe straps. No jerseys.)

One solitary ad at the very top offered "cycling jerseys." So it got my click, and I stayed.

It's worth noting that Google put that ad up top, front and center. Its performance over time in earning clicks had clearly told Google that it was relevant. The perfect match for the perfect keyword. Some smart advertiser had used peel 'n' stick the right way.

So Google rewarded the person by sticking their ad at the top (and they most likely gave them lower click prices as well—part of the benefit of a high quality score.)

Peel 'n' stick is a process, not an event. You first turn on your traffic and then do peel 'n' stick over time as you watch and see which keywords work for you and which ones yet don't.

The 95/5 rule will instantly take over once your traffic is running: Ninety-five percent of your impressions and clicks will come from just 5 percent of your keywords. So at first peel 'n' stick is just for that top 5 percent—the words that matter most.

In any ad group there are keywords that belong and keywords that don't. Some are merely mismatches for the ads you've got and will do far better in another ad group with ads of their own. Others are a waste of time and money and bring impressions with no clicks or clicks with no sales, and you're best to just get rid of them.

Here's an ad we ran back when we opened our very first Google account:

Prospecting Stinks
Telemarketing Annoys People
Guerrilla Marketing is King
www.PerryMarshall.com

FIGURE 19–2.

And here are some of the keywords we tried with it:

		Keyword	Status	Max. CPC	Clicks	Impr. ↓	CTR ⑦
		Total - all keywords			597	99,854	0.60%
	●	prospecting	Eligible	$0.40	214	20,575	1.04%
	✖	telemarketing	Deleted	$0.00	85	14,715	0.58%
	✖	sales training	Deleted	$0.00	26	7,447	0.35%
	✖	telemarketers	Deleted	$0.00	37	6,492	0.57%
	✖	marketing	Deleted	$0.00	23	5,023	0.46%

FIGURE 19–3.

You can see how many we deleted from the ad group. And you can see why: They're not used in the ad, and they're getting CTRs of far below 1.0 percent. They got peeled and stuck, so now they're in other ad groups with better ads, getting far more clicks.

What's left are keywords that *are* used in the ad in some form and which get CTRs well above 1.0 percent as in Figure 19–4 on page 141.

(Notice the keywords lower down the resulting list. Some of them don't belong, but they don't have enough impressions to matter. So we didn't bother.)

		Keyword	Status	Max. CPC	Clicks	Impr. ↓	CTR (?)
		Total - all keywords			597	99,854	0.60%
	●	prospecting	Eligible	$0.40	214	20,575	1.04%
	●	sales prospecting	Eligible First page bid estimate: $1.25	$0.45	7	199	3.52%
	●	prospect list	Eligible First page bid estimate: $3.00	$0.45	6	112	5.36%
	●	prospecting letter	Eligible	$0.45	1	89	1.12%
	●	business prospect	Eligible	$0.45	0	56	0.00%
	●	sale prospecting	Eligible	$0.45	0	18	0.00%
	●	prospecting system	Eligible First page bid estimate: $0.55	$0.45	0	18	0.00%
	●	find prospect	Eligible	$0.45	0	13	0.00%
	●	prospecting list	Eligible First page bid	$0.45	0	11	0.00%

FIGURE 19–4.

Do this right, and your CTR will go up. Your quality score will go up. Your per-click cost will go down. And Google will serve your ads more often.

Once you've done this you may find that even in your new ad groups there are *still* keywords that could use peel 'n' stick even further. I work with clients all the time for whom this is the case. Especially when they're just getting started out. They're often surprised at my suggestion.

"You mean, do this even further?"

Yes, my friend, do this even further still. Your job is never completely done. In our example above, there are a couple of terms that I bet we could write even better ads for, and get better CTRs on, such as *prospect list* or *prospecting letter*. So those are next up for testing.

When Do I Do Peel 'n' Stick?

Peel 'n' stick is for keywords that meet three criteria:

1. They get a high enough volume of impressions for it to matter.
2. They're getting a much lower CTR than they ought to be (especially if the CTR is significantly below 1.0 percent).
3. You're convinced that the right ad match will make all the difference.

How Can I Make Peel 'n' Stick Work Best for Me?

The easiest, quickest application of peel 'n' stick is to write an ad that uses your keyword in the headline. Of course, that can happen only if your keywords are grouped together as tightly as possible. Doing that will almost instantly increase your quality score.

But peel 'n' stick is not just about echoing keywords in headlines. It's about saying to your prospect what he's really thinking, which changes from keyword to keyword. Over time, you can get to know some of your keywords so well that you'll know exactly what lines two and three need to say for *this* keyword rather than for that *other* keyword over there, above and beyond what you merely say in the headline of the ad.

Let's say you were bidding on *lose 10 pounds* and *lose 10 pounds fast*. Both keywords were in the same ad group, but you did your homework and discovered that the latter searchers were largely people planning on an upcoming class reunion. You would do peel 'n' stick on the second keyword and write an ad that said,

---

Lose 10 Pounds Fast
Fit into those new clothes and
Look great at that reunion.
www.XYZWeightLoss.com

FIGURE 19–5.

Doing It Everywhere

And the magic of peel 'n' stick is that it applies everywhere. You can peel 'n' stick keywords with new ads. You can do peel 'n' stick with landing pages and start creating ad groups that send traffic to pages that are laser-targeted just for specific high-traffic keywords in your list.

Eventually, as you get into doing placement targeting as well, you'll discover that peeling and sticking placements (i.e., domain names and URLs) is virtually no different than with keywords.

And creating separate content versus search campaigns is yet another form of peel 'n' stick. Doing so gives you separate data. And as you test new ads and ideas you discover over time that "what works" slowly evolves in a different direction on the content network than on Google search.

With peel 'n' stick, what your customers are searching for they find and find instantly. That makes the cash register ring. It makes Google happy. Most importantly, it makes your customer happy.

I should know. I got my cycling jersey. If it weren't for peel 'n' stick I might still be looking.

Chapter 20

The Art and Science of Setting Bids

Your bid, or "maximum CPC," is the highest amount that you're *willing* to pay for each visitor who clicks on your ads. Take care not to confuse it with average CPC—the *actual* price you pay for each visitor (always less than your bid).

After ad copy and landing page optimization (discussed in depth in following chapters), you'll spend most of your time managing bids. It's vital that you maintain a regular review schedule because once you've eliminated the cap on your campaign budget (Chapter 25), your ad spend will vary based on available traffic. Over the course of any given month, you can expect your campaign costs to be stable. But periods of seasonality or growing demand can cause your spend to increase beyond expectations. Reviewing your campaign statistics on at least a weekly basis will help to prevent any unpleasant surprise bills at the end of the month.

However, if there's one thing more important than staying within budget, it's turning a profit. And it's almost certain your campaign will leak money if you set bids without knowing exactly what you are doing.

WHAT ABOUT BIDDING TOOLS?

There are web-based software packages that can set your bids automatically. However, I don't recommend the use of these tools. If you have a ten-thousand-keyword portfolio, it may be necessary to use bidding software to preserve your sanity. But I haven't seen any that can compete head-to-head against a skilled paid search manager and win.

Some tools do an OK job of setting reasonable bids for high-traffic browse keywords, but most shop and buy keywords defy analysis. It will take a long time to calculate a statistically sound bid price for a keyword earning just a few dozen clicks a month. By then the competitive landscape may have changed. Your bid has gone stale.

Seasonality is another problem, particularly in retail sales. In this category, good ads can turn into mediocre ones practically overnight, such as in August (back to school), September (beginning of the holiday season), and January (end of the holiday season).

Bid-management tools making decisions based on old data will be hopelessly clueless at these times.

However, if you have the budget, I do recommend the use of third-party reporting tools such as Acquisio, Marin, or Kenshoo. These tools can bring a great deal of insight to the table, and they are helpful for bringing all of your paid search statistics together into a single dashboard. All three include bid-management functionality, but even so, I would manually manage the bids for my most important keywords.

FIGURING OUT HOW MUCH TO BID

In theory, setting your bids should be quite simple. Start by putting some tracking in place to tell you how much revenue you've made from each keyword. Then set your bids low, and increase them until you start losing money. Back them down a little bit, and you're done.

If only it were that simple.

You see, your bid is just a single lever on a complicated black box made up of many interconnected moving parts. You might have heard it referred to by the mysterious names, *the algorithm* or *the auction.*

The auction determines the keywords for which your ads appear, when they appear, where on the page they appear, and how frequently they appear, or in other words, how much traffic/revenue/profits you will earn from your campaign.

Your competitors are also pushing and pulling at the same black box trying to maximize their output. People are another component as well: What they do after they enter a search phrase changes the dynamic of the auction. And let's not forget that there's always someone from the search engine themselves monkeying around in there somewhere.

How does it work? Well, the truth is that few people know *precisely* how it works. The search engines give some tantalizing clues. And through careful observation, we've learned about some of the cause-and-effect relationships. But you'll stay humble if you accept that it's a basically a black box.

Sometimes the actions you take will have predictable consequences. For instance, you probably know that if you increase your bid, your ads will appear higher on the search results page.

But other relationships are less obvious. Many paid search managers are unaware that if your competitors' quality scores are high enough, it can make it difficult for your ads to ever appear in the premium positions, even if you're willing to outbid them.

And still other dynamics are downright mysterious and practically unknown (outside of the circle of this book's readers, that is). In certain cases, if you increase your bids (and thus "graduate" from an easy spot of the auction to a harder one), your ads may stop appearing. In these situations, the only solution is to *lower* your bids in order to get the traffic to start flowing again.

The end outcome of this interplay of relationships determines whether your ad is shown and the price you pay and is calculate instantaneously by the search engine each time a visitor enters a search query you've targeted. To think that a single factor—even one as important as maximum bid price—will decide your paid search success is naïve, indeed.

Cause	Effect
Your bid	Average position
	Coverage
Your ad quality	Average position
	Coverage
	Ability to move into premium positions
Your average revenue per visitor	Maximum bid
	Optimal average position
Competitors' ad quality	Average CPC
	Coverage
	Average position
	Ability to move into premium positions
Competitors' bid	Average CPC
Competitors' average revenue per visitor	Average CPC
	Conversion rate
	Slope of the bid curve
Number of competitors	Slope of the bid curve
	Difficulty of ad copy optimization
Willingness of searchers to click ads	Number of ads shown

FIGURE 20–1. A few of the cause-effect relationships affecting the outcome of the auction.

In the previous edition of this book, I outlined a simple technique that you could use to set your bids. This method relied on a simple upward-sloping CPC curve (see Chapter 11). Unfortunately, paid search has gotten a lot more competitive over the past several years, and the simple upward-sloping bid curve is a lot harder to come by these days. If you want to succeed, you'll need a more robust technique. Still, it's a good place to start, so let's get to it.

UPWARD-SLOPING CPC CURVES

As described in Chapter 11, upward-sloping bid curves exhibit higher CPCs as average position increases. In other words, ads near the top of the page are more expensive. This was pretty typical a few years ago but has become increasingly rare.

The chart in Figure 20–2 shows a hypothetical upward-sloping CPC curve. The bottom axis indicates the position; ads shown on the bottom of the search results page are depicted to the left while premium ads are shown on the right.

Notice how both the expected number of clicks as well as the average CPC increase consistently with each position. Multiplying these two figures together gives the estimated spend for each position, which increases exponentially for ads higher on the page.

Let's pretend you are bidding on this keyword phrase. Let's also assume that your conversion rate is 0.60 percent and your average order size is $199. By multiplying the number of clicks for each position by these two figures, we can estimate our revenue and profit. This is illustrated in the table (Figure 20–3) and chart (Figure 20–4).

As you can see, we turn a very small profit at the bottom of the page. It peaks at position 4, and as we increase our bids and average ad position beyond this point, we

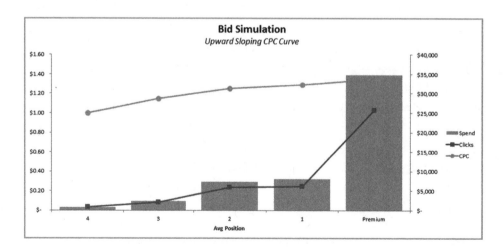

FIGURE 20–2. An example of an upward-sloping CPC curve.

Position	Spend	Clicks	CPC	Revenue	Profit
Premium	$ 34,830	25,800	$ 1.35	$ 30,805	$ (4,025)
1	$ 7,998	6,200	$ 1.29	$ 7,403	$ (595)
2	$ 7,375	5,900	$ 1.25	$ 7,045	$ (330)
3	$ 2,415	2,100	$ 1.15	$ 2,507	$ 92
4	$ 800	800	$ 1.00	$ 955	$ 155

FIGURE 20–3. Revenue and profit forecast for the upward-sloping CPC curve.

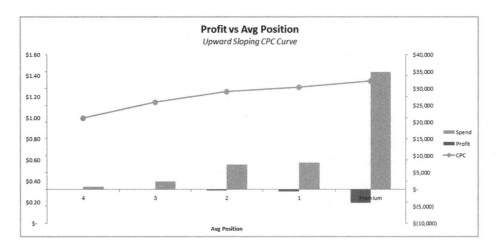

FIGURE 20–4. Spend and profit chart.

lose money. This model is pretty intuitive; as you pay more for each click, your profit declines. Pay too much, and you actually lose money.

Simple? Yes. Common? Not at all.

Upward-sloping CPC curves were commonplace a few years ago, and it's why so many books and guides recommend starting with a low bid and increasing until you get to positions 3 to 5 (depending on the source). However, I don't remember the last time I've seen an upward-sloping CPC curve. I consider it no more than a learning tool these days. But if you find one, just start bidding low and work your way up while keeping coverage at 90 percent or higher.

DOWNWARD-SLOPING CPC CURVES

Let's now consider the opposite scenario, a downward-sloping CPC curve, as shown in Figure 20–5.

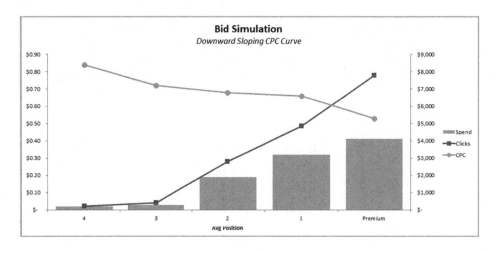

FIGURE 20–5. Downward-sloping CPC curve.

These keywords exhibit lower CPCs in conjunction with higher placements! This typically arises in two situations.

Branded search phrases such as Netflix *or* Swiffer. The advertiser appearing in the premium position is usually the brand owner and pays a very low CPC, while advertisers appearing in lower positions are often competitors who pay a much higher CPC. This is a direct result of their relative quality scores. Think about it: If you type *Walmart* into a search engine, are you more likely to click the ad for www.walmart.com or some other competitor?

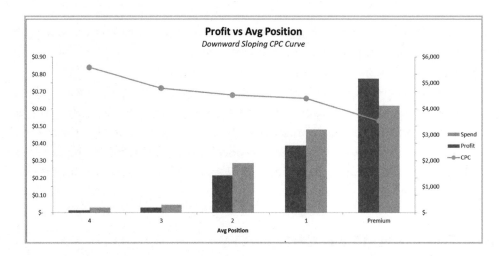

FIGURE 20–6. Spend and profit chart for the hypothetical downward sloping CPC curve.

Earned search phrases in which searchers are predisposed toward a small set of advertisers. A current example is the phrase "ipad 3," which is dominated by top electronics retailers such as Best Buy, Walmart, and Amazon.

As far as bidding goes, the strategy is pretty simple. You simply need to bid high enough to reach the first page of results. From there it's an optimization game. Improving your ad copy should push your ads up higher. This will lower your average CPC and increase your profit.

In practice, however, it's often difficult to get good placement on these terms. Ad copy is typically not the bottleneck; brand recognition is. If more searchers are clicking on a competitor's ads more than yours because they recognize their name, nothing short of an expensive brand-awareness campaign is going to help. Your ad will probably sit on the bottom of the page and show up only a small percentage of the time. If you've ever tried to bid on a competitor's brand name, then you probably know what I'm talking about.

If you suspect that you're advertising on a keyword like this, be sure to monitor your coverage. If it remains well below 90 percent despite your best efforts, you're probably better off deleting the keyword phrase from your account.

THE MOST IMPORTANT CONCEPT IN THIS BOOK

The two previous examples were simple examples. The following section will show you how to manage bids in the real world. But before we get on with that, we must cover an important concept. In fact, it is my opinion that understanding of this technique is the single most important thing that separates a world-class paid search manager from a so-so one.

From previous chapters, we know:

- As your maximum bid increases, the average position of your ads increases.
- Your quality score *relative to your competitors'* determines the actual CPC you pay.
- Your quality score *relative to your competitors'* determines your coverage (e.g., the amount of impressions your ads receive).
- Your quality score is compared to competitors appearing at about the same average position as you (quality score normalization).

Consider what happens if your ad is competing at the bottom of the page against a competitor who has a lower quality score than you, as in Figure 20–7 on page 150.

Your quality score is higher so you would expect the following:

- Your ads would appear more frequently than your competitor's (higher coverage).
- You would pay a lower CPC for the same placement than your competitor.

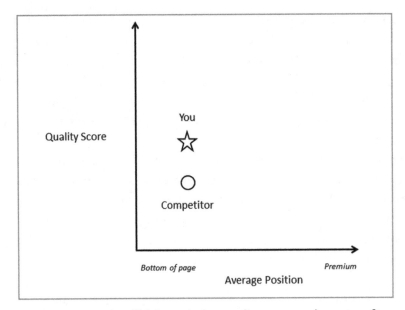

FIGURE 20–7. Impact of higher relative quality score at bottom of page.

Continuing on with the example, you now decide that you would like to improve your placement and get more traffic. For most keywords, advertisers appearing more prominently will have higher quality scores. The chart in Figure 20–8 shows such a keyword.

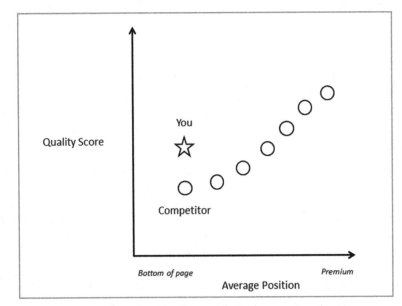

FIGURE 20–8. Quality Scores for other competitors.

You increase your maximum bid and now your ad begins to appear a few positions higher.

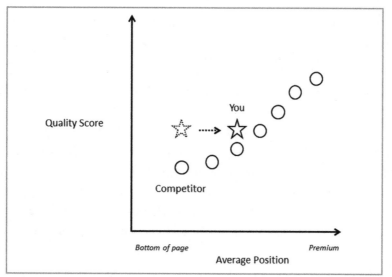

FIGURE 20–9. Relative quality score after increasing maximum bid.

Your quality score is still higher than the competitor appearing in the same position, so once again you would expect your ad to appear more frequently and to pay a lower average CPC.

But what happens if you decide to increase your maximum bid even further? See Figure 20–10.

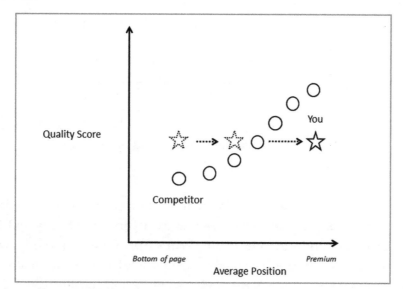

FIGURE 20–10. Relative quality score after increasing maximum bid even further.

Now you're at a significant quality score disadvantage to the competitors appearing near you. So you would now expect a different outcome:

- Your ads would appear less frequently than the other advertisers' (lower coverage).
- You should pay a higher CPC than the other advertisers.

This explains why the naïve approach of simply increasing bid prices fails so miserably in most cases. It fails because it doesn't take into account the effect of other advertisers' combined quality scores.

The chart in Figure 20–11 illustrates the same example a bit differently. In this chart, I've replaced the Y-axis (quality score) with coverage. In the first case, where we had a large quality score advantage, our ads appeared 100 percent of the time. In the second case, the quality score advantage was a bit smaller, and our ads appeared just 90 percent of the time. And finally, in the third case, we suffered from a large quality score disadvantage, and our ads captured just a fraction of the available impressions.

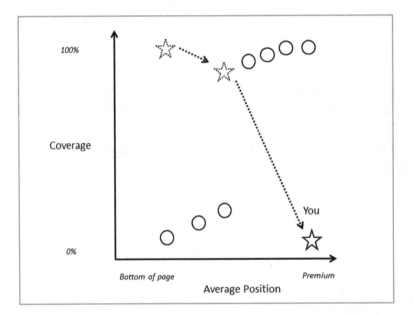

FIGURE 20–11. Impact of increased bid on coverage.

If this were to happen in a real-world situation, the solution would be to **first back down our bids to improve our coverage and then perform ad copy and landing page optimization to improve our quality score**. After we saw some improvements, we could try again. We first touched on this example in Chapter 9 but couldn't explain it fully until after the discussion of the mechanics of CPC and quality score.

IRREGULAR CPC CURVES

In practice, most CPC curves are irregular—mostly up or mostly down, with peaks or valleys in the middle or ends. A good example is the keyword *"iphone 5"* as it appeared in an AdGooroo SEM Insight report in June 2013. As expected, clicks increase with higher positions. But note how the CPC curve dips twice: once at positions 4 and 5 and again at the premium position.

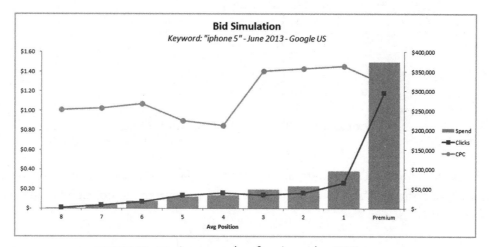

FIGURE 20–12. An example of an irregular CPC curve.

Position	Spend	Clicks	CPC
Premium	$ 374,544	294,799	$ 1.27
1	$ 95,121	65,324	$ 1.46
2	$ 56,670	39,630	$ 1.43
3	$ 48,658	34,601	$ 1.41
4	$ 33,218	39,268	$ 0.85
5	$ 29,812	33,253	$ 0.90
6	$ 18,790	17,551	$ 1.07
7	$ 8,967	8,741	$ 1.03
8	$ 2,120	2,101	$ 1.01

FIGURE 20–13. Data for the chart in Figure 20–12.

Now let's pretend you own a retail store selling iPhones, and you are bidding on this keyword phrase. As before, we'll assume that your conversion rate is 0.60 percent and your average order size is $199. By multiplying the number of clicks for each position by these two figures, we can estimate our revenue and profit. This is shown in the chart in Figure 20–14.

Position	Spend	Clicks	CPC	Revenue	Profit			
Premium	$ 374,544	294,799	$ 1.27	$ 351,990	$ (22,554)	Conversion Rate		0.60%
1	$ 95,121	65,324	$ 1.46	$ 77,997	$ (17,124)	Average Order Size	$	199
2	$ 56,670	39,630	$ 1.43	$ 47,318	$ (9,352)	Revenue per click	$	1.19
3	$ 48,658	34,601	$ 1.41	$ 41,314	$ (7,344)			
4	$ 33,218	39,268	$ 0.85	$ 46,886	$ 13,668			
5	$ 29,812	33,253	$ 0.90	$ 39,704	$ 9,892			
6	$ 18,790	17,551	$ 1.07	$ 20,956	$ 2,166			
7	$ 8,967	8,741	$ 1.03	$ 10,437	$ 1,470			
8	$ 2,120	2,101	$ 1.01	$ 2,509	$ 389			

FIGURE 20–14. Projected revenue and profit.

As you can see, we turn a very small profit at the bottom of the search results page. It peaks at position 4, and as we increase our bids and average ad position beyond this point, we lose money.

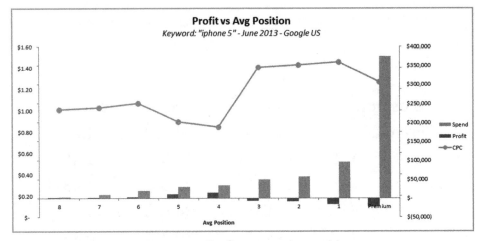

FIGURE 20–15. Profit vs. average position.

Many people might guess at a starting bid. But what's a good guess: $0.50, $1.00, or $5.00?

A more experienced search marketer might consult the AdWords Keyword Tool. At the time the above chart was created, it reported an average CPC of $1.53 for this keyword phrase. We're at least in the ballpark. But notice that this value is a bit higher than the highest price any other advertiser is paying. If you were to bid this amount, your ads would initially appear near the top of the page. Assuming that you haven't had the opportunity to optimize your ad copy and landing page yet, your coverage would be expected to be very low, your quality score will be lower than these established competitors, and you'll capture very few impressions.

So in this particular case, it would be wise to start with a lower bid than suggested by the keyword tool, but not too low. Around $1.00 seems about right. This would land you at the lower half of the page. You could then gradually increase your bids while taking care to monitor coverage to keep it at least at 90 percent. Once coverage drops below 90 percent, you'll need to begin optimizing.

So we bid $1.00, and our ads now appear around position 7. But every time we increase our bid, our coverage drops. What would happen if we optimize our ad copy? Our ad would most likely increase in position, and there would be a reduction in CPC. Note that this is precisely what just about everyone even remotely familiar with AdWords would expect.

What they might not expect is that this would get us only a few positions before we hit a wall. You can see this in Figure 20–15, where the average CPC increases dramatically from position 4 ($0.85) to position 3 ($1.41). Optimization fails to increase our average position beyond a certain point, so now we must again increase our bids in accordance with the current auction dynamics. However, if we do that, we're now going to start bleeding money.

What's the next lever at our disposal? That's right: landing page optimization. By increasing either our average order size (usually pretty difficult) or our conversion rate (usually pretty easy), we can completely change the dynamics of the auction and give ourselves the opportunity to profitably show our ads above position 4.

Let's assume that we work with the web team and manage to increase our landing page conversion rate from 0.60 percent to 0.75 percent (this is a modest and reasonable increase, assuming you haven't performed any previous optimization). Here's what our P&L looks like now.

Position	Spend	Clicks	CPC	Revenue	Profit			
Premium	$ 374,544	294,799	$ 1.27	$ 439,988	$ 65,444	Conversion Rate		0.75%
1	$ 95,121	65,324	$ 1.46	$ 97,496	$ 2,375	Average Order Size	$	199
2	$ 56,670	39,630	$ 1.43	$ 59,148	$ 2,478	Revenue per click	$	1.49
3	$ 48,658	34,601	$ 1.41	$ 51,642	$ 2,984			
4	$ 33,218	39,268	$ 0.85	$ 58,607	$ 25,389			
5	$ 29,812	33,253	$ 0.90	$ 49,630	$ 19,818			
6	$ 18,790	17,551	$ 1.07	$ 26,195	$ 7,405			
7	$ 8,967	8,741	$ 1.03	$ 13,046	$ 4,079			
8	$ 2,120	2,101	$ 1.01	$ 3,136	$ 1,016			

FIGURE 20–16. Revenue and profit after landing page optimization.

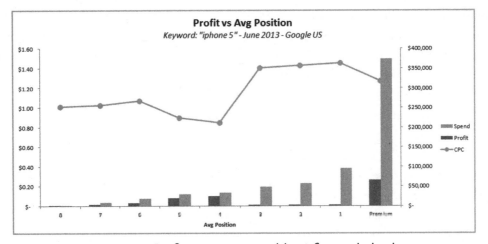

FIGURE 20–17. Profit vs. average position after optimization.

We now have plenty of room to increase our bid price. If we did so and coverage started dropping, then we'd drop our bids and get back to ad copy optimization. Meanwhile, our ads would stay in the same position, but our profits would nearly double ($13,668 to $25,389).

On the other hand, if coverage doesn't drop as we raise bids, then we may just land ourselves in the premium position (we'll find out pretty quickly because CPC prices are pretty flat in the top positions). If this happens, then congratulations are in order because we've just increased profits to $65,444, a 378 percent increase!

LOOK FOR "SUPERCONVERTER KEYWORDS"

Even with accurate bid-simulation charts, you won't be able to tell with 100 percent accuracy what is going to happen. However, there's another tell you can watch for. If your revenue per click (RPC or average order size in dollars multiplied by conversion rate) is equal to or greater than the highest average CPC paid on the page, then you may have something very wonderful on your hands: a *superconverter keyword*.

Superconverter keywords are those for which you will turn a profit no matter how high you bid, and typically, the more you bid, the more you make. They can generate 80 percent or even more of the profits in a typical campaign. However, they're not all that common. A large campaign with a thousand or so keywords may have only a few that qualify as superconverters.

Expressed mathematically, it looks like this:

$$\text{Conversion Rate} \times \text{Average Order Size} > \text{MAX}(\text{Average CPC}_{\text{Position 0-8}})$$

With regular keywords, your PPC costs will rapidly outpace your revenues. This is why it's usually the case that you can make money at the bottom of the page but not the top.

Superconverter keywords are different in that your revenues far outpace your average costs. This is almost always the result of combining a keyword that is closely related to your business with a strong landing page and order process (another reason to devote considerable resources to website optimization).

In our example above, our RPC before optimization was just $1.19 (0.60 percent x $199). Because this was lower than the highest average CPC predicted by the bid simulator ($1.46), we would not be able to bid up to the premium ad positions and turn a profit.

However, *after* optimization, our RPC was $1.49 (0.75 percent x $199). This was greater than the highest average CPC predicted by the bid simulator so we would expect that our maximum profit would be realized in the premium ad positions.

AVERAGE POSITION AND CONVERSION RATES

There is an interesting phenomenon in paid advertising that we call *searcher fatigue*. This term refers to the fact that people tend to click on more ads during the first stages of their search, but, as they refine their terms (moving from browsers to buyers), they become more selective and spend more time on the websites they visit.

In other words, the ads at the top of the page sometimes do a better job of educating the visitor than selling to him.

Most of the time, it won't make a difference. But we've found a measurable trend in a small percentage of keywords that we've studied (most of these being broad keywords), so you must be aware that your conversion rate might vary depending on where your ad is found on the page.

For high-traffic browse terms, the conversion rate tends to be higher at the bottom of the page. For low-traffic shop and buy terms, the conversion rate tends to be lower at the bottom of the page.

The chart in Figure 20–18 on page 158 shows an example of a keyword in which there was a trend. Notice how the conversion rate decreases from position 3.5 to 2.5.

If you have extra time to spend on your campaign and you can reliably track conversions, this might be worth exploring for some of your higher volume keywords.

TAKING DOWN TOUGH COMPETITORS

For some terms you may be able to greatly increase your quality score relative to your competitors. If so, there's a way to take down—sometimes permanently—weaker

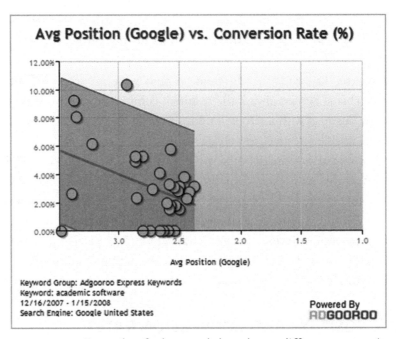

FIGURE 20–18. Example of a keyword that shows different conversion
rates by position.

competitors who aren't paying attention to their coverage. This is the only tactic I know of that can be used offensively against specific competitors.

Here's an actual example of this at work. On June 30, we were ranked behind four other competitors for the phrase *keyword research*. Here's how we stacked up (names have been removed from the charts and graphs for obvious reasons):

Advertiser	Rank	Coverage	Avgerage Position
Competitor B	1	97.1%	0.0
Competitor A	2	97.1%	0.4
Competitor C	3	97.1%	1.0
Competitor D	4	97.1%	1.4
AdGooroo.com	5	94.3%	1.4

FIGURE 20–19. Average position and coverage in late June.

The chart in Figure 20-20 shows how this looked graphically (our website is represented as a star and located in the upper right).

According to our AdWords account, our quality score was seven. In addition, our coverage for this term at the time was nearly 100 percent, suggesting that we

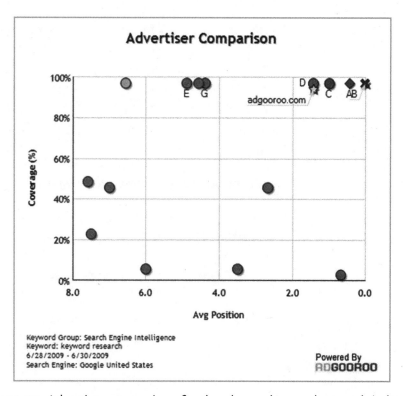

FIGURE 20-20. Advertiser comparison for the phrase, keyword research in late June.

potentially had a quality score advantage over nearby advertisers. If so, a small increase in bid would potentially be enough to dislodge one or more of the competitors appearing near us.

We were bidding $1.60 at the time, but our actual CPC was just $1.35. Over the next week, I slowly raised our bid to $2.00. We moved up substantially in the rankings, taking position 2. Competitors B, C, and D retained their relative positions. Competitor A, however, lost about 80 percent of their search traffic for this term. The combination of their higher bid and lower quality score allowed us to turn them into a gladiator bidder!

What's more, our clickthrough rate rose from around 0.4 percent to 1.48 percent and our average CPC increased only to $1.55! See Figure 20-21 on page 160.

Advertiser	Rank	Coverage	Avg Position
Competitor B	1	91.7%	0.0
AdGooroo.com	2	91.7%	0.5
Competitor C	3	91.7%	1.0
Competitor D	4	91.7%	1.8
Competitor E	5	91.7%	3.4
Competitor A	11	16.7%	0.3

FIGURE 20–21. Average position and coverage in early July.

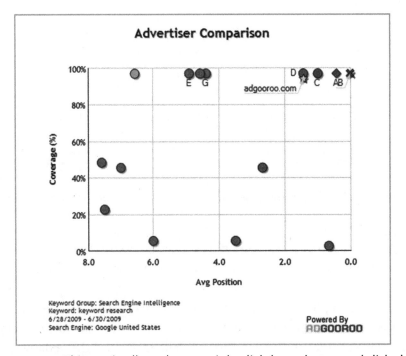

FIGURE 20–22. This tactic allowed us to triple clickthrough rate and dislodge a well-established competitor at minimal cost. Notice that Competitor A lost 80 percent of their impressions from this keyword as a result of our actions.

SUMMARY

Once you've covered the basics, you should be in the top 5 percent of all search advertisers. To break into the top 1 percent, you'll need a solid understanding of the interplay between coverage, average position, and relative quality score as described in this chapter.

Chapter 21

Drag Visitors to Your Site with Killer Ad Copy

Financial considerations often require us to place our ads in the lower positions on the search results pages instead of the more desirable upper positions. Although these bottom-of-page placements are usually profitable, they don't generate nearly as much traffic as the higher ones (see Figure 21–1 on page 162). By writing better ad copy, we can increase our clickthrough rate and in turn improve our quality score. This results in increased coverage, higher positions, and sometimes even reduced CPC prices. It's not uncommon to see traffic gains of 50 percent resulting from better ads!

The process of testing alternate ads for the purpose of finding the most effective one is called *ad copy optimization*. It is an offensive tactic, in that it forces advertisers appearing above you to pay more, as well as a defensive tactic, in that it helps to minimize the CPC pressure resulting from advertisers appearing just below you.

For all of these reasons, ad copy optimization is one of the best opportunities you have to outperform the competition. It is the cornerstone of achieving a long-term competitive advantage on Google AdWords.

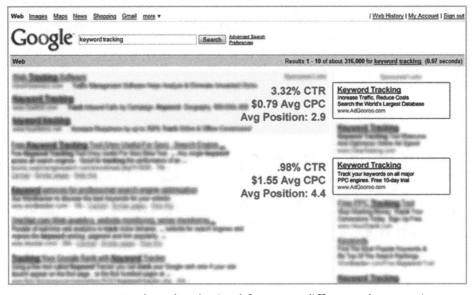

FIGURE 21–1. Actual results obtained from two different ads appearing on the same keyword.

WRITE YOUR ADS TO MIRROR YOUR VISITORS' INTENTION

Ads work best when they are aligned with the visitor's search query. Too many advertisers simply ignore this advice and use generic ads for all or most of their keywords.

But if you invest the time to identify the customer life cycle category for each of your keywords, you'll be far ahead of the pack when it comes to crafting powerful ads. Here are some general considerations to keep in mind.

Browsers

Browsers are looking for information. Your ads should offer them educational articles, technical advice, white papers, and so on. Don't focus on price, delivery, or guarantees, because many of them won't care and may actually be turned off by aggressive pitches. A good strategy here is to educate potential consumers about your product or service category while capturing their email address. If you succeed, you'll be able to stay in touch for free, and they'll be more likely to return to your site again in the future.

Shoppers

Shoppers are closer to a purchase decision but are generally looking for comparative information about different products. Descriptive terms work well (e.g., *best, cheapest,* or *review*) as do head-to-head comparisons, feature lists, third-party testimonials, and so

WRITE ADS THAT MIRROR THE ORGANIC SEARCH RESULTS

If you're looking to break through the clutter, try testing ads that mirror the top organic search results.

on. Your goal should be to convert shoppers to buyers. An effective means of doing this is with email capture immediately followed up with limited-time promotions.

Buyers

These visitors have committed themselves to making a purchase, so you can make an aggressive pitch without worry of turning off the customer. As with shoppers, promotional offers work well. You could cater to their purchasing needs: fast shipping, high quality, low price, and so on.

Not Sure of the Keyword Category?

Some keywords don't fall neatly into a single bucket, so try split-testing multiple ads. The best performers will often tell you the category to which the keyword belongs. If your split tests don't determine a clear winner, then try experimenting with negative matching to eliminate ad impressions for clearly off-target search queries.

Another powerful technique is to use the organic search results to guide your paid search ad copy. Although the organic search results generally cater to a different demographic, in many cases the top results will give you a strong indication of what searchers are looking for. Try incorporating these factors into your ad copy.

TEN QUICK TECHNIQUES TO INCREASE YOUR CLICKTHROUGH RATES

Search ads are short. You have only the following to work with:

- Headlines contain 25 characters.
- Two lines of copy contains 35 characters each (70 characters total).
- A display URL (which doesn't have to match the clickthrough URL).

To succeed, you must be concise. But there are plenty of other rules you can follow to write more effective ads. If you read the first edition of this book, don't skip this part!

The rules have changed since then, and some of the old recommendations no longer work or can actually hurt your clickthrough rate!

In late 2012, AdGooroo analyzed 20 million paid search ads appearing in the United States to identify best practices you should follow when writing your copy. Our top ten findings are below. Please be aware that a specific rule may or may not work in every situation. *Always split test when changing your ad copy!*

1. Use "www" in Your Domain Name

Your domain name is found at the end of every paid search ad. You can use either the long form with a preceding "www" (for instance, "www.adgooroo.com") or a short form that omits the prefix ("adgooroo.com").

The longer version was found to increase clickthrough rate by nearly 16 percent.

	www.example.com	Example.com	Improvement
Clickthrough rate	2.56%	2.20%	+15.8%

2. Avoid Numbers

Many paid search ads contain at least one number, for instance:

> **50th birthday gift ideas**
> A free service to help you find
> creative 50th Birthday Gifts.

Or "buy" ads, like:

> **Save 45% On Abrasives**
> Grind & Cut Wheels, Discs, Belts
> Quality Same Day Ship on Stock Item

This is a widely recommended practice. However, our data suggests that it doesn't work for most advertisers. We noted that ads with no numbers performed nearly 20 percent better than those with them.

	Without Number	With Number	Improvement
Clickthrough rate	2.66%	2.22%	+19.8%

3. Avoid Exclamation Points

Another practice many advertisers follow is to include exclamation points in their ad copy.

> **facilitate this!**
> Effective and dynamic meeting
> facilitation and skills training

We found that ads with exclamation points performed 9 percent worse than ads without. Perhaps Google has caught on to this tactic.

	Without Exclamation Point	With Exclamation Point	Improvement
Clickthrough rate	2.60%	2.38%	+9.2%

4. Avoid Overused Call-to-Action Phrases

When writing new ads, it's often a good idea to test a call-to-action ("Buy now," "Try now," "Download now"). However, Google frowns on certain terms, and so this tactic isn't nearly as effective as it was a few years ago. Ads with the word "now" in them actually underperformed all other ads by 7 percent.

	Without "Now"	With "Now"	Improvement
Clickthrough rate	2.45%	2.29%	+7.0%

Here are some other common call-to-action phrases you might try testing in your ads:

- Get official quote
- Shop and save
- Learn more today
- Get tips!
- Order today for quick delivery
- Request info
- Read this

5. Offer Something for Free

After finding that some of the most reliable ad copy tactics were no longer effective, we were surprised to learn that including the word "free" still seems to work like a charm. Ads with this word performed 9 percent better than ads without.

	With "Free"	Without "Free"	Improvement
Clickthrough rate	2.55%	2.34%	+9.0%

6. Save Space with Ampersands

Space is tight with paid search ads, so anytime you can save a character or two, it's welcome news. The ampersand (&) not only works well for this, we also found that it increases the average advertiser's clickthrough rate by 8 percent.

	With "&"	Without "&"	Improvement
Clickthrough rate	2.57%	2.38%	+8.0%

7. Don't Include the Price

Many search marketers include the price in their ad copy on the basis that by doing so, they will avoid unnecessary clicks from those who are looking for either a higher or lower price offering. While this does work (and will save you money), it will also lower your clickthrough rate by a whopping 17 percent, ensuring you get hit with a quality score penalty.

	Without Price	With Price	Improvement
Clickthrough rate	2.43%	2.07%	+17.4%

8. Be the "Official" Site

Although Google has quietly eliminated most affiliates from its advertiser list, some advertisers are still using "official site" in their ad copy. Only a small percentage of ads in our database included this word, but it makes a big difference. "Official" ads have a 71 percent higher clickthrough rate on average.

> **Shop For iPod Nano**
> Official Site. Free Shipping on orders
> $24 & up or pick up in store

> **Tiffany & Co. (Official)**
> Shop the Official Tiffany & Co.
> site for exclusive Tiffany designs.

	With "Official"	Without "Official"	Improvement
Clickthrough rate	3.68%	2.15%	+71%

9. Incorporate Trademark symbols

Trademark symbols (™, ©, ®) may be required only for legal reasons, but they can dramatically boost your paid search results. We discovered that these unusual characters improved clickthrough rates by nearly 90 percent!

	With TM Symbols	Without TM Symbols	Improvement
Clickthrough rate	4.00%	2.11%	+89.6%

10. Use All the Space You're Allowed

Sometimes you might not need a lot of space to say what you've got to say. Take a look at this pithy ad:

> **Books**
> Buy a book
> Read and become smarter
> www.books.com

Other advertisers try to be cute with their ads:

> **Postcards**
> No Way!
> Can't be true?
> www.postcardsrus.com

Avoid this tactic and use as much of the available space in your ad as you can. We tested both short and long ads and found that on average, longer ads have 64 percent higher clickthrough rate.

	Long Ad	Short Ad	Improvement
Clickthrough rate	2.20%	1.34%	−64.2%

SEVEN APPROACHES TO WRITING BETTER ADS

The previous list included quick fixes for your existing ads, but you'll also need to write ads from scratch. Here are seven more approaches to inspire you.

Use Action Words

Use simple and enthusiastic action verbs in your ad copy: *discover, enhance, get, learn, receive,* and so on.

Capitalize Every Word

Capitalizing every word is a common ad copy tactic that many advertisers swear by (including me). You can also experiment with ads that make creative use of capitalization in the title ("WOW Big Sale"). These ads draw the eye, but take care not to appear spammy.

Include a Brand Name

Anecdotal evidence suggests that including well-known brand names in the ad copy can substantially boost clickthrough rates. In the most competitive categories (such as travel), this may be the only way to compete successfully on Google.

Out-Target the Competition with Localized Ads

In some cases, a mediocre local ad can outperform well-written national ads. For instance, here's an ad that displayed for the keyword "buy digital printer."

> **Minuteman Press**
> Quality, cost-effective printing
> "We're as close as your phone"
> [domain name removed]
> Chicago, Illinois

Despite the ad not being well aligned with the keyword, it outranked many national ads that incorporated the words "digital" and "printer" in the headline, possibly because of the increased clickthrough rate resulting from the fifth line containing the city.

Capture the Lead to Boost Your Conversion Rate

In competitive fields, trying to make the sale directly from the ad may be a tough proposition. Often, it's better to offer information for free, capture the lead, and attempt to sell via other means such as email marketing. This is a common tactic in such competitive fields as:

- Travel—free destination guides
- Online education—degree information
- Pharmaceuticals—prescription info
- Hair restoration—free transplant info

There's another benefit to email capture as well. Keeping visitors on your site a bit longer will boost your landing page quality score.

Don't Forget Niche Keywords

Despite being more profitable, many advertisers overlook longer niche phrases and instead pay too much attention to their high-cost broad keywords. Given their profit potential, we recommend that you allocate some time to improving them. (This is much easier if you regularly monitor coverage for all of your keywords.)

For instance, on a recent search for "teen car insurance," I saw just three ads out of eleven that actually had the word "teen" in the ad copy. Another search for the phrase "credit online report identity theft" returned 11 ads but just two of them had anything to do with identity theft (the rest advertised credit score reporting). A savvy competitor could easily improve performance in these niche phrases with even the most cursory ad copy optimization.

Guess the Intention on Broad Keywords

One vexing problem with search advertising is that broad searches (typically one word) generate the most traffic but offer little clue as to what the visitor is searching for. Relying on the search phrase alone often results in low clickthrough rates.

One tactic that appears to work is to run shop ads for these broad keywords. The intent is to turn a browser into a shopper, potentially beating other competitors to the punch. An example for the keyword *spyware* will help to illustrate this. Rather than running ads with the title "Spyware," advertisers are enticing searchers with offers for more information:

> **Top 5 Spyware Removers**
> Compare and Download the 5 Top
> Spyware Virus Removers for Free.

> **Which Spyware Remover?**
> Don't download any Spyware removers
> until you read this article.

EIGHT WAYS TO WRITE TERRIBLE ADS

Now that you know what works, you should also be mindful of what doesn't. Here are eight mistakes commonly made by paid search marketers.

Blindly Using Keyword Insertion

Keyword insertion is an advanced AdWords feature that allows you to insert the keyword that triggered your ad directly into the ad copy. To use it, you place a short piece of code into your ad text. Each time the ad shows, the code will be replaced with the targeted keyword.

For instance, the following string will attempt to insert the keyword that triggered your ad into the line of text. If it doesn't fit, it will insert the phrase "Buy widgets" instead.

{keyword: Buy widgets}

This works out pretty well if your keywords have been chosen appropriately. For instance, if you are targeting the phrase "Erase Internet History," and you use keyword insertion in the headline, the displayed ad could look like this:

> **Erase Internet History**
> Erase your internet history
> Fast, easy, and secure. Free trial!
> www.SurfSecret.com

However, some advertisers get it wrong, resulting in comical ads such as the following, which I recently found for the term, "spyware":

> **Spyware**
> Protect your system with Dell
> and save on Spyware today!
> www.Dell.com

Use keyword insertion only for ad groups with carefully chosen keywords.

A NOTE ABOUT DYNAMIC KEYWORD INSERTION

When you use keyword insertion, the keyword in your campaign that triggered your ad will be inserted into the text, *not* the user's search phrase.

Relying Too Much on Broad Keywords

Broad keywords appeal to a wide audience, but they suffer from the disadvantage that it's difficult to adjust ad copy based on searcher behavior.

Is the person who typed in *plasma TV* looking to buy a specific plasma television? To learn about the different types of flat-panel displays? Or to compare prices? There's no way to tell for sure, and that's why conversion rates are so low for this keyword. Conversely, traffic is very high, so you end up spending a disproportionate amount of your ad budget to generate relatively few sales.

Broad keywords also suffer from low clickthrough rates. AdGooroo recently ran test advertisements on the shareware for Google. Our ad produced a single click in about 1,700 impressions and was quickly disabled. Is this a big deal? You bet. The two factors of high volume and low CTR deliver a double whammy to your historical stats, dragging your entire campaign down. This can result in your ads for all of your other keywords being penalized!

If you want to be a dominant advertiser, you can't avoid targeting broad keywords: But one technique that could help is negative matching (Chapter 18).

Forgetting to Spell Check Your Ads

No matter how long you've been in business or how great your reputation may be, misspellings make your company look unprofessional. Furthermore, ads with obvious misspellings in them often convert at a lower rate. Double-check all your ad copy before hitting the save button.

Using Abbreviations to Save Space

Not everyone, especially nonnative English speakers, will understand the following abbreviations:

- lb
- ea
- qty
- ASAP
- INC
- ext
- w/o

Sometimes you can't avoid using abbreviations because of space considerations, but you should generally try to write without them.

Using Technical Jargon

Jargon can be useful but generally only in niche B2B categories. If you aren't selling to specialists (for example, scientists or mining engineers), avoid industry jargon. If, on the other hand, you are running a frequency campaign designed to differentiate your product in the minds of expert users and the space is very competitive, technical jargon is worth trying. I suspect that most of the time you will be disappointed, however, because the truth is that people buy what makes them feel good, and technical terminology doesn't speak well to that part of our brains responsible for emotion.

At the end of the day, people buy benefits, not features. And benefits can usually be stated in clear, nontechnical terms.

Including Your Company Name in the Headline

Unless you are advertising on behalf of a well-known brand, your company name probably doesn't belong in the title.

Using Superlatives

Superlatives such as *best, greatest, #1,* and so on generate a sense of suspicion in most people. Avoid using these terms at all costs. We ran a series of ads that touted our "amazing" new software and had dismal clickthrough rates. The software really was amazing, but searchers didn't respond to this particular claim.

That said, you should always test superlatives in your ad copy. We found that some do work, but it is highly dependent on your business category.

Don't Promise What You Can't Deliver

Not only do people resent being sold a bill of goods, but Google's editors will remove your ad if they learn that you are making unjustifiable claims. Even if you do have the lowest prices, making this claim is a bad idea for a variety of reasons, unless you are credibly positioned as a value company (Southwest Airlines, Walmart). You will probably get more effective results by clearly stating the price in your ad and letting people judge for themselves. On a related note, does it need to be said that if you can't deliver the goods then you shouldn't advertise them? This is not only a great way to waste your ad budget, it's also unethical and potentially illegal.

PAINT A BULL'S-EYE ON YOUR ADS

Howie Jacobson
Author, *AdWords for Dummies*

The animal inhabitants of the Costa Rican rain forest spend most of their time and energy looking for food and trying not to become food. They've evolved an amazing array of predatory and defensive strategies in the never-ending battle for survival. For example, bird species that feast on insects have a huge array of choices—thousands of different potential meals. It's more overwhelming than the dinner menu at the Cheesecake Factory.

PAINT A BULL'S-EYE ON YOUR ADS, CONTINUED

But not all of the insects are edible. Some are poisonous to birds. Some are yucky-tasting (a scientific word meaning "unpalatable"). And a whole bunch of yummy bugs have evolved to look like the poisonous ones.

So what's a hungry bird to do? Before you answer, think about these two constraints:

Constraint 1: Too Much Information

When my family and I hiked in a Costa Rican rain forest for four hours, we saw exactly one animal: a hairy tarantula standing in the middle of the path, with a "You want a piece of me?" expression. The animals were there; we could hear them and even see their pictures in the laminated card we got at the gift shop, but the place looked like a greenhouse ghost town. Everybody was hiding or camouflaged in the varied and verdant environment.

Finding the animals was like playing "Where's Waldo?" Except that instead of hundreds of people in red and white stripes vying for our attention, the multiplicity of leaves, mosses, ferns, and barks obscured the hundreds of animals evolved to hide in plain site.

I tip my hat to those insectivorous birds who choose to make the rain forest their home and restaurant. Anyone looking for animal protein in that place has got to have amazing eyesight.

Constraint 2: Limited Processing Power

Birds have small heads, which means limited cranial capacity, which means their brains are, well, bird-brained. Small. Not a lot of processing going on in there. Think about the computer you bought in 1994 trying to run *Second Life* and YouTube.

THE STRATEGY: SEARCH IMAGING

To recap: The birds can see tons of stuff—about seven times more detail than humans—but can't deal with all the information because there's more stimuli than capacity to process it. (Sound like us on the internet?)

Even though there are lots of palatable species of insect available to them, the birds focus on one or two at most because they lack the brain processing power to take in

PAINT A BULL'S-EYE ON YOUR ADS, CONTINUED

and evaluate the entire visual landscape. So they create a "search image" in their head before they start looking for food and only pay attention to what matches that search image.

They miss a lot of potential dinners (having no capacity for opportunism) but rarely go hungry. That's how your prospects are looking at Google's search results.

They are overwhelmed by the sheer size of the web. By the amount of information available on every single topic. Websites, articles, videos, audios, PDFs, emails, banners, popups, blog posts, blog comments, tweets, SMS, voice mails, argghhhh . . .

So when they search, they are not looking for more information. They are looking for LESS. To eliminate everything that isn't breathtakingly relevant, interesting, and important.

And they search with an image in their mind—a search image that allows the brain to ignore almost everything that doesn't match the image.

How do you know what their search image is?

They tell you—by typing it.

Keyword = Search image

If someone is searching for "industrial clean room," they see the following Google ads:

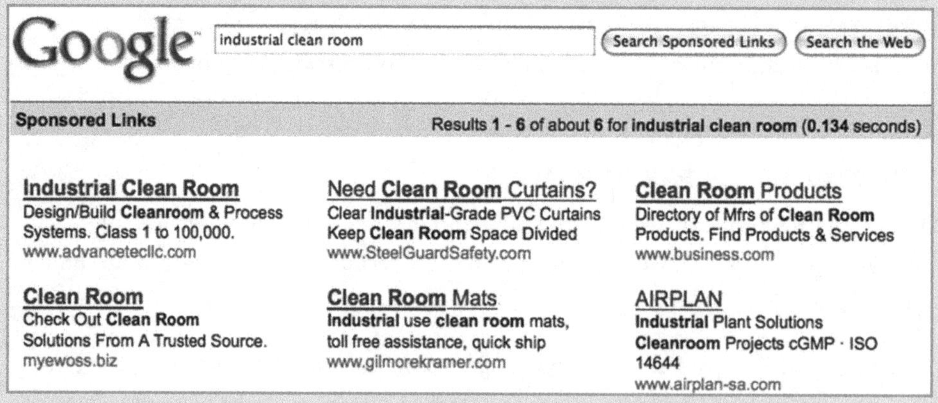

FIGURE 21–2.

PAINT A BULL'S-EYE ON YOUR ADS, CONTINUED

Which headline matches the search image? Only one: "Industrial Clean Room." It captures the eye immediately, because that click requires less thought, less expenditure of processing energy, than any of the others.

Now, are the other ads also relevant to the search? You might argue that the word "industrial" is superfluous: All clean rooms are industrial. So why bother showing it in your ad?

Because your prospect has told you exactly what their filter is. They want industrial, you give them industrial. Otherwise they will tune you out.

Opportunism—clicking on a "Gee, this might be interesting" ad—is not a preferred strategy in an environment of information and opportunity overload.

In a perfect world, you might suppose, your ad would mirror the search image for every keyword in your AdWords account. But that's not realistic or even desirable. (Your long-tail keywords belong in groups, if only to garner enough traffic to determine split-test winners.)

The best practice here is to isolate and reflect the search image for your "money" keywords—the high-traffic, high-converting words that keep you in business. Each deserves its own ad group and its own ads, perfectly keyed to the prefiltered desire of your prospect.

Don't Be Mechanical

I don't want to give the impression that you should always paste the search term into the headline. A lot of the time you should but not always.

The main exception is when everyone else is doing just that. If the prime directive of search marketing is relevance, then the subprime directive is uniqueness. If you want to be seen, you've got to stand out.

More on this later. For now, just remember that your prospects aren't just searching. They're hunting. With eyes that can see more than their brains can process. If you want to get caught (and you do), then match your ad to the search image they're already carrying.

AD EXTENSIONS

In addition to standard text ads, Google also offers variations called "Ad Extensions." There are many different types of Ad Extensions, and they are constantly changing as old formats are retired and new ones are introduced.

Because there are so many different formats, any attempt to show you how to set them up would become quickly outdated. At a high level, however, you can activate these ads on the "Ad Extensions" tab found in your AdWords account. Please note that many ad extensions are not available through the AdWords interface, so you may need to contact your Google representative to get them activated.

Why should you consider using Ad Extensions? One reason: higher clickthrough rates. As you'll see from the examples below, many of these ads stand out and are simply more engaging than the standard text ad. One type in particular, Product Listing Ads, are so effective that we have devoted Chapter 28 to them.

Here are some of the more popular Ad Extensions in use at the time of this writing (September 2013).

Comparison Ads

Compare **Mortgage** Rates		Sponsored link
5/1 ARM from 3.375% (3.137 APR) 15-year fixed from 4.000% (4.130 APR) 30-year fixed from 4.500% (4.960 APR) google.com/comparisonads/mortgages	What is the purpose of the loan? ○ Buy a home ○ Refinance	Compare rates

FIGURE 21–3. Comparison Ad Extension found on mortgage search.

Calculate **Mortgage** Amount		Sponsored links
5/1 ARM from 3.375% (3.185 APR) 15-year fixed from 4.000% (4.167 APR) 30-year fixed from 4.500% (4.965 APR) google.com/comparisonads/mortgages	Approximate home price Select one ▾	Compare rates

FIGURE 21–4. Another Comparison Ad Extension. Note that the ad is asking for different information from the user.

Call Extensions

FIGURE 21–5. A Call Extension found on a mobile phone.

Credit Cards (UK)

FIGURE 21–6. Credit Card Extension (UK version).

Credit Cards (US)

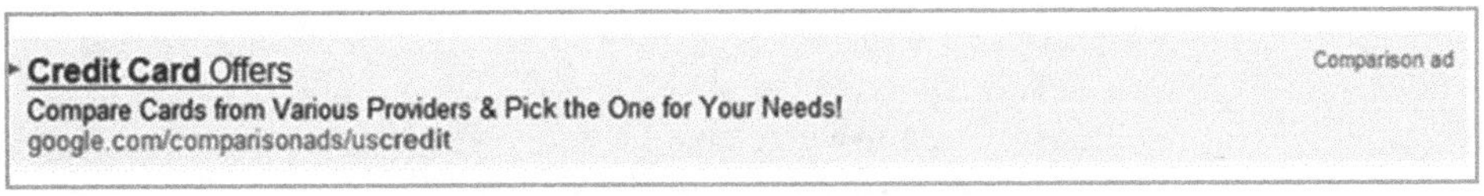

FIGURE 21–7. Credit Card Extension (US version).

Pharmaceutical

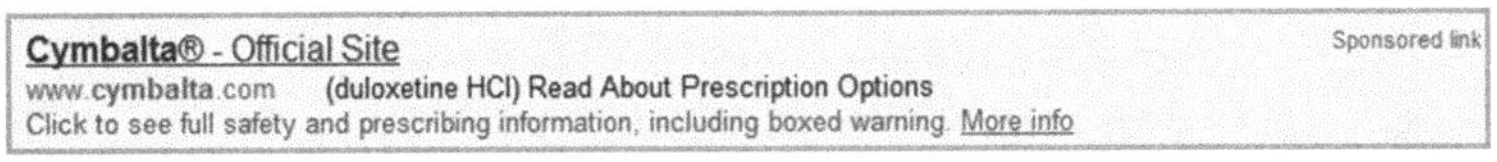

FIGURE 21–8. Pharmaceutical Extension. Note the product warning found at the bottom of the ad.

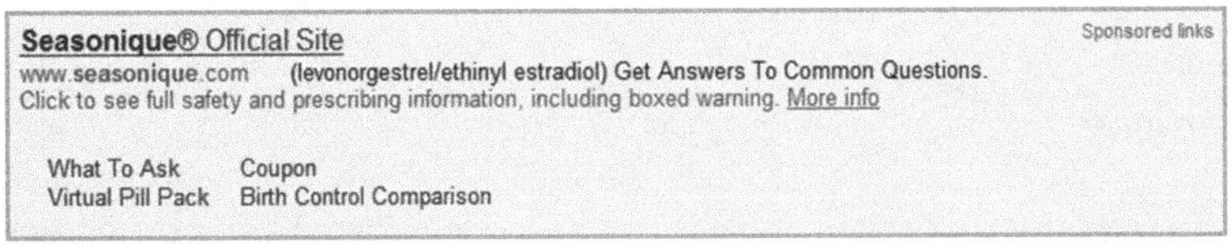

FIGURE 21–9. Pharmaceutical and Site Link Extensions found in a single ad.

Site Links

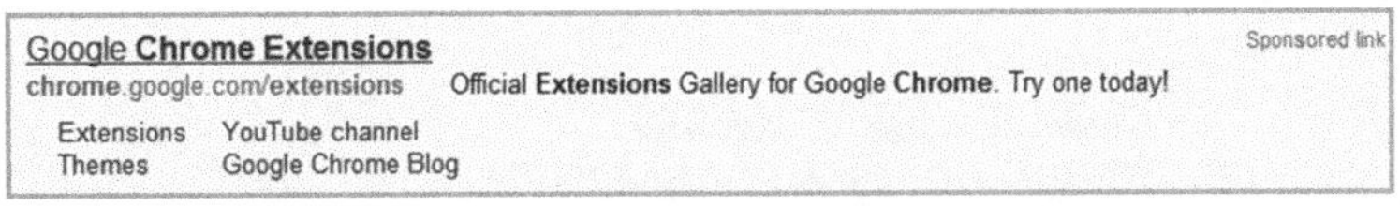

FIGURE 21–10. Site Link Extensions include multiple links.

Dell中国唯一官方网站
www.Dell.com/China　欢迎访问 www.Dell.com.cn 官方网址 采用2010英特尔®酷睿™ 访问官网
新品上市！VOSTRO3000系列笔记本电脑　戴尔OptiPlex 380,功能强大价格优惠
戴尔多重大礼引爆世界足球盛宴 5/28 - 6/24　全新Inspiron14笔记本 详询800-858-0863!

赞助商连结

FIGURE 21–11. Site Link Extensions are found in all regions, including China.

Local Extensions (Address and/or Phone)

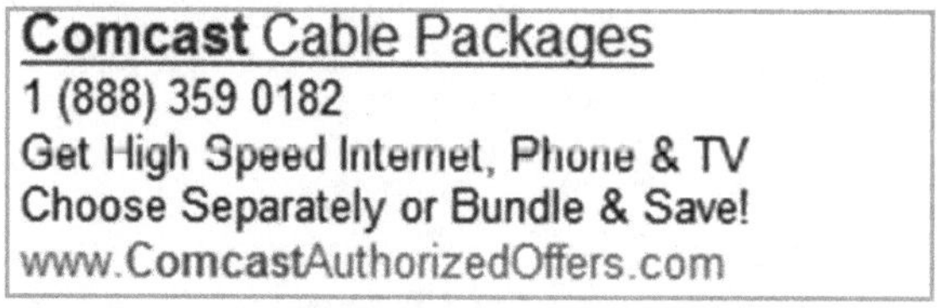

Comcast Cable Packages
1 (888) 359 0182
Get High Speed Internet, Phone & TV
Choose Separately or Bundle & Save!
www.ComcastAuthorizedOffers.com

FIGURE 21–12. Local Extension showing phone number.

Royalcaribbean.com
Huge Savings on **Royal Caribbean**
Cruises. Lowest Prices on the Web.
RoyalCaribbean.Cruises.com
Illinois

FIGURE 21–13. Local extension showing advertiser location.

Rating Extensions

Cheap Tickets　Sponsored link
www.CheapTickets.com　The Official **CheapTickets**.com Site Makes Finding **Cheap Tickets** Simple!
CheapTickets.com is rated ★★★★☆ on Google Products (91 reviews)

FIGURE 21–14. Rating Extensions show the average customer rating from
Google Shopping.

Discount Flight **Tickets**
Compare Airlines For Cheaper Rates.
Travelocity Guarantees Low Prices.
www.Travelocity.com/Flights
Travelocity.com is rated ★★★★☆

FIGURE 21–15. Another Rating Extension. Note that there is no link to the
Google Shopping reviews page.

Offer Extensions

FIGURE 21–16. Offer Extensions allow advertisers to promote coupons and special deals to searchers.

Google Places

FIGURE 21–17. Google Places Extensions link to the business location on Google Maps.

Media Ads

FIGURE 21–18. This Media Ad Extension includes a link to a movie trailer.

FIGURE 21–19. Media Ad Extensions are often used for other media, including video games.

Communication Extension

FIGURE 21–20. Communication Extensions can be used to acquire email addresses directly from AdWords.

Social Extension

FIGURE 21–21. Social Extensions link to Google+ pages.

"BORROW" THE BEST ADS

One of the quickest ways to achieve breakthrough improvements in your clickthrough rates is to identify top companies from different industries and repurpose their ads.

For instance, I once split-test an ad on a high-traffic keyword for over six months and was unable to come up with a single variation that outperformed the original. However, by borrowing an ad concept from a successful stock photography company, I was able to triple my clickthrough rate in just 24 hours.

Borrowing an ad is one thing. Finding the right ad to borrow is a whole different ballgame. Grabbing ads at random from your browser doesn't cut it for a number of reasons:

- There are usually too many candidate ads to test. For instance, there are currently over 5,000 unique ads containing the phrase, "identity protection." There's not enough time to test that many variations.

- There's no way to guess which ads are likely winners. Your competitors are probably not going to give you access to their AdWords accounts to find out.
- You miss a lot of ads, both because of personalization as well as geo-targeting. It also tells you nothing about the frequency or average rank of competing ads, important clues to how effective they are.

So while you might be able to stumble across some gains by testing ads you've grabbed at random from your browser, a paid search intelligence service such as AdGooroo will help you generate endless candidates for split testing. However, there are just too many ads for you to test all of them, so you'll need to narrow them down.

I regularly use three filters to identify candidate ads for split testing.

Ads with the Highest Spend

Most advertisers are lazy and use too few ads. However, they do split test those ads, and the most effective variants tend to get the most spend.

Ads with Highest Coverage

In the previous chapter, we showed how coverage can act as a proxy for quality score. Those ads with the highest coverage are always the most successful ones.

Ads with Higher Average Position

Quality score is loosely correlated with average position so limiting your search to the highest placements will also eliminate many underperformers.

Within the AdGooroo SEM Insight interface, it's easy to apply one or all of these filters to narrow down a candidate list of ads. Navigate to the "Keyword Creative" report, and click the "Filter" button at the top of the page. Create your chosen filters using the dropdowns and textboxes. Once you're done, you can also save this filter so you can instantly select it later (see Figure 21–22 on page 182).

Once you apply the filter, only the ads matching your criteria will be shown (see Figure 21–23 on page 182).

This technique is excellent for seeding your own ad copy efforts and rapidly improving your quality scores. Virtually every ad you discover using this technique will have a high clickthrough rate, and with it, you can create new campaigns with high-performing ads in a few hours and have a positive history from the very beginning. While most advertisers struggle with building their campaign for months, my initial efforts almost always capture a high percentage of the available impressions. The keyword chart shows a new campaign that I started in a high-competition category. In just two

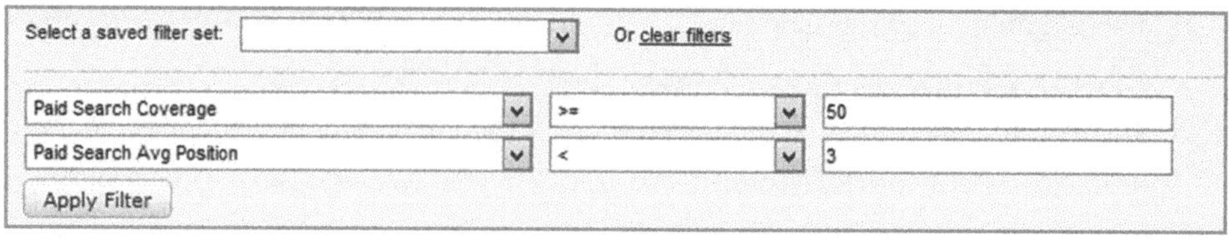

FIGURE 21-22. Setting up an advanced filter to narrow down the most effective ads.

Advertiser	Text Ad	Spend	Impressions	Clicks	CTR	CPC	Avg Position
bestbuy.com	iPhone 5 from Best Buy® *www.bestbuy.com/iPhone5* Get Connected With The iPhone 5 From Best Buy®. Shop Now!	$5,092	86,134	2,959	3.43%	$1.72	1.3
verizonwireless.com	iPhone 5 - Verizon 4G LTE *www.verizonwireless.com/iphone5* Now available at the official Verizon Wireless site. Shop now.	$1,421	86,134	1,001	1.16%	$1.42	1.8

FIGURE 21-23. The resulting report contains only ads deemed to be most effective.

weeks, most of their most important keywords were appearing at 90 percent and better coverage. It's rare for a new account to achieve high coverage so quickly (see Figure 21-24 on page 183).

The next chart compares different advertisers. Surfsecret.com went from virtually unknown to fifth in the category in just two weeks (see Figure 21-25 on page 183).

When starting a new campaign, it's normal for traffic to ramp up slowly. In this case, clicks stayed low for just six days before Google took the breaks off. This happened primarily because we started out with such great ad copy. (See Figure 21-26 on page 184.)

SPLIT TESTING

Search marketing has a great advantage over most other forms of advertising in that it delivers feedback on ads very quickly. Create a successful print or television ad generally requires extensive marketing research, copy tests, focus groups, and so on. But with search, you can simply let two ads run side by side for a certain period and choose the one with the higher clickthrough or conversion rate.

This feedback is so valuable that you should always be testing at least two ads simultaneously using an A/B split test. This can tell you with great confidence if one ad is more effective than the other over the same period.

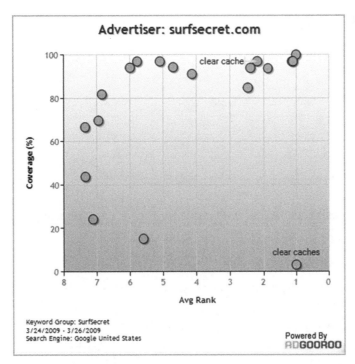

FIGURE 21–24. An example of an account launched with high-performing ads. Icons represent individual keywords.

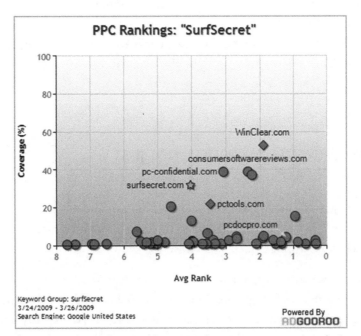

FIGURE 21–25. Another chart showing how SurfSecret compares to their competitors, taken two weeks after launch. Icons represent individual advertisers.

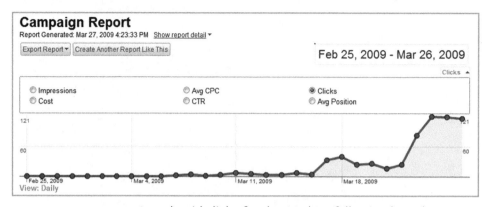

FIGURE 21–26. Actual paid clicks for the 11 days following launch.

How Long Should You Test an Ad?

When you are testing ads, it's important to get enough traffic to be confident of the results.

How many clicks do you need? There are complex statistical formulas (see the "Calculating Z-Value") you can use to tell you exactly how much data is needed, but the simple answer is that it depends on the difference in clickthrough rates between your ad variations.

If one ad is pulling in 2.00 percent CTR versus another that is pulling in .65 percent, you'll be quite confident that there is a long-term difference in as few as 10 or 20 clicks.

On the other hand, if your two test ads are pulling 1.75 percent and 1.65 percent, respectively, then it may take several hundred clicks to gain a good degree of confidence in your results. This is why split testing tends to take longer as your ads get better.

OPTIMIZE INCREMENTAL PROFIT, NOT JUST CONVERSION RATE

If you're using conversion tracking on your site, you can also measure the conversion rate for each ad and choose the variant that maximizes your profits (new sales less advertising costs). This measure is known as incremental profit.

When testing, be sure to keep an eye on both of these metrics. It's easy to write ads that generate high clickthrough rates but low sales (just include the word *free*). If you're in a high-traffic vertical and can generate enough conversions to measure incremental profit, then by all means use it. It's a far better metric.

CALCULATING Z-VALUE

Calculate a z-value for the two clickthrough rates, and compare it to the percentiles of a standard normal distribution. If p is the clickthrough rate and n is the number of clicks, the formula is

$$z_1 = \frac{\hat{p}_1 - \hat{p}_2}{\sqrt{\dfrac{\hat{p}_1(1 - \hat{p}_1)}{n_1} + \dfrac{\hat{p}_2(1 - \hat{p}_2)}{n_2}}}$$

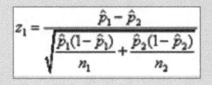

MEASURING RESULTS

After your testing period is over, compare the clickthrough rate (or incremental profit) for each ad to determine which was most effective. Disable the losing ads, and either start a new test or let your winning ad continue to run by itself. The best-performing ad is sometimes known as a control.

Our control ad today is producing a 3.2 percent CTR in an extremely competitive keyword. The average cost-per-click is only $0.12. How did we do it? Careful side-by-side testing of multiple ads performed over a sufficient length of time.

Chapter 22

Landing Page Design

A d copy optimization is just one half of the equation. As we've seen, improving your ads can result in a position bonus, a CPC discount, and a boost in coverage. However, in many cases you'll be targeting keywords where you simply can't afford to bid as high as competitors. This is when you'll need to turn to *landing page optimization*.

Improving your landing pages increases your conversion rate, which in turn increases your average revenue per visitor. When this metric exceeds the highest average CPC seen on your targeted keyword, you'll be able to affordably show your ads in the premium placements (see "Look for Superconverter Keywords" in Chapter 20). This will bring in a flood of profitable traffic.

What's more, landing page optimization can further increase your quality score, resulting in the same kinds of benefits as ad copy optimization. This is why the top 1 percent of paid search advertisers take these two activities very seriously.

Landing page optimization can easily take an entire book to cover completely, and in fact, there are several good books on the subject. So instead of trying to tackle the subject in its entirety, this chapter will touch on the most important principles of good landing page design.

OPTIMIZATION GOALS

When testing landing page variants, many marketers focus solely on conversion rate or total revenue. Keep in mind, however, that for paid search, the average visit duration is also important. The longer a visitor stays on your site before returning to the search results page, the higher your perceived landing page quality score will be.

EVALUATING YOUR LANDING PAGE DESIGN

When designing landing pages, you should keep the following eight principles in mind:

1. Single conversion goal
2. Eyeline
3. Anxiety
4. Length
5. Friction
6. Congruency
7. Load time
8. Incentives

The Eight-Fold Path to Conversion Nirvana

Use this checklist to evaluate your landing pages.

Single Conversion Goal

- ❑ Does every page in your sales funnel have a primary call to action?
- ❑ Can a typical visitor understand the page's purpose in less than five seconds?
- ❑ Is the page's intended goal clearly spelled out in a headline?
- ❑ Is the page's purpose clearly visible "above the fold"?

Eyeline

- ❑ Do the shapes and colors of the page clearly lead the eye to the desired call to action?
- ❑ Are you using no more than two columns in your page layout?

FIGURE 22–1. Eight core principles of landing page design.

The Eight-Fold Path to Conversion Nirvana, continued

Anxiety

❏ Are you asking for data the visitor may not want to give?

❏ Are you offsetting the user's anxiety with a payoff?

❏ Can you use testimonials?

❏ Can you use third-party trust seals to improve credibility?

Friction

❏ Are there too many elements on the page?

❏ Are there too many links or navigation elements?

❏ Is there sufficient white space on the page?

❏ Are you using a font appropriate for your visitors?

❏ Are form fields aligned with one another?

❏ Are links and buttons used appropriately?

❏ Are you asking for unnecessary information?

❏ Do the labels on form fields clearly convey what is required of the visitor?

❏ Are you limiting the use of Flash or other third-party technologies?

❏ Can you use dynamic HTML to eliminate unnecessary page reloads?

Page Length

❏ Is the page copy of the appropriate length?

❏ Are there ten or fewer form fields on the page?

Congruency

❏ Does the page look similar to the ones immediately before and after it?

❏ Is the page hosted on a third-party domain?

Load Time

❏ Does the page load in less than five seconds in Internet Explorer, Chrome, and Firefox?

❏ Is the page size under 150k?

Incentives

❏ Can you use incentives to boost response rates?

❏ Is your incentive something that would be useful to your ideal customer?

FIGURE 22–1. Eight core principles of landing page design, continued.

Let's consider each of these eight principles more fully.

Single Conversion Goal

The first and most important rule of conversion optimization is that every important page on your site must have a single goal, or call to action.

Not two. Not three. Just one.

With few exceptions, every sales funnel page must be assigned a singular, positive outcome. Here are some examples:

- Subscribe to your opt-in email newsletter list
- Add a product to the shopping cart
- Accept a special offer
- Complete a contact information form
- Confirm the order

Relatively few websites heed this advice. In the course of an average day, I come across many pages on popular websites that either have no clear purpose or have too many of them competing with one another.

Furthermore, the purpose of the page must be clearly conveyed to the visitor within a very short period of time: no more than five seconds. This is usually accomplished through headlines and supporting graphics.

This does not mean that the page should be entirely devoid of navigation or other links (like the spammy, single-page, long-copy websites that were popular in 2003). Rather, the most important action of the page should stand out so the casual visitor doesn't have to think about what to click. Other actions that can potentially complete with the primary goal should be de-emphasized (visitors looking for them will be more motivated to hunt for them).

Some examples will help to illustrate this important principle. Figure 22–2 shows a landing page that demonstrates a clear, singular conversion goal. The headline is well above the fold and is easily distinguished from the rest of the page. The button reading "Buy The Full Version" hammers home the next step that visitors should take.

In contrast is the page from a competing site, shown in Figure 22–3. This page also has a "Buy Now" button, but there are two other competing call-to-action areas on the page. The low-contrast button is overwhelmed by the various other high-contrast graphics on the page, and as a result, it practically hides in plain site.

This page could be dramatically improved by eliminating the two alternate offers, toning down the red graphics, and making the button larger.

Of course, you can't always have a single conversion goal on a page. Online shopping sites present a challenging example because browsing is an important customer activity.

FIGURE 22–2. An example of a landing page with a single conversion goal.

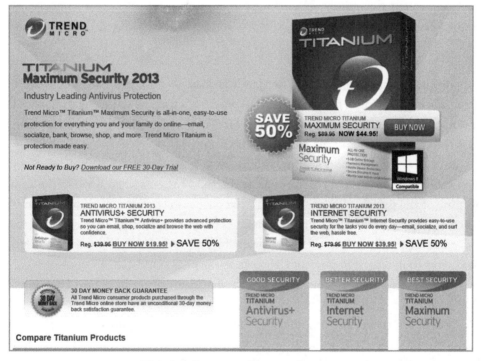

FIGURE 22–3. This landing page has no clear conversion goal.

How can these sites present a variety of products to their visitors, while still following this principle?

J.Crew shows us how (see Figure 22–4 on page 192). Their landing page, which was served for the phrase "black pumps" on Google, has a matching headline, and

FIGURE 22–4. J.Crew's landing page for women's heels has a clearly defined purpose.

the purpose of the page is clear: The visitor is there to browse a selection of women's "heels & wedges." Notice that other page elements such as the site navigation have been de-emphasized in such a manner that minimizes their distraction from the page content (this will come up again in the section on friction).

In contrast, the corresponding landing page from Piperlime (Figure 22–5) buries the headline ("Sandals") in reverse-type at the top of the page. And while the primary purpose of the page is to browse sandals, the page also encourages visitors to "Narrow it down" (in very small type). While the images of the shoes are probably enough to save this page, it could be improved dramatically by simply changing some of the font sizes and colors to make the important elements of the page stand out.

There is absolutely no confusion about what the website in Figure 22–6 is asking their visitors for.

In contrast, this page from one of my favorite local pizza joints has no clear call to action on the page (see Figure 22–7 on page 194). The headline reads, "Order Online!" but there is no button or link to click. How am I supposed to place an order here? On Facebook?

The need to choose a single goal for every page can be a frustrating exercise at times, particularly so with larger organizations. The need to accommodate multiple stakeholders is one of the primary reasons the websites of certain large corporations tend to do a poor job of converting visitors into customers.

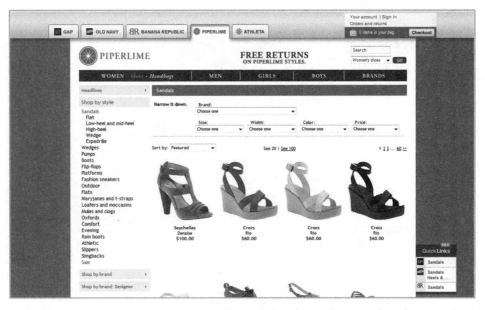

FIGURE 22–5. Visitors have to work much harder to browse this shoe site.

FIGURE 22–6. This page from Domino's Pizza has a single, well-defined purpose.

Figure 22–8 on page 194 shows an example of how conflicting priorities can undermine a website's effectiveness. This is a landing page from several years ago for AmericanAirlines.com. At the time, the page was cluttered with a variety of links,

FIGURE 22–7. You'll really be hungry by the time you figure out how to order pizza from this website.

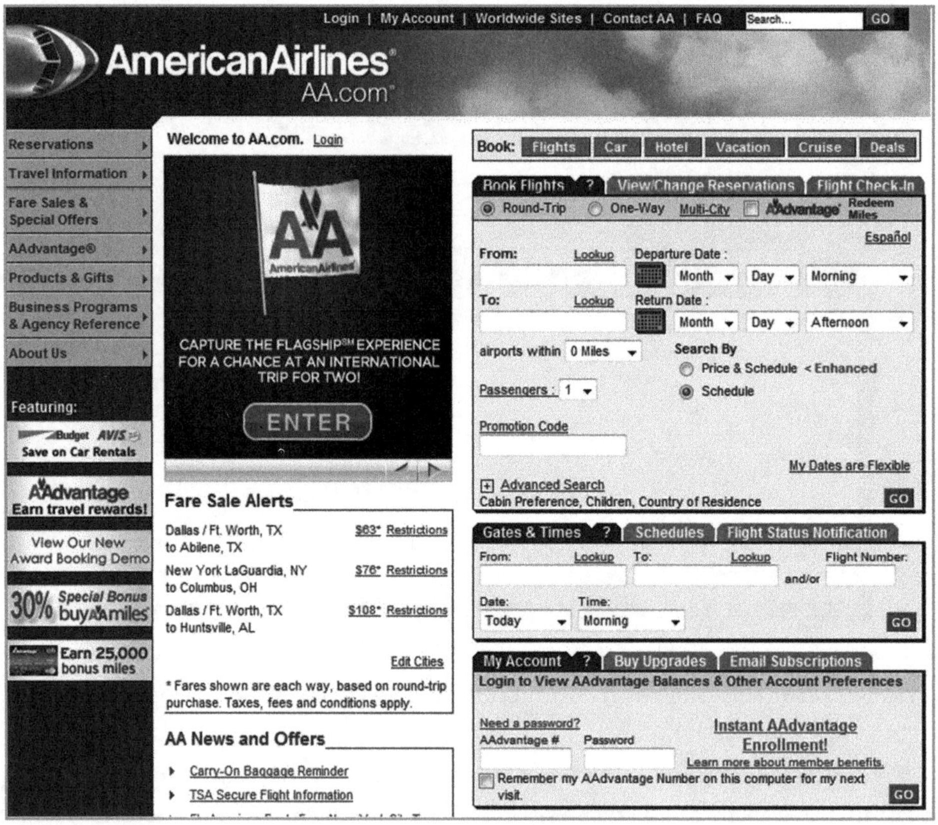

FIGURE 22–8. This American Airlines landing page consists of a confusing array of options. There are too many conversion goals on this page.

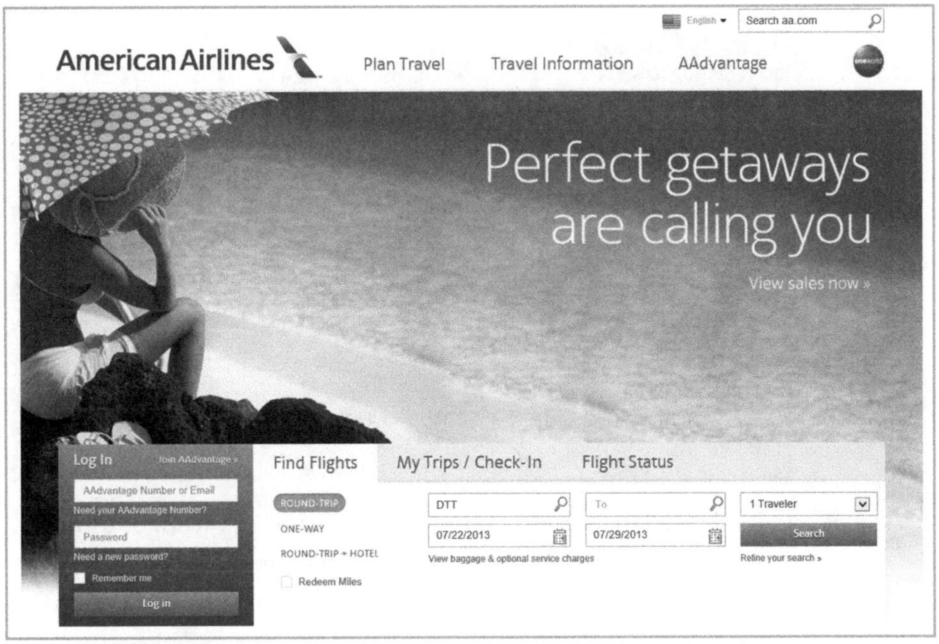

FIGURE 22–9. A much improved American Airlines landing page.

navigation, discounts, and alerts. This is typical of corporate landing pages, which are designed to please executives more than customers.

Since then, American Airlines has made some major improvements. Notice how much simpler and easier the new page shown in Figure 22–9 feels. While they still haven't succeeded in narrowing the landing page down to a single conversion goal, they have at least focused it on a primary goal ("Find Flights") while de-emphasizing other options. This is a major improvement, but they could take it even further. As a paid search landing page, many of the other options such as "Log In," "Check-In," and "Flight Status" could be eliminated.

Eyeline

Eyeline is the path that your visitors' gaze and mouse clicks naturally follow as they skim a page. It is guided by the use of color, contrast, and visual interest. Through careful use of these elements on your pages, you can subtly direct visitors to your desired action.

To see where the eyeline leads on a page, start at the top left of the page and follow the line of color. On most sites, the logo is found in the top-left corner, and after years of training, most of us begin reading there (of course, if your visitors read from right to left, you would start at the upper right.)

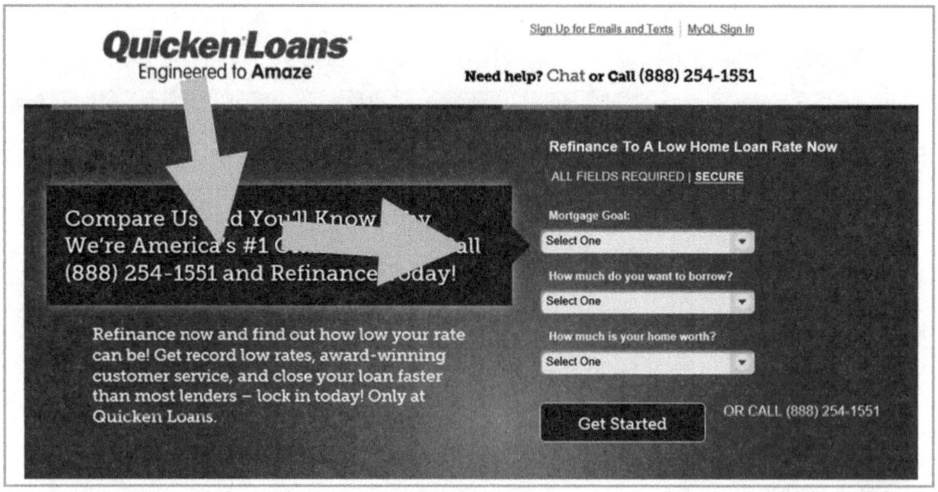

FIGURE 22–10. The eyeline on this landing page leads from the logo, through the text box, and into the action area.

Here are three examples. These were all taken from the mortgage industry to illustrate how looking at competitive sites within a particular category can help to uncover important principles.

The eyeline on this page from Quicken Loans starts at the top left. From there the dark brown box proceeds downward and then points right toward the call-to-action area. This small area consists of three fields that the visitor fills out to receive their mortgage quotes. There is absolutely no doubt what visitors should do when they arrive at this page.

Photographs are often used for the purpose of directing eyeline due to the high visual interest, color, and contrast, as demonstrated in the page from click-n-loan featured in Figure 22–11. The eyeline starts at the upper left, moves down into the copy below, and is then drawn to the right by the photograph. Finally, it is anchored in place by the high-contrast orange call-to-action button below.

Again, here's still another example of how to put this technique in action in a slightly different manner (see Figure 22–12). This page eliminates virtually all horizontal eye movement and instead directs the visitor's gaze straight down into a prominent, single-field form. This page also has the advantage that it will display cleanly on small mobile devices.

Finally, this page from Xerox (Figure 22–13 on page 198) was put together with little thought given to eyeline. Starting at the upper left, the visitor's eye is dropped at the navigation bar and abandoned, as neither the headline nor "start saving" button have sufficient contrast or interest. Not only do these elements blend into the page, they are competing with the bright, interesting photo off to the right.

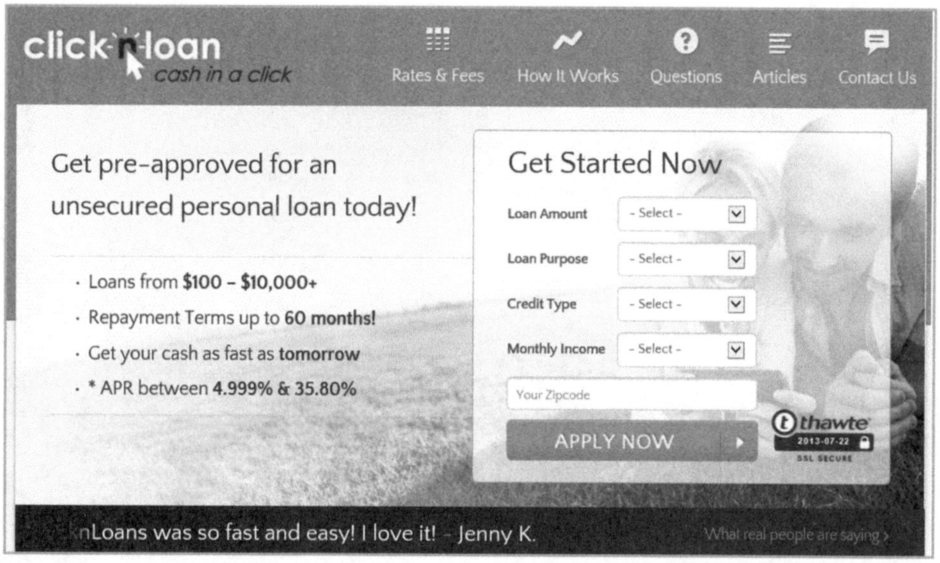

FIGURE 22-11. This landing page uses a photo to draw the eye to the action area.

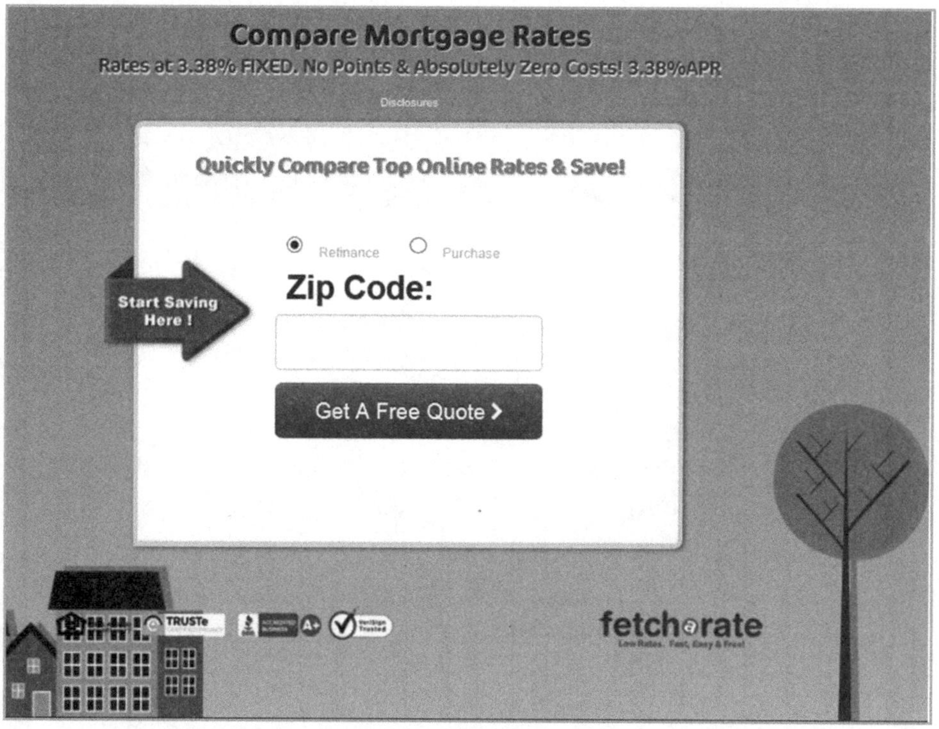

FIGURE 22-12. This lead-generation form eliminates virtually all horizontal eye tracking.

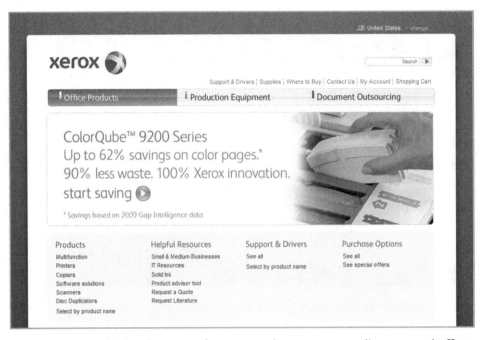

FIGURE 22–13. This landing page from Xerox does not use eyeline to good effect but could be improved dramatically with just a few minor tweaks.

The page could be improved dramatically with just a few minor tweaks (see Figure 22–14). By simply moving the photo to the left of the copy area and increasing the

FIGURE 22–14. Here's the same page with a few minor changes.

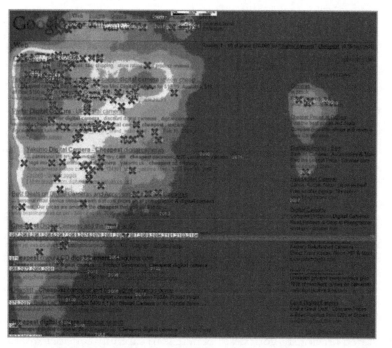

FIGURE 22–15. Heat mapping is a useful tool to see where your visitors are looking (and clicking).

contrast of the headline and button, I'd expect to realize a 20 to 30 percent improvement in clickthrough rate.

It takes a fair amount of practice to be able to correctly spot the path of least visual resistance through a page, so some companies opt to have their pages tested by usability labs. These labs produce heat maps—graphic visualizations of where their visitors are paying the most attention (see Figure 22–15).

This type of study is rather expensive, so years ago I created a software package that could track both mouse movements and clicks on my pages. Although it couldn't track where users were actually looking, this information still proved incredibly valuable in my testing efforts.

Today, you can do the same thing on the cheap with a tool called CrazyEgg (www.crazyegg.com). This service starts at $9/month, putting it within reach of virtually every internet marketer (see Figure 22–16 on page 200).

Anxiety

Anxiety refers to your site visitors' reluctance to provide personal information. While designing your sales pages, you should be sensitive to the concerns visitors may have when you ask them for their address, phone number, email address, and, of course, credit card data.

FIGURE 22–16. CrazyEgg is an inexpensive tool you can use to generate click maps, an inexpensive substitute for heat maps.

As we stated previously, your best bet here is to carefully consider what information you require for visitors to complete an action on your site. Eliminate all but the most necessary data fields.

However, you cannot eliminate anxiety from your pages completely! In order for prospects to buy from you, they must provide some payment information. If you want visitors to sign up for a newsletter, they must provide their email address.

Therefore, you need to offset their anxiety in some manner. The best way to do this is to establish your credibility. Here are some common techniques for reassuring visitors to your site that their personal information is safe:

- Prominently display company phone numbers.
- Provide a contact page with a mailing and email addresses.
- Place (authentic) customer testimonials in sidebars.
- Include a privacy policy on your site.
- Allow customers to submit and browse product reviews directly on the site.
- Link to third-party reviews of your products and services.
- Provide live chat capabilities.
- Display third-party trust seals on checkout pages.

And here are some common mistakes that can harm your credibility:

- Fake testimonials
- Use of certain third-party trust seals; certain ones can actually hurt sales because they make your site look cheap

- Poorly written copy that makes outlandish or unbelievable claims
- Use of false addresses or PO boxes; with the advent of Google street maps, anyone can check to see who's really at your address
- Off-shore phone support and live chat

Figure 22–17 shows a site that manages to break many of these rules. The homepage copy is poorly written and makes use of logos unrelated to the business (why is there an NFL logo on an auto transport website?). Even the Better Business Bureau logo (which is normally a good thing) has been faked. An actual BBB lookup shows that this company has received nothing but complaints from dissatisfied customers.

Clicking through to the "Contact Us" page shows a physical address but no email or phone number. Google street maps shows that there is actually a mailbox store at this address. Run, don't walk, from this website (see Figure 22–18 on page 202).

Visitors get (rightfully) scared when asked for credit card information. This is an area where you should spend time reassuring them. The checkout page at Back to Basics Toys (Figure 22–19 on page 203) uses a third-party trust seal from McAfee to let customers know their credit card information will be transferred via a secure connection. This

FIGURE 22–17. This site has many signals that it can't be trusted.

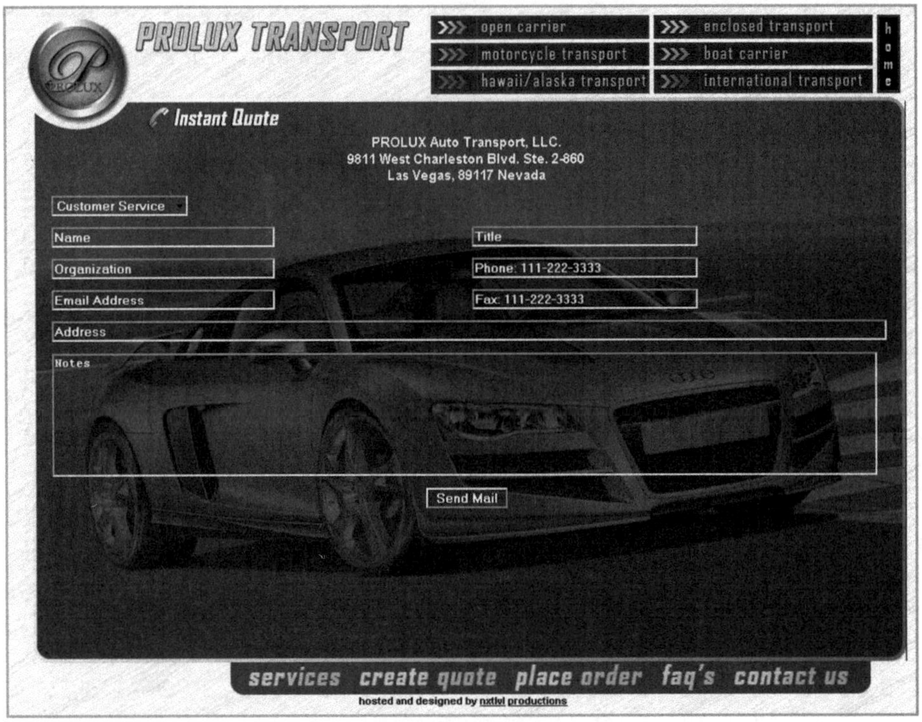

FIGURE 22–18. The contact page shows a fake address for this business.

page is pretty good, but it could be improved further by including testimonials from customers who were happy about how their orders were handled.

Friction

Friction can be thought of as page elements that cause confusion for visitors and increase the likelihood that they will abandon the page.

There are many ways in which poor design can cause friction for visitors, so I'll cover only the most common ones. Low-friction pages aren't particularly instructional, so this concept is best illustrated through bad examples.

The first and by far most common way that sites confuse their visitors is by including too many elements (links, navigation items, and form fields) on a page. This is often compounded by poor use of eyeline.

The American Airlines site mentioned earlier has this problem, but the worst offender I've come across is HavenWorks.com (see Figure 22–20).

Even pages with relatively few links can cause major confusion for visitors. If you're serious about website optimization, you should avoid the use of clever, "metaphor"

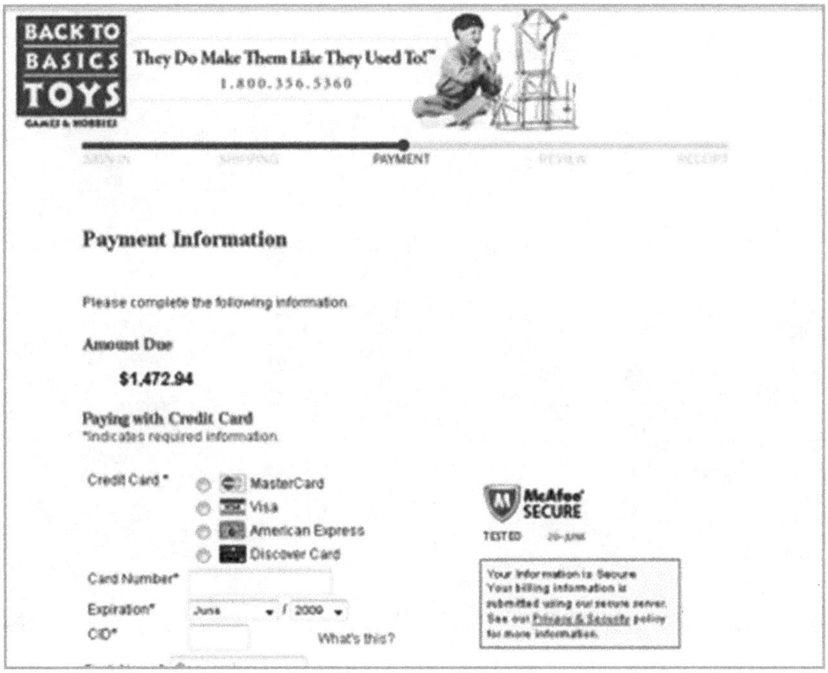

FIGURE 22–19. Reassure customers using third-party trust seals. This site would also benefit by placing testimonials on this page.

FIGURE 22–20. Havenworks.com: A case study in friction.

FIGURE 22–21. Keep your designer on a tight leash or you may end up with a navigation scheme like this one.

navigation schemes such as that shown in Figure 22–21. Internet users have navigation pretty well figured out these days; no need to reinvent it.

The website of Sarasota Tampa Express (www.stexps.com, Figure 22–22) provides some more examples of what not to do. The page makes use of annoying flashing graphics, including a circa–1996 effect that displays a text message wherever the mouse cursor moves. Navigation is included at the top, left, and bottom of the page. And for the trifecta, every page on the site plays MIDI-style classical music.

Many sites fail to use hyperlinks in the proper way. Either through "creativity" or neglect, these sites end up making navigation extremely difficult for their users.

Here are some basic rules you should follow when using hyperlinks on your site:

- Links should be clearly labeled with meaningful and understandable names.
- Use underlines to distinguish links from other elements on the page. Avoid using underlines anywhere else, because this only serves to confuse visitors.
- Most of the time, you should use text, rather than graphics, for links. If you opt to use graphics for your links, split test them against text-only versions because this often has a profound impact on sales.
- All links on your site should have the same format so that visitors can distinguish them from other elements on the site.

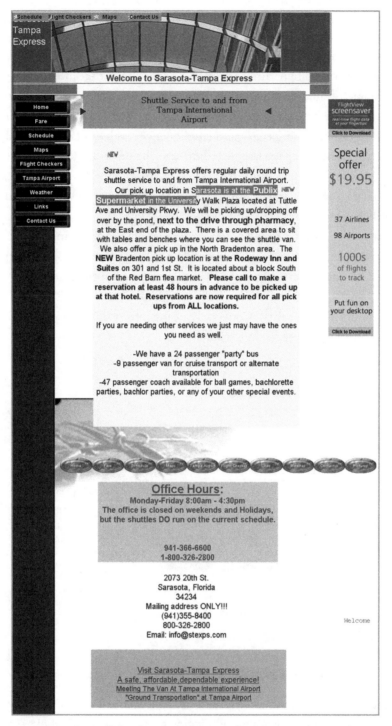

FIGURE 22–22. One of the few websites on the internet that makes use of triple navigation bars.

Another common (and important) question that comes up in optimizing your web page design is whether to use links or buttons. The rule of thumb I follow is that if clicking the link will complete a transaction of some sort, use a button. Otherwise, use a traditional underlined hyperlink. The rationale for this is that most people experience a certain degree of anxiety when clicking a button, much more than they feel when clicking links. Therefore, use buttons only when you want to signal to your users that they will be doing something that has a consequence (such as placing an order).

Figure 22–23 shows a page that uses buttons when it should be using links.

Figure 22–24 shows an example from Dell that makes good use of buttons and links. Although the page is packed with information, the buttons give visitors a hint of where they should click next.

An area that should be tested far more extensively than you may think is the font style and size. Many sites use a font size that is either too small or too large for their target audience. For instance, if your B2B site caters to executives, your font size should be no less than 12 pixels in height (many people past the age of 35 have difficulties reading fonts smaller than this). Conversely, using a font size greater than 15 pixels on page copy can convey unprofessionalism.

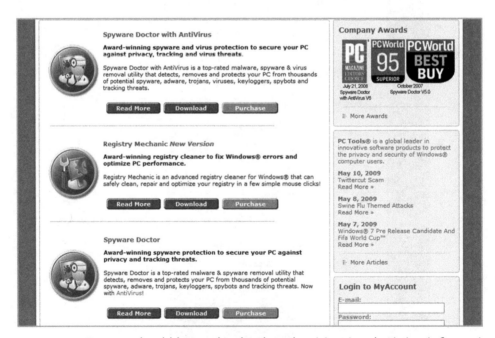

FIGURE 22–23. Buttons should be used only when the visitor is submitting information or completing a transaction. Replacing these buttons with links would probably lift sales.

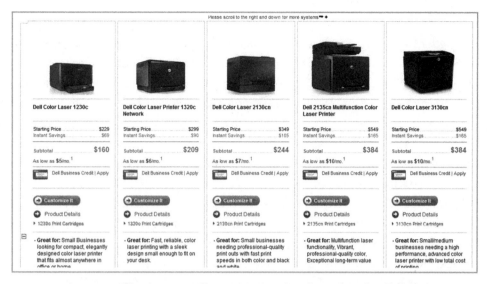

FIGURE 22–24. Effective use of buttons on a landing page for Dell printers.

Friction may also stem from the technologies that your developers use behind the scenes. For instance, Flash is a favorite technology with many designers. However, it has some serious drawbacks:

- Flash can increase the overall size and load time of the page.
- Flash animations often add a few seconds of rendering time to the page, especially for those visitors using slower computers.
- Flash is not available on certain mobile devices (most notably, the iPhone). Its use may also be restricted in corporate environments.

For these reasons, I almost always shy away from the use of Flash with the exception of product demo videos and, even then, only after split testing against static HTML versions of the same page.

Modern web development platforms such as JQuery can be useful in landing pages, but be careful to test it on a wide variety of platforms and browsers. I have personally seen cases where dynamic pages worked fine in Chrome and Internet Explorer but were broken in Firefox. The problem went undetected for months because most users were able to interact with the page normally.

The final source of friction can be traced back to minor cosmetic issues on your pages. Seemingly trivial problems such as misaligned text boxes or insufficient white space can depress conversions to a small degree, so again, be sure to thoroughly test your site on a wide variety of browsers.

Page Length

The length of your pages and sales funnels will dramatically affect conversions.

First, your ad copy length should be appropriate to the product or service that you're offering. Note that this doesn't mean copy needs to be as short as possible. On the contrary, high-commitment transactions often require lengthy copy in order to sell. This is because copy length (generally) needs to be proportional to the price of the product. An email newsletter signup form should require no more than a few sentences to convince visitors to subscribe. A seminar costing $700 will probably require five or more page lengths of copy.

Next, your pages should each have no more than ten data entry fields on them. When longer forms are unavoidable, try splitting them out on separate pages, or use modern web design techniques to maximize completion rates.

Incidentally, if you do end up splitting your pages out, one way to reduce the perceived length of your sales funnel is through the use of a progress indicator at the top of the page (see Figure 22–25).

Another very important optimization task is to reduce the height of your important sales funnel pages. Your conversions will jump dramatically if you can squeeze your content in "above the fold" in a 1024 x 768 pixel browser resolution. Your options here are (again) to reduce the number of fields you ask your customers to fill out or to use double-column format. If you use Google Analytics, you already have access to a nice

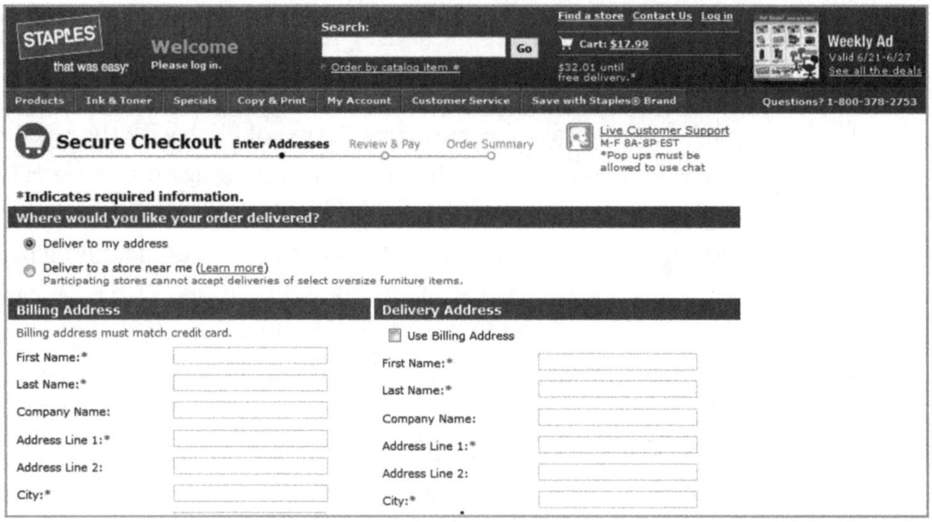

FIGURE 22–25. Staples.com uses a progress indicator to reduce the perceived length of the checkout process.

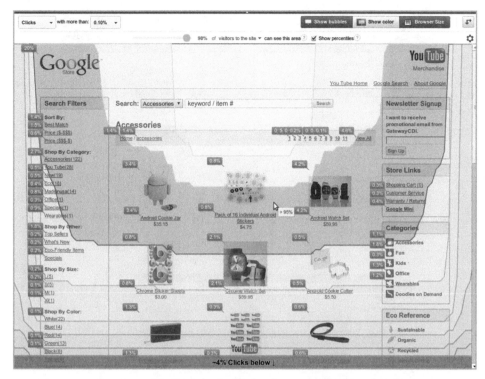

FIGURE 22–26. Google Analytics browser size simulator.

tool that can help with this (see Figure 22–26). To use it, navigate to the Content section and click "In-Page Analytics."

Staples.com fits the most important fields above the fold on their checkout form but then negates the benefit by following it up with three pages of additional fields (see Figure 22–27 on page 210).

Finally, take a look at the actual size of your pages in bytes (in Firefox, right-click the page and select "View Page Info"). Page size should be as small as possible, certainly no more than 150k. We'll touch on the reasons for this shortly.

Congruency

All of the pages in your sales funnel should share as many common elements as possible (with the exception of the content areas, of course). When visitors see dramatic changes in page layouts, they are far more likely to abandon your site.

These common elements consist of the page header, sidebars, navigation menus, and, to a small extent, footers.

Another common cause of lost conversions is due to the use of third-party shopping carts, particularly those hosted on a separate domain. Nothing kills sales faster than

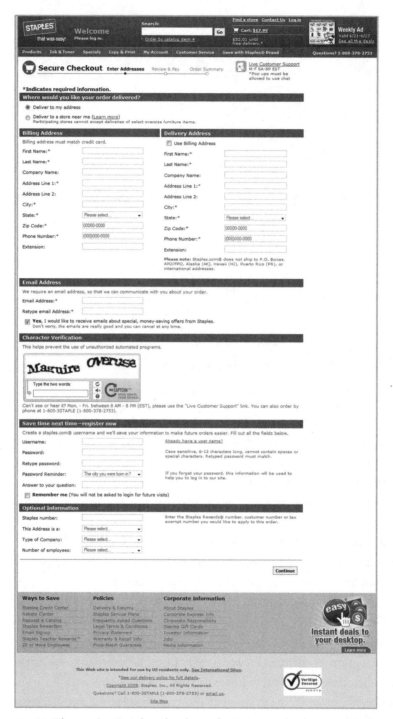

FIGURE 22–27. The entire Staples checkout form is nearly three pages long and includes many unnecessary fields. Eliminating several of these sections as well as the footer could dramatically improve online sales.

when customers are abruptly switched from your site to a third-party domain with a completely different look and feel. If you have a choice, keep the shopping cart hosted on your own domain.

Load Time

Your pages' load time will have a profound impact on your conversion rate. Your clickthrough rate will start taking a hit after five seconds. After eight seconds, most visitors will abandon the page (unless they've already filled in a good number of data fields on prior forms).

Many marketers make the mistake of assuming that if a page loads quickly on their own computer, that it will load quickly for most or all of their visitors. This is a mistake because page-load time is dependent on a wide variety of factors.

- *Database calls made by the page.* The effect of database calls and other page logic is usually apparent to all users (even ones at your corporate headquarters), so this is usually optimized away by the developers.
- *Total page size in bytes.* This will affect visitors with slow internet connections and those who are geographically far away.
- *Number and order of external files (CSS, Javascript, and images) referenced by the page.* This will tend to affect visitors more or less randomly based on their network latency, bandwidth, and even the type of browser they are using.
- *The HTML Doctype that the page adheres to (such as HTML 4 Transitional, HTML 4.01 Strict, XHTML, and so forth).* This seemingly minor detail will have a profound impact on your page-load speed and is particularly dependent on the browser version your visitors are using.

Your developers and designers should be well informed on this subject. Here are some general guidelines to follow, however:

- *Minimize the total page size in bytes.* You can see how large your pages are by right-clicking them in Firefox and selecting "View Page Info" from the popup menu. Ask your developers to remove unnecessary code from the page, and consider switching your website to a CSS-based design, such as XHTML, if you haven't already.
- *Minimize the number of external files referenced by your page.* An easy way to do this is by combining all of your Javascript code into a single, global include file. The same can be done for your CSS files. Even images referenced by your site can be merged into a single sprite file to minimize load time. Your designers will know how to do all of this.

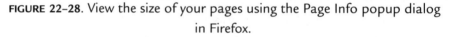

FIGURE 22–28. View the size of your pages using the Page Info popup dialog in Firefox.

- If you do have multiple Javascript files, group them together on the page and reference it before any CSS. This will allow the javascript files to be loaded in parallel and will speed up page rendering.

- Utilize design tricks such as loading indicators, AJAX, and (subtle) animations to reduce the perceived page-load time your users experience. Note that this won't reduce the actual page load time, but users will perceive it to run a little faster.

- If you're using ASP.Net to host your website, ask your developers to devote attention to minimizing the view state data contained in the page. By default, ASP.Net uses far more storage within view state than necessary. This adds considerable bloat to the page and can seriously increase your page-load times (both perceived and actual). At AdGooroo, we use ASP.Net only for our internal reporting pages because these tend to be more complex. For the external marketing pages, we stick with lightweight languages such as PHP and Perl.

- Don't go overboard with dynamic HTML (AJAX, jQuery, etc)! Keeping in mind what was said in previous chapters about the benefits of using dynamic HTML to reduce your sales funnel length, many sites use far too much of it. This can be annoying to users, prevent your pages from being indexed properly, hurt your quality scores, and significantly increase the size of your pages. Use it sparingly.

One of the best tools for speeding up your pages is the Google Page Speed add-on for Chrome and Firefox (https://developers.google.com/speed/pagespeed/ insights_extensions). This free plug-in analyzes your pages and generates specific recommendations that your developers can implement to reduce your load time.

Urgency

A classic sales technique for improving close rates is to create a sense of urgency. This works on landing pages as well!

The technique is simple: Offer something of value to your potential customers to encourage them to complete the conversion process. This generally works well, but you have to be careful, because it can also increase the number of bogus orders.

Contrary to popular belief, incentives work just as well with B2B websites as they do B2C ones. The key is to ensure that the incentive provides value to your target audience. While corporate executives are unlikely to be swayed by a pen or plastic toy, they do respond to proprietary research studies.

We make use of this technique at AdGooroo. We experimented with many types of incentives, ranging from corporate schwag to free subscriptions. The most successful incentive turned out to be a copy of my previous book, *Mastering Search Advertising*. Not only did this incentive increase free trials by 48 percent, it also helped to educate many new search advertisers, some of whom later came back as subscribers.

A REAL-WORLD CONVERSION OPTIMIZATION EXAMPLE

The next screenshot (Figure 22–29 on page 214) is the actual email newsletter signup form from the Methuselah Foundation as it looked in the beginning of 2009. Work through the checklist in Figure 22–1 on pages 188 and 189, and see how many optimization opportunities you can find.

During the optimization process, I performed this same exercise by marking up a printout of the page. Here are some of the problem areas I found:

- The page doesn't appear to have a single purpose. Rather, it's a confusing collection of links, images, navigation bars, and form fields.
- The form is nearly three pages in length.
- Login area (along the top of the page) competes with the rest of the page elements.
- Menu items above photo offer the user conflicting choices and push the important areas further down the page.
- A second left-hand navigation menu competes with the top menus.

FIGURE 22–29. The Methuselah Foundation email newsletter signup page as it looked prior to optimization.

- A third column is required to contain the left-hand navigation menu. This breaks up the eyeline.
- The form and "Join Now" button are below the page fold at a standard 1024x768 resolution.
- A large, red "Donate Now!" button sits prominently above the fold .
- The photo is interesting, but it drags the eyeline to the right (directly into the "Donate Now!" button).

- Copy is three paragraphs in length. This may be too much for an email newsletter signup page.
- The newsletter thumbnail graphic to the right pulls the eyeline right, away from the form fields.
- The primary headline ("Membership") does not clearly convey the purpose of the page.
- A secondary headline ("Receive the latest news in anti-aging research") does a better job of describing the page but is in small type.
- The area containing the form fields has a red background. This may increase anxiety on the part of the user.
- This simple email newsletter signup form is asking for too much personal information. The following fields could be eliminated:
  - Login
  - Password
  - Password verification
  - "HTML Email Please!" checkbox (all emails should be sent in both HTML and plain text)
  - Phone number
  - Country
  - All address fields
- More competing links ("Press Kit" and "Contact Us") are found at the bottom of the page.

My notes gave me a clear direction for where I wanted to take this page (see Figure 22–30 on page 216). I eliminated everything that I felt wasn't necessary and rearranged the remaining elements to come up with the testing candidate shown in Figure 22–31 on page 216.

Figure 22–32 on page 217 shows both pages placed next to each other for comparison.

How Well Did the New Page Work?

The original page scored a conversion rate of 23.6 percent. This sounds like a pretty incredible completion rate for an email newsletter signup page, but because the page was so hard to find, relatively few people saw it. And those that did find it were highly motivated to do so. This skews all of our conversion rates upward.

We were blown away by the results. The new page had an astonishing conversion rate of 60 percent. Imagine what results like this could do for your pay-per-click campaign!

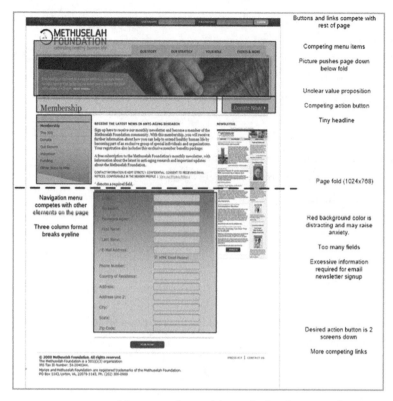

FIGURE 22–30. My notes from this optimization exercise.

FIGURE 22–31. The redesigned email newsletter signup page.

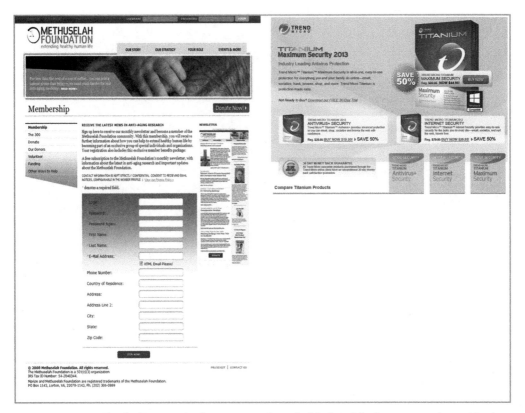

FIGURE 22–32. The before-and-after pages placed side by side for comparison. Notice how much shorter and cleaner the new page looks.

Chapter 23

Monitoring Your Campaign Performance

You wouldn't run your business without occasionally looking at your income statement and balance sheet, would you? Yet, you would be surprised at how many small business advertisers rarely take more than a casual look at their online advertising campaigns.

The next few chapters will focus on the numbers side of pay-per-click advertising. If math isn't your thing, don't worry! We'll boil it down to only the essential statistics that you'll need to keep an eye on to properly manage your campaign.

WHY IT'S IMPORTANT TO STAY ON TOP OF YOUR CAMPAIGN DATA

Knowing your overall campaign data will help you answer questions like:

- What's a reasonable clickthrough rate to expect for my ads?
- Am I spending too much (too little) on advertising this month?
- How much revenue could I possibly earn each month from my paid search campaign?
- Is my advertising in this particular keyword hurting or helping me?

There's no way to answer these questions without having a working knowledge of how your campaign has performed in the past. And, believe me, these things are important to know.

The first thing a high-priced agency or consultant will do is analyze your past data to get an understanding of what you've done and how much better they can do in the future (and how much they can charge you).

Along with the behavioral model, this data serves as the foundation for everything that comes later. Without it, you'll never be able to make an informed decision about your campaign. With it, your eyes will open to problems and opportunities that were invisible before.

KEY STATISTICS TO WATCH

- Your average daily and monthly campaign spend
- Your average impression share and coverage, i.e., the percentage of search engine users who are seeing your ads (also known as reach)
- The number of visitors (clicks) you typically receive on both a daily and monthly basis
- Your average clickthrough rate, or CTR, meaning the percentage of people who see your ads and actually click them
- Your average conversion rate, or the percentage of visitors to your site who buy from you
- Your spend relative to your competitors' (optional, but highly recommended)

Typical Daily and Monthly Spend

The two most important statistics you need to track are your daily and monthly campaign spend. I can't tell you how many advertisers I've talked with who can't tell me how much they spend on paid search.

This will help you answer questions such as:

- Are you spending $10 a day or $100?
- How has your campaign spend changed over the past month?
- What does a normal month look like?

Start by looking at your absolute dollar spend every day (or try to). If you don't do this, you may be in for some rude surprises.

You never know when this data point will come in handy. A few years ago, I was mining my server logs to find new keyword phrases to target. One of the keyword phrases was "Flooder.AKE," a computer virus that was rapidly spreading over the internet. After noticing that no other advertisers were targeting this phrase, I added it to my campaign with a modest $0.15 bid.

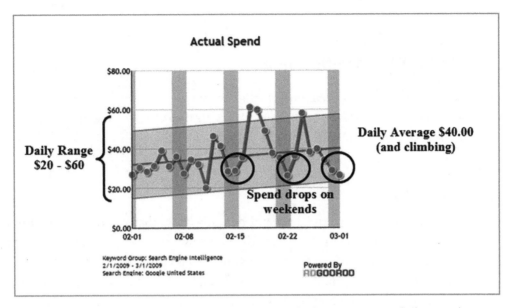

FIGURE 23–1. Use monthly spend charts to find your average daily spend, the normal range, and trends.

Three days later, I discovered that my tactic worked too well, and my site was flooded with new visitors. My campaign spend increased from $200 per day to over $2,500! Had I been more diligent I would have saved myself a massive AdWords bill.

It's also a good idea to maintain a trending chart. This will help you distinguish between normal daily fluctuations and abnormal ones. A typical trending chart is shown in Figure 23–1. With it, you can see that the costs are usually highest in the first half of the week and trend down into the weekends (indicated by the shaded vertical bars). The chart also tells us that while our typical spend is $40, it's perfectly normal for daily costs to fluctuate between $20 to $60. Anything outside of that range should set off the alarm bells.

Coverage and Impression Share

Impression share is the percentage of the available search impressions in which your ads appear across all of your keywords. Coverage is similar, except that it doesn't take traffic into account and can be used on individual keywords. These metrics tell you how much traffic you're leaving on the table and are so important that we devoted an entire chapter to them earlier in the book.

Impression share is a nice-to-have, but coverage is indispensable because it tells you exactly where the problems lie by revealing places where your quality score lags behind your close competitors.

HOW TO USE IMPRESSION SHARE

I use impression share for one purpose: to monitor my campaign's overall health. If it drops below 70 percent, I know it's time to roll up my sleeves and figure out what's going wrong.

Daily/Monthly Clicks

You'll also want to track both the daily and monthly clicks that you're receiving from your PPC campaigns. Just as we discussed with campaign costs, you need to be able to distinguish between normal daily fluctuations and trends either up or down.

Here's an example of a monthly chart showing clicks. They are highest in the beginning part of the week and trend down into the weekend. Clicks often mirror costs, but not always. If they diverge significantly, you should drill into your historical CTR to see if there are any interesting patterns there.

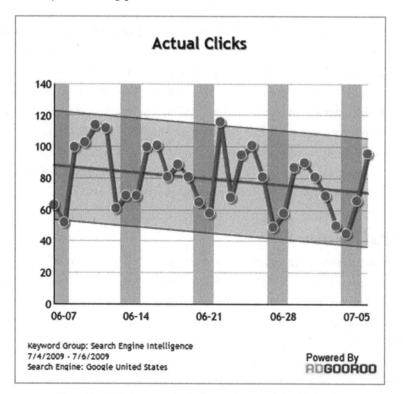

FIGURE 23–2. You should also track daily and monthly clicks from your paid search campaigns.

Average Clickthrough Rate

Having charts of your costs and clicks is helpful, but it doesn't give you the whole picture. It's very easy to miss important changes in your campaign if you try to eyeball the charts against one another. For this reason, we also want to track the average daily clickthrough rate.

In this next sample chart, you can see that the daily clickthrough rate is decreasing (the blue band indicates a statistically significant trend). This isn't at all obvious from the previous two charts. This indicates that something may possibly be wrong with this campaign, and we need to dig deeper to find the root cause.

Average Conversion Rate

The final one of our must-have statistics is our average website conversion rate (attributed to PPC traffic). This figure adds color to your overall website sales.

If your website pulled in twice the revenue this month than last, you might just pat yourself on the back and move on. Before you do, though, be sure to check out

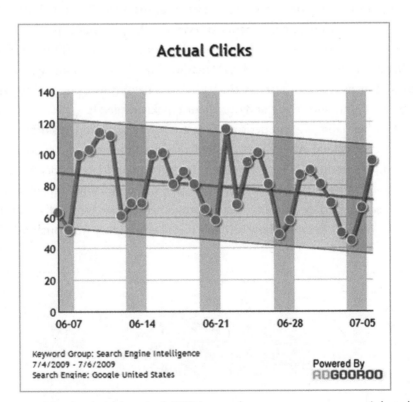

FIGURE 23–3. Monitoring historical CTR is another way to spot potential problems in your campaign.

the average conversion rate. If it lags behind your sales, you may be missing out on something big.

I once worked on a site that was generating over $15 million a year in sales from paid search. One weekend, the average conversion rate in the United Kingdom dropped dramatically while the overall website sales remained in the normal range. Upon further investigation, it turned out that a minor development change on the website resulted in endless loops in the shopping cart, but only for that country. I never would have noticed this problem had I not been paying attention to the average conversion rate.

Competitors' Spend

This last metric has recently bubbled into the top tier of statistics I keep a close eye on. As we'll see in the next chapter, dramatic changes in your competitors' spend often provide valuable insights into their businesses.

If you see a long-time competitor increase their bids, it's often a sign that something is working (the same does not hold true for brand-new competitors, who may simply be trying to figure out the optimal position for their campaigns). Check their landing pages for new products, feature improvements, or even new layouts and copy.

Not too long ago, we saw a client's primary competitor rapidly increase their ad spend after a period of relative stability. When we dug into their campaign, we saw that the increased spend was attributed to the launch of a new online coupon campaign. This campaign was wildly successful, and our client quickly copied it.

On the other hand, if a competitor's bids and/or budget drop, it's often a sign that something isn't working. At one time, we had a fierce competitor who suddenly reduced their AdWords spending. They began with day parting and later added a budget cap, which was evident because their keyword coverage was uniformly capped at around 50 percent. A year later, they quit advertising altogether. Today, we hardly hear anything from them. This data was incredibly valuable to us because they were pushing a business

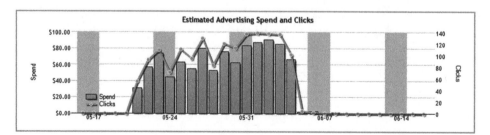

FIGURE 23–4. By monitoring your competitors' spends, you can learn what works and what doesn't much more quickly than you could through firsthand testing.

model that seemed promising at the time, but their poor subsequent performance in the marketplace convinced us that it was a losing strategy.

Figure 23-4 on page 224 shows an example of another one-time competitor who activated their AdWords account for only 15 days before shutting it down. We learned a lot about what doesn't work by investigating their website.

Aside from the strategic advantage this data gives you, it's also very handy for benchmarking your own campaign spend and traffic versus that of your competitors. This helps ensure that you can at least achieve parity with your rivals.

SPEND BY COUNTRY

If your campaign spans multiple markets, you simply must track your spend by country. However, the method for doing so isn't very obvious. As of this writing (early 2013), you can do this within AdWords.

- Select the "Campaigns" tab from the top menu bar.
- Select the "Dimensions" tab.
- Select "geographic" from the "View" dropdown.
- Customize your columns to show only the breakdown by country. Do this by selecting the "Customize Columns" from the "Columns" dropdown and removing "Region," "Metro Area," "City," and "Most Specific Location."

SPEND BY CHANNEL

Most marketers we ask are not aware that Google AdWords includes both display and search advertising totals within its reporting interface by default. You can separate them by scrolling to the bottom of the "Campaigns" tab. On the bottom of the main report, you'll see two rows: "Total—Search" and "Total—Display Network."

If you're like most advertisers, you'll find that display makes up the majority of your impressions but relatively few clicks. This means that if you don't take the time to separate the two, you will end up with a distorted view of your campaign clickthrough rate.

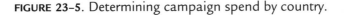

Country/Territory	Clicks	Impr.	CTR	Avg. CPC	Cost
United States	266	100,086	0.27%	$1.47	$391.65
United Kingdom	141	191,800	0.07%	$1.29	$181.42
Canada	56	83,947	0.07%	$1.66	$92.92
Australia	31	32,174	0.10%	$1.38	$42.91

FIGURE 23-5. Determining campaign spend by country.

SPEND BY COUNTRY AND CHANNEL

Why would you want to break display and mobile spend down by country? One reason is that it allows you to gauge the effectiveness of your search and display campaigns by geography. Another common reason is to compare your actual campaign spend with estimates produced by competitive intelligence services.

One approach to do this is to first run the two reports described above and then apply the display/search ratio for each country. Unfortunately, this method leaves a lot to be desired because your display and search campaigns will almost certainly vary significantly by country.

The only truly accurate way to get these figures is to create a separate search account for each country. Unfortunately, this adds up to a lot of management overhead so I can recommend it only for the largest accounts.

WHAT ABOUT COVERAGE?

Earlier I stated that nearly all of the data you need is available within your AdWords or Microsoft Ad Network reports.

Coverage is the exception. Coverage, the percentage of the time your ads appear to search engine users, is not a widely available statistic. And yet, it's absolutely indispensable. In the land of the blind, this metric will make you the king.

The only way to get coverage is through a third-party monitoring solution. This data provides valuable feedback about the advertising marketplace, and with it you'll be able to run circles around your competitors.

DON'T BLOW IT OFF!

Look, I know you're busy. But if you don't think you have time to check in with your campaign on a regular basis, then you're probably better off not running a paid search campaign. Successful advertisers just don't get lucky in paid search. They work their tails off and exploit every advantage they have to get to the top. That's what you're up against.

That said, the payback on regular campaign reviews is huge.

Here's an exercise that could pay for this book in spades. Download your campaign statistics into an Excel spreadsheet, and figure out how many keywords were responsible for 80 percent of your campaign spend for the past month. Now compare that with how much revenue these keywords produced. If you've never done this before, you'll probably find that the Pareto Rule is in effect here: Most of your revenue will come from relatively few keywords.

The first time I did this exercise back in 2004, I was shocked. I found that over 80 percent of my budget was spent on a single keyword (to the tune of $800 per day).

And this keyword generated less than 5 percent of my total revenues. I immediately dropped my bids and improved my ad copy, resulting in immediate improvements in my campaign return.

I repeated this exercise in 2007 while writing the first version of this book. I discovered that two keywords were generating nearly 70 percent of our traffic, but the conversion rate was running at about 10 percent of the site average. In that case, we used a negative exact match (Chapter 18) to drop our campaign costs by half while not losing a single sale.

I repeated the exercise again in 2009 (with a heavily optimized AdWords campaign) and still found that just 10 keywords generated over 50 percent of the revenue on our site, while accounting for only 16 percent of the total campaign cost.

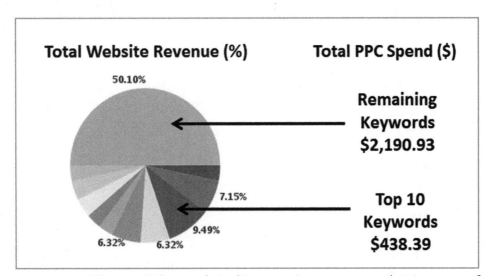

FIGURE 23–6. The top 10 keywords in this campaign represent only 16 percent of total campaign costs but generate 50 percent of the revenues.

Hopefully this example demonstrates to you the value of devoting even a little time to digesting your campaign metrics. The payoff can be huge.

Chapter 24

Put the Competition to Work for You

The days when you could run your pay-per-click campaigns in a silo, completely oblivious to the impact of other advertisers, are long gone. The search engines' increasing focus on relevance as well as high demand for ad placement means that advertisers are judged against one another to determine which ads will be shown and which will not.

If you want to take a bigger bite of the apple than your competitors, you have to keep close tabs on them. This practice is known as search intelligence. In this chapter, I'll show you a number of ways you can use search intelligence to outwit your competitors and take advantage of their mistakes.

PRIORITIZE OPTIMIZATION EFFORTS

You can't be everywhere at once. This is why you need to know when and where competitors are making improvements to their quality score through ad copy and landing page optimization so that you can prioritize your own efforts. As competitors improve their placements on specific keywords, your relative quality score will be diminished, your coverage and traffic will suffer, and your CPC costs could even go up. Having even one competitor close the gap can put the hurt on your campaign. Having a few do it can be catastrophic. This is why campaigns that are put on autopilot tend to decline after a few months.

You can see the effect of quality score shifts pictured graphically in Figure 24–1. As quality scores improve at the top of the page, remaining advertisers are pushed down. If you aren't vigilant, your position can—and will—eventually be taken over by other advertisers as they struggle to remain relevant. Just imagine this taking place across your entire campaign.

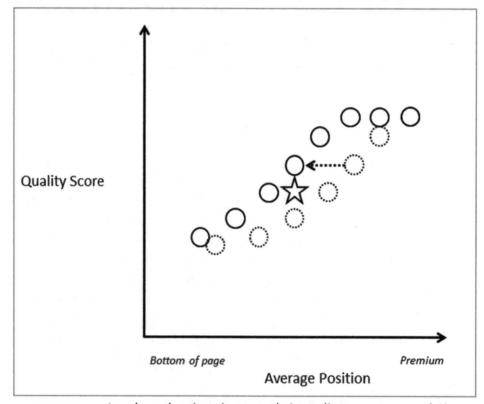

FIGURE 24–1. As other advertisers increase their quality scores, your relative Quality Score will decrease.

PEEK INTO COMPETITORS' BUSINESS MODELS

Paying attention to competitors' paid search efforts can pay off in less obvious ways as well. Because PPC is so measurable, many companies test new products, features, and services on the search engines prior to widespread launch. You can get advance notice of these changes if you're watchful.

You can also use paid search to peek inside of your competitors' business models. If a competitor launches a new pricing model or brand while aggressively increasing

CPCs, keep a close eye on them for a while. If they later drop CPCs and/or pull the model, you've found something that didn't work. Our competitors have saved us countless times at AdGooroo from launching features that the market truly didn't want.

BENCHMARK AGAINST THE COMPETITION

You also need to keep a close eye on your competitive benchmarks, or statistics that show how your performance compares to your close competitors.

It is very easy to become complacent in paid search, especially after spending several months tuning your campaign and experiencing some success. Your client (or your boss) may be thrilled with your results, but if you can't prove that you are delivering best-of-class results, it's just a matter of time before your account (or job) is up for review. In fact, my experience is that client churn is highest among agencies that aren't paying attention to this data.

However, if you have access to competitive data, you are far more likely to notice problems or new threats much earlier and respond much more quickly.

As an example, let's look at Figure 24–2, a prominent advertiser in the credit card vertical. The chart shows that their campaign spend (and traffic) has been steadily declining for eleven consecutive months and is now down nearly 50 percent from a year ago.

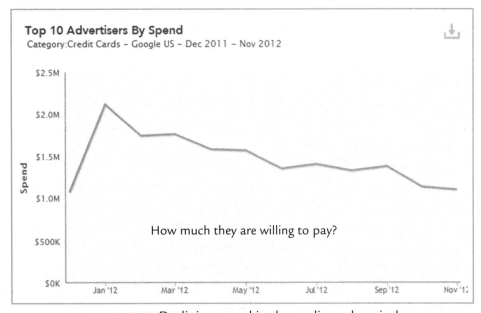

FIGURE 24–2. Declining spend in the credit card vertical.

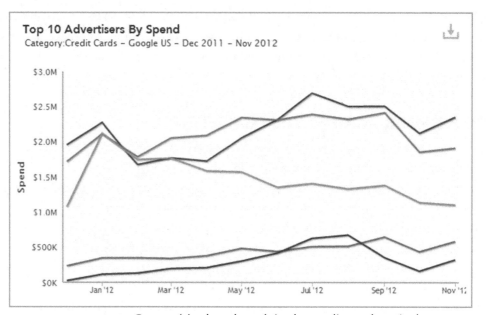

FIGURE 24–3. Competitive benchmark in the credit card vertical.

Maybe this isn't so bad. After all, there are worse things that could happen than reduced spend. Unfortunately, the picture isn't quite so rosy when you compare this advertiser to a few of their competitors. This company is quite literally being eaten alive by the competition, and they don't seem to know it. Take a look at Figure 24–3.

Although I chose not to include the names of these companies, it's worth mentioning that none of them are "mom-and-pop" advertisers. The spends shown above belong to major credit card companies that you read about and see on television all of the time (and you probably have one of their credit cards in your wallet right now). Loss of market share is a "big company" problem.

While competitive benchmarks don't provide solutions, they do alert you to the fact that there are problems afoot. This is another important data point that serious search advertisers don't try to do without.

If you are self-managing your campaigns and your boss (or CFO) asks if you can live without it, ask them if they are OK leaving a significant portion of potential revenue on the table.

If, on the other hand, you outsource your paid search efforts, ask every potential consultant or agency if they monitor competitive benchmarks and if they will provide you with direct access to this data. Reputable paid search agencies will happily do so because this will clearly demonstrate their value. Less reputable firms will discourage this because it invites unwanted accountability.

PLAN NEW CAMPAIGNS

One of the best uses of search intelligence is in the planning stages of a new campaign. With it, you can answer questions such as:

- How much traffic can I expect?
- How much should I budget?
- How much revenue can I expect to generate (both short-term and long-term)?

It's important to realize that only the roughest of estimates can be made without actually having either an active search campaign or sophisticated computer modeling techniques at your disposal. If you don't absolutely need to plan your campaign ahead of time, then I advise you to simply start your campaign and see what the numbers tell you after a week or two.

On the other hand, if you need to get approval for your budget in advance, you'll probably want some sort of defensible estimate to fall back on. However, you should set reasonable expectations: *There is no such thing as a perfect estimate.*

A GOOD ESTIMATE IS HARD TO FIND

Whenever you rely on the preliminary data that the search engines provide with their keyword or traffic estimator tools, be sure to take it with a grain of salt. As we say in search marketing, this data is as good as bad data gets.

It's not that their data is wrong. It's simply based on system-wide averages, and your campaign will (hopefully) be anything but average. The statistics you get from the search engines ignore the effect of duplicate keywords, ad coverage, optimized copy, landing page quality scores, and historical clickthrough rates so your actual campaign results may vary wildly from your initial estimates.

So use the data as a directional indicator only. If you estimate that there are 580,000 searches in the United States in your industry in a given month, don't be surprised if you actually see 150,000 or 2,000,000. In practice, if you can get within 300 percent, you've done a pretty good job.

There are many reasons why the data you pull from the search engines might be wrong. Here are some of the most common.

Traffic Sources

The traffic estimates as reported by the search engines may or may not include traffic from partner sites. For instance, the Google AdWords API includes traffic from Ask.com and AOL. Not only is this traffic highly volatile and difficult to predict, your quality scores play a large part in determining how much of it you'll get access to.

Quality Score Issues

Your actual search results will vary tremendously based on your quality scores. For instance, if your ads and landing pages are considerably better than most advertisers out there, you can expect your average position (and thus clickthrough rate) to be higher than anticipated while your average cost-per-click may end up far lower.

Conversely, if your landing pages or ad copy aren't very good, you may receive little or no traffic at all.

Seasonality

Search data also varies widely depending on when it was collected.

For example, at the time of this writing Google reports an average of 720 searches per month for the term, "Chicago flower delivery." But the February 2013 estimate was 1,600 (February is the biggest month of the year in the online flower industry). If you inadvertently create a yearly forecast using the February estimate, your final figure will be overstated by 122 percent.

Mobile Traffic

As of this writing, the Google Keyword Tool is slated to be replaced by the Keyword Planner. Unlike the Keyword Tool, the Keyword Planner doesn't offer you the ability to filter out mobile traffic. This limitation means that for most advertisers, the actual traffic you receive from AdWords will be lower than reported.

One-Time Events

Another source of error is that one-time occurrences such as news articles, press releases, and offline advertising campaigns can temporarily push traffic well above normal levels.

Declining Markets

All markets experience periods of growth and decline. If you're entering a market in decline, you may find that your search traffic comes nowhere near the levels you initially estimated. This happened in 2005 to the antispam software category as well as in 2011 to the mortgage category.

Keyword Matching

If you follow my recommendations for using both phrase and exact matching in your keyword lists, your paid search clicks will likely end up far higher than the "average" estimates provided by the search engines. This is because the vast majority of advertisers don't make use of these keyword-matching techniques.

Keyword matching is very difficult to factor into traffic estimates. Not only will your clickthrough rates be higher, your traffic and cost-per-click will tend to be lower when matching is used extensively.

Niche Terms

If you've done a good job at keyword expansion, you'll be making use of hundreds or thousands of niche terms. Because there is relatively little traffic for these phrases, AdWords will not report estimates for many of them.

Geo-Targeting

Another subtlety that can throw off your estimates is failing to use the geo-targeting filter when retrieving traffic data. If your campaign is targeting the United States, then be sure to exclude traffic from the rest of the world from your estimates.

Day Parting

If you plan on day parting, be aware that you will capture only a portion of the available traffic. You'll need to guess how much of the available traffic you'll miss out on and adjust accordingly. Day parting is explored further in Chapter 27.

With this discussion out of the way, let's move on to some of the more useful data points you can gather about your category and competitors.

ESTIMATING SEARCH VOLUME

Earlier we began constructing a spreadsheet to contain our keyword research data. You can also add a column to capture the monthly search volume for your keywords. This data will not only help you plan your PPC campaign, you can also benefit greatly from it by incorporating it into your SEO campaigns. This data is available from the AdWords Keyword Planner (https://adwords.google.com/ko/KeywordPlanner/Home).

ESTIMATING IMPRESSIONS

There is a common perception that the search volume estimates provided by Google tend to be inaccurate, but we've found their reported search volume estimates are reliable, provided that you account for the various sources of error discussed above.

For the most part, this perception is based on the fact that marketers don't typically earn as many impressions as the AdWords tools suggest.

Some of the reasons for this include:

- Your ads may not be displayed on the first page of search results (where most of the search volume is generated) due to low bids or quality score issues.
- Your ads may appear on the first page of search results but may only capture a small percentage of the available impressions (low coverage).
- The AdWords tools do not filter out fraudulent impressions. These impressions are filtered from your AdWords account (although sometimes with a lag of several days).

For these reasons, you need to discount the search volume to come up with an impression estimate. One rule of thumb you can follow is that 99 percent of advertisers receive less than 20 percent of the available impressions. If you are serious about search marketing, however, you stand a good chance of capturing a higher amount. Fifteen percent is easily attainable in most markets, while 30 to 50 percent is about the highest an advertiser can hope for, unless they have serious chops.

ESTIMATING CLICKTHROUGH RATE (CTR)

Producing reliable clickthrough rate estimates without sophisticated computer models is well nigh impossible.

However, if you absolutely, positively need to generate an estimate for some reason, you can do so with the best-guess estimates based on the customer life cycle category:

- Browse keywords—.8 percent
- Shop keywords—1.5 percent
- Buy keywords—2.0 percent

Just keep in mind that if you use these estimates, they won't be very good (forget being in the ballpark; you'll be lucky if you're in the same state).

Estimating Cost-Per-Click (CPC)

Forecasting CPC can be done in a variety of ways—in order from most to least accurate:

1. Use computer simulations to generate CPC estimates for individual keywords, then adjust these estimates for various factors (such as average position of your ads).
2. Use the CPC estimates provided by the search engines (e.g., use the engine's traffic estimator tools or connect programmatically via their APIs).

3. Use generic CPC estimates for all keywords:
   - $3.50 for broad keywords
   - $1.50 for lower-traffic keywords
   - $0.10 for a branded keyword you own

ESTIMATING CONVERSION RATE AND ORDER SIZE

Forecasting these metrics makes the above clickthrough rate and cost-per-click calculations look like an exact science. They are completely dependent on the credibility of your brand, how fine-tuned your sales funnels are, seasonality, overall demand in your category, and hundreds of other factors.

In other words, any estimate is little better than a guess.

If you have an existing website, you may be able to use your sitewide conversion rate as a starting point. If not, you can use these best-guess ranges based on your website conversion strategy:

- Email capture—20 percent
- B2B lead generation—3 to 5 percent
- Sale of a common low-priced consumer goods (under $40)—1 to 2 percent
- Sale of common high-priced consumer goods (over $40)—.5 percent

The above figures assume that you are making use of targeted keywords, superior landing pages, and sales funnels. If for some reason this isn't a safe assumption, you should cut them by 80 percent.

Order size can be trivial to estimate, or it can be virtually impossible. If you are selling a single product, such as $19 ebooks, it's pretty straightforward. If you are capturing leads, then you'll need to devise a proxy value per lead. If you have a catalog site with hundreds of categories, you'll probably need to hook into your financial systems directly.

ESTIMATING COMPETITORS' TRAFFIC

A number of tools will help to give you an idea of how much traffic (from all sources, not just paid search) competing websites are receiving each month. This can be very helpful for both planning a new website as well as forecasting traffic and sales of an existing one.

There are a number of other questions for which experienced paid search managers typically need answers:

- How many competitors are advertising in a particular market?
- Who are the biggest threats?

- What's the most effective ad copy in a particular category or even individual keyword?
- Which landing pages are most effective?
- How much traffic is my competitors generating from paid search?
- What gaps are in my competitors' campaigns?

The search engines do not (and in fact, cannot) provide you with this information. This is where third-party toolsets enter the picture.

Third-Party Tools

Among the many third-party tools that can provide some of all of this data, here are a few of the best.

Alexa
(Alexa.com)

Alexa is one of the first places most people go to get an idea of how their competitors stack up in terms of raw traffic. Simply type in the domain name to generate traffic statistics. The most interesting one is Reach, which indicates the percentage of global internet users who visit that site in a given month (Alexa doesn't report estimated visitors).

Alexa collects its data using toolbars that are installed on millions of computers all over the world. It is, unfortunately, not as accurate as it once was.

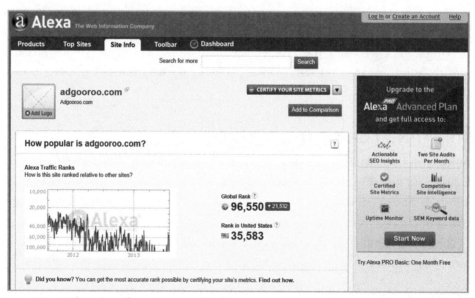

FIGURE 24–4. Alexa is a free resource that you can use to estimate competitors' traffic.

CONVERTING ALEXA'S REACH ESTIMATES TO ACTUAL TRAFFIC

Although Alexa doesn't report actual traffic estimates, if your site primarily targets English-speaking visitors, you can convert Alexa's reach figure into a monthly traffic estimate by multiplying it by 670,000,000.

AdGooroo Industry Insight
http://www.adgooroo.com

AdGooroo Industry Insight is an easy-to-use subscription service that provides comprehensive paid and organic search data for virtually every advertiser in 50 countries throughout the world. This data includes search spend, traffic estimates, clickthrough rates, keyword lists, and ad copy.

This data is not collected through a panel but rather through frequent statistical sampling of ads, which is then joined to other data sources, including the APIs provided by the search engines (or for the ultimate in data accuracy, clients' own advertising accounts). Statistical modeling is then used to adjust for variations in performance due to branded terms, position, quality score, and so on.

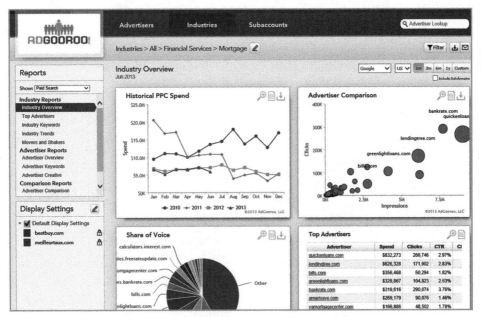

FIGURE 24–5. AdGooroo Industry Insight.

This approach is superior in that it provides accurate estimates for virtually every advertiser in the world, avoids privacy issues, and eliminates the error resulting from sampling small populations of tagged internet users.

Compete Pro
http://www.compete.com/products/compete-pro/

If you are looking for site analytics on competing sites that includes all traffic regardless of advertising channel, then check out Compete Pro. Compete generates traffic estimates using a panel consisting of millions of internet users. They offer a greater variety of statistics than Alexa, including traffic estimates. However, as with all panel companies, the data accuracy falls off for smaller sites. Compete also offers behavioral segmentation analysis, which can provide incredibly valuable insight into a particular website's audience.

Compete data is available in the United States, United Kingdom, and France.

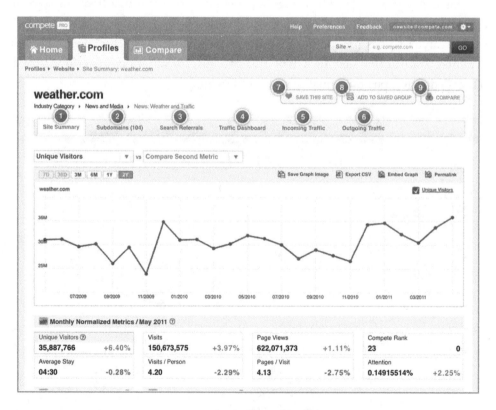

FIGURE 24–6. Compete Pro

UNDERSTAND WHERE THE DATA COMES FROM

While all of these services are valuable in some way, take the time to understand how they acquire their data as well as the strengths and weaknesses of each. This will help you avoid drawing erroneous conclusions.

I once received an email from an internet marketing "guru" describing how to find "winning landing page ideas" by watching for dips in Alexa traffic and then looking for changes on their sites using Internet Archive (http://archive.org). Anyone with a cursory understanding of Alexa's methodology could see that this technique is worthless because Alexa doesn't drill down into landing pages.

Limitations of Panel Data

A "panel" is simply a group of people who have given permission for a company to track and report on their internet activities. This approach dates back to the 1920s, when Arbitron began tracking radio listeners.

Panel data provides valuable insights into the behavior of a particular website's audience. This data is most reliable when it is aggregated into large population samples and can provide insights including:

- How many people visit a particular site each month?
- What is the demographic and/or behavior composition of that site's visitors?
- How long do visitors stay on that site?
- Where do they go immediately before/after visiting that site?

However, as the samples get smaller, the data accuracy declines to the point where these insights are no longer valid. This can impact you in two ways:

- Smaller sites tend to be misrepresented—or completely missing—from many panel sources.
- Few specifics can be provided about any particular of traffic to a site.

The takeaway is that panel data cannot provide reliable clickthrough rate estimates, keywords, or other data specific to paid search.

This does not diminish the value of these services in any way. Just realize that clickthrough or conversion rate estimates based on small samples are not reliable, and you shouldn't believe them. Total traffic estimates and demographic/behavioral information provided by these services, on the other hand, do seem to be reliable.

SUMMARY

Search intelligence has become a critical component of modern pay-per-click strategy. Advertisers who rely on it are faster and more nimble and can defend against their competitors' efforts to chip away at their campaign performance. If you're facing off against larger, well-funded competitors, this may be the only advantage you have against them.

Chapter 25

Don't Starve Your Campaign

Most of us don't have an unlimited budget. The search engines know this, so they give us a way to make sure we don't exceed our budget by allowing us to specify a reasonable maximum daily spend. In this chapter, you're going to see why you should never use this feature. We'll also touch on bid management, and I'll show you a do-it-yourself system that could save you thousands in bid management fees.

HOW TO SET YOUR MAXIMUM DAILY BUDGET

Log in to your AdWords account, and select your campaign in the "Campaigns" tab. Above it, you'll find an "Edit" button. This is where you can specify your maximum daily budget. See Figure 25-1 on page 244.

HOW THE MAXIMUM DAILY BUDGET FEATURE WORKS

When you set up your paid search campaign, you're asked to specify a maximum daily budget. The search engines will allocate this amount across your various keywords, and they typically do a good job ensuring that you spend no more than the specified amount each day. In other

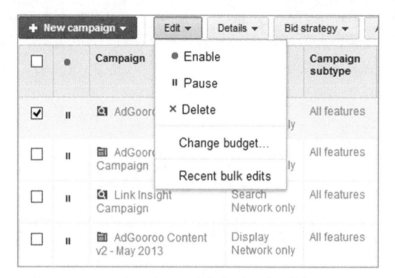

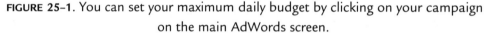

FIGURE 25–1. You can set your maximum daily budget by clicking on your campaign on the main AdWords screen.

words, if you specify a $75 daily campaign limit, then, over the course of a month, you will have spent on average $75 each day. There may be days you go over or under, but it averages out over time.

This sounds like a good thing, but really it's not.

Would You Let a Stranger Run Your Marketing?

That's exactly what you do when you set a low daily budget limit on your campaign.

The problem arises when the potential amount you could be spending on search marketing goes over your daily budget limit. In other words, if you could potentially spend $2,000 a day on your search campaign but you specify a $75 daily limit, then you're going to run into problems.

The reason this is a bad thing is that it's in the search engines' best interest to conserve the shelf space of ads. In other words, they have a limited inventory of advertising they can sell each day. This means that to generate the most revenue, they need to sell as much premium shelf space to the advertisers with the largest (or unlimited) budgets to capture that revenue.

So what about your $75? Doesn't the search engine want it? Yes, and they'll usually get it by selling you less-desirable ad inventory.

Advertisers who specify a high maximum budget have a better chance of getting placement in higher-traffic keywords, because this traffic is more predictable and thus allows the search engines to maximize their revenue reliably.

HOW SEARCH ENGINES USE YOUR BUDGET CAP

You can learn more about how budget plays into the AdWords algorithm by reading the academic paper, "AdWords and Generalized On-line Matching" (Mehta, Saberi, Vazirani, and Vazirani, http://www.stanford.edu/~saberi/adwords.pdf).

While not a light read, it goes into great depth about how the search engines can use your daily budget figure to throttle your ads and maximize their revenue.

The real kicker is that you've ceded control over a critical part of your campaign (where to show your ads) to a complete stranger (a strange computer program, actually). This computer program generally makes poor decisions on your behalf, because it doesn't know or care about your profit margins or your ROI. It's optimized to spend your campaign budget as quickly as possible within the parameters you've given it.

In contrast, if you don't specify a budget, you've taken this control away from the search engine. You've in essence told them, "Please maximize my impressions wherever possible, without exception." This removes a major source of uncertainty from your marketing efforts and allows you to pursue your goal of reaching 100 percent coverage more easily.

Let's look at some examples of how limiting your budget can hurt you.

Missing Out on High-Traffic Periods

Figure 25-2 on page 246 shows the daily cost for a campaign that did not have a maximum budget. As you can see, the daily spend was lumpy. On a few days, total spend was over $200, but it averaged $118/day overall. This advertiser received the benefit of getting more exposure on those high-traffic days. An advertiser with a budget restriction would probably miss this opportunity.

In contrast, look at one of their competitors who had a maximum budget cap (Figure 25-3 on page 246). As search volume increased in their category, their costs stayed flat because they hit their maximum budget. But notice how their coverage declined over the same time period.

As you can see, campaigns with low daily budgets do not automatically adapt to changing market conditions—just one more thing that can go wrong during the course of a typical AdWords campaign.

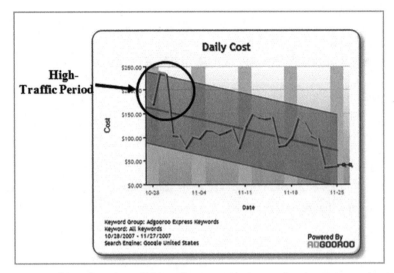

FIGURE 25-2. This advertiser did not have a maximum budget set and was able to take advantage of a high traffic period.

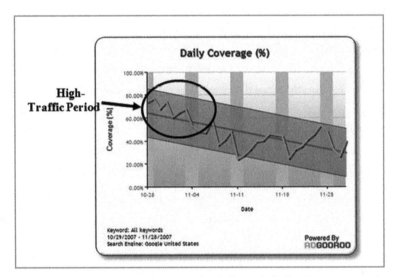

FIGURE 25-3. This competing advertiser had their daily budget set too low. As a result, their ads were throttled and their coverage dropped during the same high-traffic period.

Diverting Your Budget to Low-Profit Keywords

In the scatter plot shown in Figure 25-4, each icon represents a keyword in our AdWords campaign. Coverage is shown on the y-axis and indicates the percentage of the time that the ad was seen by searchers. During the time period of this chart, we specified a daily spending limit, so our ads were shown only about 75 percent of the time. This is typical of a campaign that is budget starved.

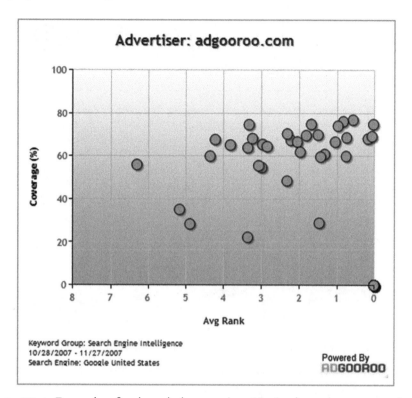

FIGURE 25–4. Example of a throttled campaign. Notice how the coverage is not equally distributed across all keywords.

If all keywords were throttled equally, this might not be such a bad problem. However, you can see from the chart that the impressions weren't prorated evenly across all of the keywords. Rather, a number of keywords were given impressions less than 50 percent of the time, including some very profitable keywords with very high bids.

A computer program determines the actual coverage you get for each keyword when operating under a fixed budget. It incorporates many variables, and nobody outside of the search engines can say with authority what those variables are. But we do know that these algorithms don't take into account your profit margin for each keyword, so the chances are very high that some of your budget will be shifted away from high-profit keywords into low-profit ones, which is not good.

Advertisers with unlimited budgets don't experience this problem nearly as often. Here's an example of how our campaign looks today. There are actually 107 keywords represented in this chart, and all but a few have coverage values near 100 percent.

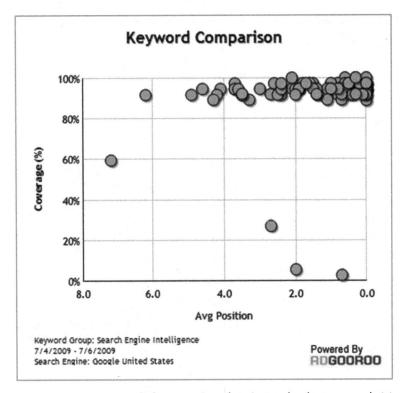

FIGURE 25–5. A pay-per-click campaign that is not budget starved. Most keywords appear with high coverage.

SUMMARY

Putting control over your campaign spend in anyone else's hands is a bad idea. If you instead clear the maximum daily budget setting on your account and control your campaign at the keyword level, you'll eliminate several problems that drag down the efficiency of many paid search campaigns.

Chapter 26

Don't Blindly Trust the Search Engines

Sometimes you just can't trust what the search engines tell you.

You may think your ad is appearing when it's not. You may think it's not, when it is. Sometimes your campaign reports are, well . . . just downright wrong.

It's not their fault, really. If you think about all the possible ways an ad can get triggered (various match types, synonyms, plurals, maybe even affiliates bidding on your same terms with identical ads, etc.), it's easy to see how your search reports might say one thing, while your customers are seeing another.

Figure 26-1 shows an example taken from one of my campaigns today. In the screenshot below, you can see that Google is reporting that my ads aren't appearing for the phrase "keywords search." According to this, I've received exactly zero impressions in the past seven days.

FIGURE 26–1. AdWords reports that this keyword has had no impressions in the past week.

The supposed reason is a "low quality score." Clicking the magnifying glass takes me to the AdWords Keyword Analysis page. Here it says that I have a problem with my landing page.

Keyword Analysis: keywords search

Your ad is rarely showing for this keyword because the keyword's Quality Score is poor.
See the 'Quality Score' tab for details.

Your bid: $1.15 Max CPC

| Ad Showing? | Quality Score: Poor |

⚠ **Quality Score: Poor (1/10)** ②

What should I do?
Improve the quality of your landing page, which is negatively impacting your Quality Score. In addition, your keyword and ad text can benefit from some general quality optimizations.

Try to:

- Make your landing page useful, honest, and easy to navigate. Strive to create a happy and meaningful user experience. You can also select a more relevant landing page for your ad. Learn more

- Edit your keyword and ad text so they clearly relate to each other and accurately describe your landing page. Learn more

FIGURE 26–2. AdWords reports a "Poor" quality score for this same keyword.

However, my ads are appearing. In fact, according to AdGooroo, in the past three days my ads have appeared exactly 93.9 percent of the time in the United States at an average position of 1.3 for this very same keyword.

Show Advertisers	**Show Ads**	PPC Campaign Stats			
Displaying 1 - 47 of 47 items		First | Prev | Next | Last		Display 50 ▼	items per page
Ad	% Served ▼	Avg Rank	Destination URL		Keywords
Find Keywords for AdWords Discover thousands of profitable keywords! World's largest database www.adgooroo.com	93.9	1.3	http://www.AdGooroo.com/products /adgooroo_express.php		keywords search (93.9%)

FIGURE 26–3. However, our ads appear about 94 percent of the time for this keyword.

A casual Google search also confirms this. I found my ad on the first search results page.

Why does AdWords clearly say that my ad isn't appearing while at the same time serving it to end users?

The key is to look at the ad text. In the AdGooroo screenshot, we see an ad that starts with, "Find Keywords for AdWords." Yet the AdWords reporting interface shows that the ad below is the one we're attempting to serve.

Search 5,000,000 keywords Increase Traffic, Reduce Costs Search the Largest Keyword Database www.AdGooroo.com	Edit	Active	0.0%	0	-	0.00%	$0.00	0.0%	$0.00	-

FIGURE 26–4. Here's the ad we are trying to show for this keyword.

After searching through my campaign, I finally discover that the ad served is being targeted to the broad term, "keyword." This triggers the ad for "keywords search."

Amazingly, both ads have the same exact landing page. So while the AdWords quality bot has for some reason decided that the combination of a niche keyword, highly targeted ad, and a well-crafted landing page wasn't up to snuff, it simultaneously decided that a broad keyword, generic ad, and the same landing page was a pretty good fit. Good enough to show my ad in the top spots of the search results page.

Does it make sense? No.

Do you have to settle for it? No, not if you triangulate your data using third-party tools.

Had I believed the AdWords reporting interface, I would have (incorrectly) thought that my ad wasn't showing. But it was. Near the top of the page, in fact.

This is why it's important to look at your keywords exactly as your customers do. They are probably seeing things a lot differently than you may think.

Chapter 27

Open All Night (Day Parting)

High up on the list of overhyped pay-per-click practices is day parting, the practice of increasing bids during the hours of the day when conversions are at their highest. At other hours of the day (usually during the wee early-morning hours), bids are lowered or keywords may be paused altogether.

This idea is a holdover from the world of broadcast ("push") advertising. In the traditional media world, day parting is the practice of dividing the day into several parts, each of which caters to a different audience. Television and radio stations could then charge different prices based on the audience that was expected to see an ad at any given time.

This not only gives media buyers the ability to stretch their ad dollars, they can also use it to better reach the people who are most interested in their products. This is why commercials for family products run during the day (better demographic targeting) and infomercials run at night (the ad spots are cheap).

Unfortunately, neither of these concepts translates well into pay-per-click marketing.

THE DEMOGRAPHIC MARKETERS

Day parters tend to fall into two camps. Let's consider the first: demographic marketers. These marketers use day parting in an attempt to maximize the number of impressions they are serving to their target audience. They believe that because there are more sales when traffic is highest, this is a sign that their target demographic is more active. Thus, they raise their bids or activate their campaigns during the busiest hours of the day.

However, pay-per-click allows us to directly measure the correlation between searchers' interest in a product and their decision to buy. We no longer have to make guesses about our audience using the indirect relationship that exists in broadcast advertising. We can measure this relationship directly.

And measurement almost always shows that there is no direct correlation between the time when things are busy and when people are ready to buy. These days, people may be ready to buy at noon during their lunch break, or they may be ready to buy at 2 A.M. when they can't sleep because they are so worried about their problems (which your product will solve, right?).

The internet is an instant-gratification medium. Advertisers who try to use day parting to segment their audience just don't get this fundamental fact.

This doesn't mean that you shouldn't try to better target your ads. It just means that you should be using proven methods that work (such as keyword matching).

THE COST CUTTERS

The other camp of day parters consists of those who use it as a means of cutting costs (and conversely, increasing ROI).

They argue that if conversion rates are lower at night, then money they save by pausing their campaigns at that time outweighs the opportunity cost of the sales they missed. This results in an effective net profit.

This argument holds a lot more water than the first, to be sure. But just because a boat has smaller holes doesn't mean it will float.

Here are a few of the reasons why day parting doesn't make for an effective cost-cutting measure.

Day Parting Ignores "Assists"

Not every one of your keywords will appear to be a winner. There may be dozens of keywords to which you can never attribute a sale, but as soon as you remove them from your campaign, your conversions drop like a rock.

When a visitor fails to buy the first time they click on one of your ads but does so later after clicking another ad, it is known as an assist. These keywords assist other keywords in doing their job. They are the Scottie Pippen to your Michael Jordan.

Unless you install special tracking, however, you will fail to see the assist at work. And herein lies the reason why so many people mistakenly try to cut costs during low-conversion hours. They fail to see that many of those late-night visitors come back the next day with their wallets out, ready to buy from that site they found the night before, especially for businesses with a traditionally offline component. I have personally researched automobiles and contractors at night, left my browser window open, and called them in the morning.

Day Parting Doesn't Cut Costs as Much as You Think

You've already seen how CPC prices are determined in no small part by the overall demand for a keyword. Because demand for ad placement goes down at night, CPC prices tend to drop during this time. In addition, traffic volumes are much lower at night.

The combination of low search volume and reduced average CPC means that the total cost savings realized by pausing campaigns during nonpeak hours is often small in comparison with the spend during peak hours. It almost doesn't seem worth it.

Day Parting Helps Your Competitors

Conversely, when you pause your campaigns, you reduce the competitive bidding pressure for the remaining advertisers. I'm taking it for granted that you're a high-quality/high-coverage advertiser. When you drop out of the auction, you're actually giving your competitors a fighting chance.

In essence, you're increasing the efficiency of their campaigns, probably far more than your own.

Day Parting Adds Management Overhead

All three of the big search engines offer day parting in their feature set these days, so the cost overhead of buying a third-party solution to manage day parting has largely gone away. However, there are still some lingering complications that require your attention.

Chief among these are the differing ways in which the search engines handle day parting. With Google, day parting is based on the time zone where your campaign was set up. If you're a California advertiser who's day parting your campaign from 8 A.M. to 5 P.M., your ads will actually appear from 11 A.M. to 8 P.M. in New York. It's for this reason that day parting becomes far less useful as the geographic footprint of your customer base grows. (Note that Bing works the way it should; its day parting is based on your visitors' time zone.)

As the pay-per-click algorithms evolve over time, you'll need to assess the impact of any changes on your day parting strategy. For example, Google used to use your absolute clickthrough rate (regardless of the position of your ads) when calculating the relevance of your campaign. If you used day parting to lower your bids, your campaign-level quality score would have been negatively impacted. This is no longer the case, but there will always be subtle complications that you need to stay on top of.

But Sometimes Day Parting Works . . .

Although I recommend against the use of day parting for most advertisers, there are a few situations where it makes sense.

First, certain types of audiences do tend to exhibit a demographic skew at various times throughout the day. For instance, there tends to be a pronounced bias toward corporate buyers in most B2B categories during regular business hours (7 A.M. to 6 P.M.). Conversely, entrepreneurs and small business owners tend to predominate during the evening and early morning hours.

Second, day parting becomes more valid if your budget is limited and you've determined that assists aren't playing a prominent role in your campaign. This may be the case with one-step digital buys, such as software and ebooks.

And finally, day parting is practically required for local advertisers with regular business hours (such as dentists, plumbers, local retailers, etc.), due to the nature of local search. Many local searchers will simply go down a list of ads and choose the first business that picks up the phone. If nobody is there to answer (weekends, holidays), then you might consider pausing your ads so you don't incur the cost for wasted clicks. Just keep in mind that you'll miss out on your more patient buyers.

SHOULD YOU ADVERTISE ON WEEKENDS?

These same arguments apply to "weekend parting" as well. If your local business is only open Monday through Friday, you may want to consider pausing your campaign on Saturday and Sunday.

SUMMARY

Day parting is a strategy that most advertisers should avoid, but it does serve a valuable role in a few niche categories as well as for local advertisers. If you do decide to incorporate it into your campaign, be sure to stay on top of changes to the paid search algorithms, because even seemingly minor tweaks can have a big impact on your traffic and conversions.

Chapter 28

Product Listing Ads

Product listing ads, or PLAs, are one of the most exciting innovations to come out of Google in a long time. This alternative ad format uses images to give retailers a way to actually show their products to consumers.

FIGURE 28–1. A sample of Product Listing Ads.

The thought process behind them is simple: You search for a product, you see a picture of it, you click on it, you buy it. No ad copy to worry about. Image, price, vendor, and an occasional special offer become the main ingredients of a successful ad.

However, the digital shopping model discussed in Chapter 13 suggests that it's not *that* simple. This is because in the real world, most people consult a variety of sources before making a purchase, such as social media, retail sites, brand sites, price comparison engines and so on. PLAs are not the only game in town. Far from it. They are a tiny part of a huge, potential advertising mix.

And furthermore, we saw in Chapter 14 that search engine users fall into three main purchasing categories: browsers, shoppers, and buyers. PLAs appeal primarily to buyers (recall that price and special offers are key influencers in this segment). They *should* appeal to shoppers, but in practice, that is often not the case because a block of eight PLA ads usually shows wildly different products. This makes shopping difficult. And forget browsing; it's pretty darn difficult to accomplish this task using these ads.

A HISTORY OF PLAS

In 2002, Google launched its combination search and shopping engine, Froogle. Advertisers uploaded their product feeds to this website using an unstructured database called Google Base.

In 2007, Froogle received a makeover and was renamed Google Product Search. A few years later, Google Base was downgraded to the Google Merchant Center (and accompanying APIs).

Finally, in May 2012, Google Product Search was rebranded as Google Shopping and converted to a pay-to-play model (that's right, folks—those clicks used to be free). The initial outrage quickly subsided when advertisers learned that Google Shopping was a really effective advertising model.

WHO SHOULD USE PLAS?

PLAs are clearly a retail play. If you're selling B2B services, pharmaceutical, financial products, or hundreds of other things—anything but retail—you can pretty much ignore them.

However, if you are a retailer, you should be taking a close look at them. The following chart (Figure 28–2) ranks various product categories by the number of PLA impressions generated from March to May, 2013.

It's also instructive to note which advertisers are making the most use of PLAs. The following table (Figuer 28–3) shows this data for the time period of March to May, 2013.

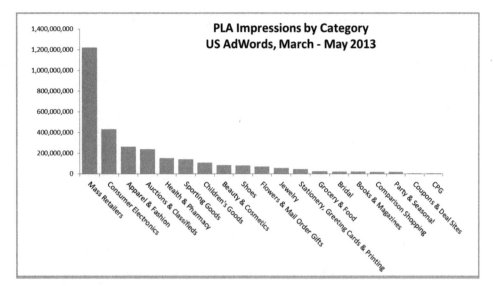

FIGURE 28–2. PLA impressions by category.

	Top 20 PLA Advertisers by Total U.S. AdWords Impressions, March-May 2013			
	Website	No. of Impressions	No. of Unique Products Advertised	No. of Unique Ads*
1	walmart.com	408 million	129,381	262,588
2	ebay.com	187 million	479,855	659,333
3	target.com	180 million	39,946	76,387
4	bestbuy.com	109 million	6,744	15,179
5	overstock.com	98 million	74,567	150,565
6	newegg.com	84 million	47,010	74,646
7	macys.com	81 million	29,363	124,859
8	staples.com	73 million	28,953	48,219
9	homedepot.com	53 million	33,570	62,258
10	drugstore.com	48 million	23,910	84,972
11	walgreens.com	47.6 million	13,526	44,209
12	etsy.com	47 million	109,854	142,956
13	toysrus.com	40 million	15,598	33,767
14	soap.com	37 million	13,571	39,882
15	sears.com	36.6 million	49,955	74,659
16	lowes.com	36 million	16,936	38,435
17	bhphotovideo.com	34 million	22,380	50,852
18	rakuten.com	33 million	37,320	97,924
19	globalindustrial.com	32 million	33,235	51,681
20	store.apple.com	31 million	822	1,803

AdGooroo, 2013

FIGURE 28–3. Top 20 PLA advertisers for Google US, March–May 2013 (*Source*: AdGooroo Blog, http://www.adgooroo.com/blog).

SETTING UP PLAS IN YOUR ADWORDS ACCOUNT

Getting PLAs set up in your Google AdWords account can be a pretty mysterious process. Fortunately, Google has implemented a lot of improvements since the initial rollout so it's now pretty easy (once somebody shows you how). Here's a rough overview of the process:

1. Start by signing up for a Google Merchant Center account (http://www.google. com/merchants).

2. Once you log in, you'll need to verify your ownership over the domain name as it appears in your ads.

3. Then create and upload a product feed. This is a text file that contains a list of your products and various important attributes (such as price).

4. Once this is completed, you can set up PLA ads. Log in to AdWords and create a new "Search Network Only" campaign. On the next page, you'll be given a chance to choose the type of campaign. Select "Product Listing Ads."

5. Finally, chose appropriate settings from the remaining fields on the page. Some options you'll want to pay special attention to are target location and bid price. By default, AdWords will choose when and where your PLAs are shown. If you would rather override this and select your keywords manually, deselect the checkbox in the "Ad Extensions" area that reads, "Use product information from Google Merchant Center to create and target ads."

Due to the fast-changing nature of PLAs, the exact setup instructions are likely to change over time. However, there is an excellent guide with up-to-date setup instructions here: http://cpcstrategy.com/product-listing-ads/.

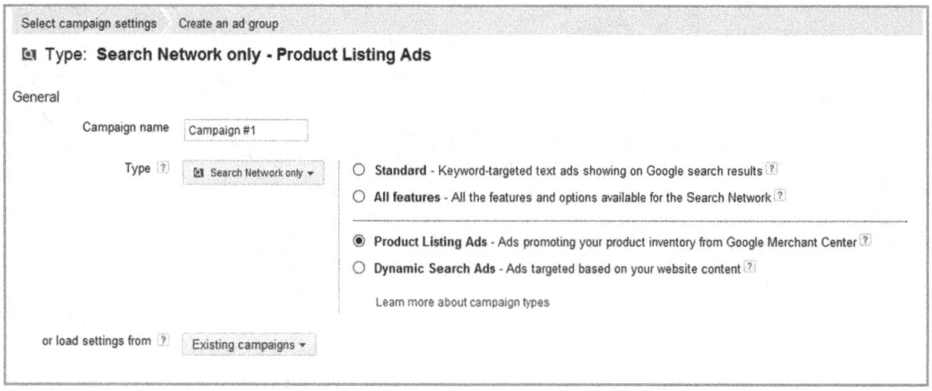

FIGURE 28–4. Setting up a new PLA campaign.

TARGETING OPTIONS FOR PLAS

PLAs have a lot of promise. But, unfortunately, targeting is currently an issue. Unless a searcher types in a specific SKU, it is very likely they will see a variety of products and prices in the PLAs shown. In the search shown below, two types of Pampers are shown with prices ranging from $11.69 to $47.19.

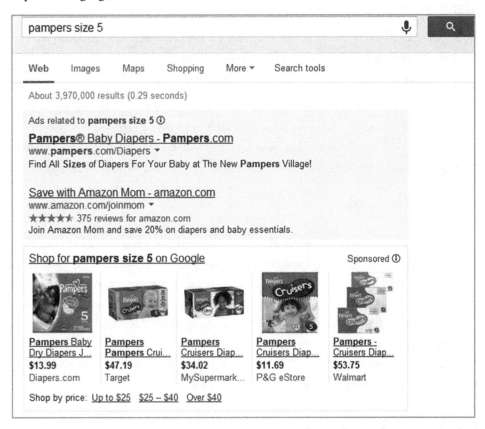

FIGURE 28–5. A typical PLA query (note the range in prices).

By default, AdWords will crawl your product feed and decide which products to show for a given query. This might work well . . . or it might not.

You may want to consider taking your top 10 or 20 bestsellers and target them manually. Do this by setting up a different campaign and turning off the default targeting option (as explained in step 5 above). You can then assign products to specific keywords.

Another little-known method that can help to improve your placements is to use negative keyword matching.

WHY MANUALLY TARGET SPECIFIC KEYWORDS FOR PLAS?

Targeting specific keywords for PLAs can be a lot of work, but there is a major payoff: campaign efficiency.

As in other areas of paid search, there is usually a high hidden cost associated with allowing Google to determine your placements. Specifying certain placements can result in a major improvement in your advertising ROI.

Along with this efficiency comes increased transparency. AdWords will not report keyword-level data to you when you use their default targeting settings. However, when you take over, AdWords will report your PLA statistics down to the individual keyword, allowing you to see which keywords are working and which ones should be deleted.

Finally, the order in which your PLA appears can have a big effect on your results. You can boost your CTR by testing different images, product descriptions, and promotions. Bid price is also important because it can affect your average position (but at a minimum, it should be high enough to ensure your ad appears regularly).

All of these techniques, however, require a third-party data feed in order to learn where and when your products are appearing.

This is a dynamic marketplace. Things change fast. What worked this month might not work next month so you have to stay on top of things.

ANECDOTAL RESEARCH

At the time of this writing, there isn't much hard research available about what works and what doesn't with PLAs (be sure to check the AdGooroo blog occasionally, because that's where we'll put it). There are a few things we've learned so far, though:

- Clickthrough rates for PLAs tend to be a bit higher than their corresponding text ads. A range of 2 to 4 percent is common, but even higher clickthrough rates are possible.
- Cost-per-click prices are all over the board. Some advertisers report wildly lower CPCs while others report that their PLA ads cost more. It is likely that this depends heavily on position, price, image, and promotion, not just of your own ads but also your competitors'.

Finally, you should be aware that the same advertiser can appear multiple times within a block of PLAs, resulting in coverage greater than 100 percent. This is highly desirable because every time your ad appears, a competitor's does not. The following screenshot shows an example of a PLA block containing three separate Walmart ads.

FIGURE 28–6. Example of multiple PLA ads appearing for the same advertiser.

Chapter 29

Mobile Search and Enhanced Campaigns

M obile advertising has been a hot topic lately. According to eMarketer, the mobile ad market is expected to reach $16.65 billion in 2013, with Google capturing over 50 percent of that revenue.

The mobile revolution is clearly underway. But for our purposes, the real question is: **Should paid search advertisers care?**

The majority of mobile advertising revenue is derived from mobile display, mobile apps, and YouTube advertising. This means that only a relatively small amount is being generated from mobile search. According to our computer models, mobile AdWords is on track to generate approximately $1 billion in revenue in 2013. Growing? Yes. But still small in comparison with desktop and tablet search.

Google is taking steps to change that. Recognizing the greater role that mobile is playing in our lives, in July 2013 Google launched Enhanced Campaigns. An unassuming name, this new platform actually represents a big change in the way advertisers will now be managing their campaigns.

So like it or not, mobile paid search will affect you in one way or another.

In order to find out how, we must first take a step back and look at mobile search from the top down.

DOES MOBILE SEARCH REALLY MATTER?

To answer this question, we applied our computer models to the mobile advertising market. We discovered that mobile is still pretty small. As of 2013, mobile makes up just 7.6 percent of total U.S. AdWords spend and just 8.2 percent of U.S. Bing spend.

And as you might expect, the effectiveness of mobile varies widely based on business vertical. "Shopping & Classifieds," "Lifestyle," "Automotive," and "Travel" are the biggest categories on AdWords (Figure 29–1). On Bing, "Automotive" has much less mobile traffic, while "Business" is much larger than it is on Google (Figure 29–2).

Note that on both mobile advertising platforms, "Computers and Internet" runs high; this is primarily due to advertising for mobile apps (for instance, Google Play ads that run on Android handsets).

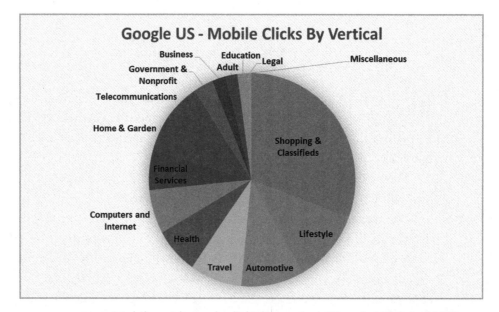

FIGURE 29-1. Mobile paid search clicks by vertical (Google US, July 2013).

However, the total volume of mobile clicks is very low in comparison to desktop search (note that desktop includes laptop and tablet devices as well). Figure 29–3 on page 267 and 29–4 on page 268 show the division of clicks between the different platforms on both AdWords and Bing.

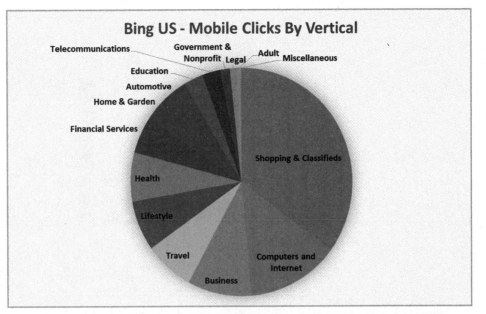

FIGURE 29–2. Mobile paid search clicks by vertical (Bing US, July 2013).

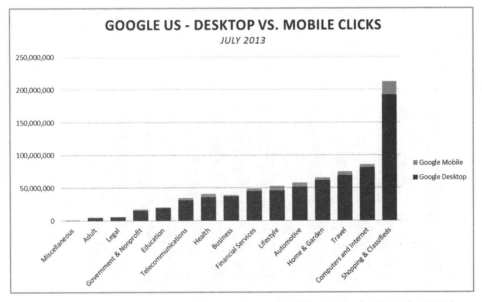

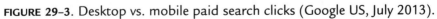

FIGURE 29–3. Desktop vs. mobile paid search clicks (Google US, July 2013).

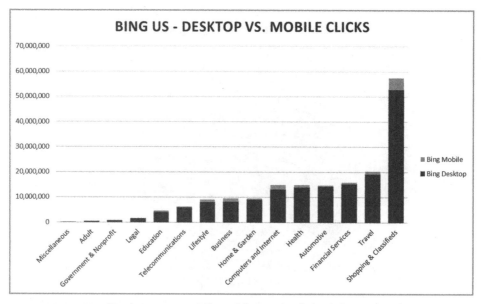

FIGURE 29–4. Desktop vs. mobile paid search clicks (Bing US, July 2013).

Another way of comparing mobile and traditional paid search is as a percentage of traffic. Figures 29-5 and 29-6 show mobile clicks as a percentage of total search traffic by vertical. For most categories, mobile search generates less than 10 percent of paid advertising clicks.

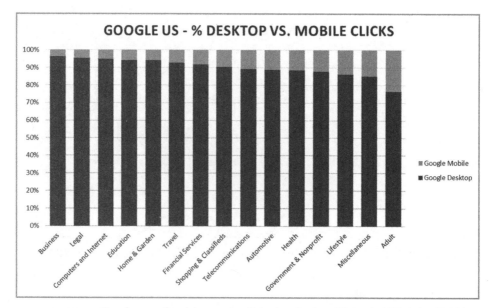

FIGURE 29–5. Breakout of paid search clicks by device (Google US, July 2013).

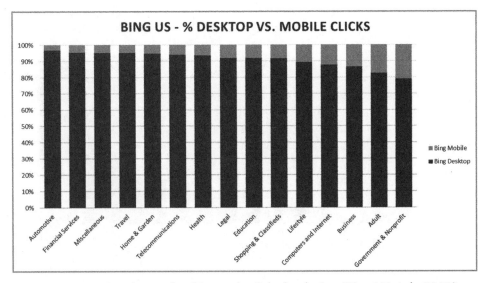

FIGURE 29–6. Breakout of paid search clicks by device (Bing US, July 2013).

With mobile paid search traffic averaging just 10 percent across all categories, you can expect total mobile paid search spend to be low. The next two charts depict desktop and mobile spend by category.

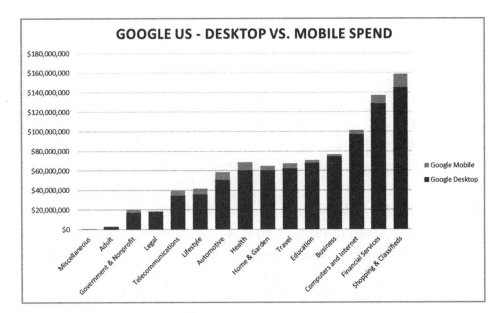

FIGURE 29–7. Mobile paid search spend by vertical (Google US, July 2013).

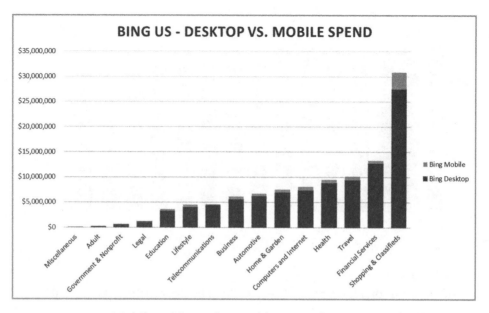

FIGURE 29–8. Mobile paid search spend by vertical (Bing US, July 2013).

WILL MOBILE SEARCH OVERTAKE DESKTOP SEARCH?

Mobile paid search is still a small segment of the total search advertising market. If it were to continue to grow at the rapid pace seen in 2012 and 2013, it would overtake desktop search in just a few years. However, there are several reasons why this is unlikely to happen.

Mobile Search Generates Much Less Traffic Than Desktop Search

Mobile devices are great. We can't live without them. But in comparison to tablets, laptops, and desktops, they are slow, hard to read, and difficult to browse the internet with. They are ultimately *convenience devices,*—i.e., we use them when we're bored, stuck in line, or have nothing better to do. Most of us prefer to search on larger screens.

Mobile CPC Prices Are Typically Lower Than Desktop Prices

For most categories, advertisers are not willing to pay as high of a price for mobile traffic as they are for desktop and tablets. There are exceptions of course; Automotive and Travel are the two biggest. But even for those categories, CPC prices aren't drastically higher. Figures 29-9 and 29-10 show relative CPC prices on Google and Bing.

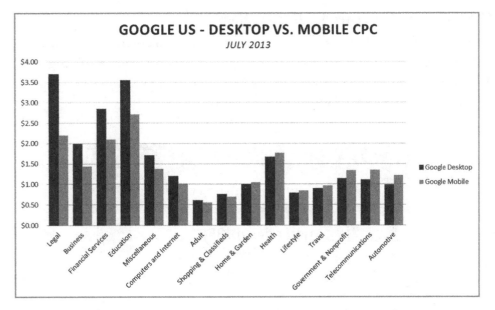

FIGURE 29–9. Mobile vs. desktop CPC prices (Google US, July 2013).

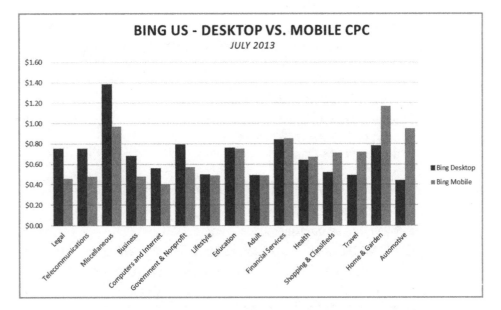

FIGURE 29–10. Mobile vs. desktop CPC prices (Bing US, July 2013).

Mobile Devices Show Fewer Ads Than Desktops

Ultimately, however, the real reason that mobile search won't overtake desktop is due to real estate. Desktop and tablet devices show up to 12 ads on a search result page. Mobile devices show a maximum of three (Figures 29–11 and 29–12).

Fewer ads means fewer impressions and clicks.

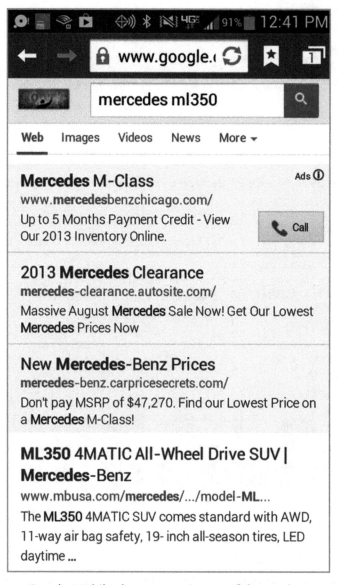

FIGURE 29–11. Google Mobile shows a maximum of three ads per results page.

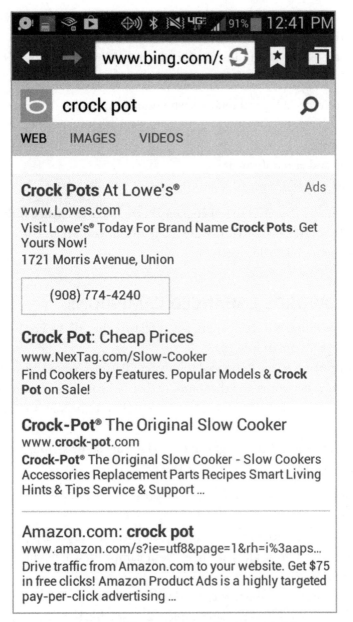

FIGURE 29–12. The same goes for Bing Mobile.

SO SHOULD YOU CARE ABOUT MOBILE SEARCH?

The answer is: not usually. Most advertisers can opt out of mobile without fear. In fact, when one factors in the cost and complexity of management overhead and that mobile clicks tend to convert at a much lower rate, advertisers who opt out may actually come out ahead of their more ambitious competitors.

However, there are some industries for which mobile makes a lot of sense:

- Automotive (particularly local dealers)
- Retailers (especially local retailers who offer coupons)
- Travel
- Mobile apps
- Lifestyle and entertainment
- Small local businesses

A general rule of thumb is that if consumers are likely to engage with your business on a mobile device (for instance, they are likely to call you), then you should probably look further into mobile paid search.

GOOGLE ADWORDS ENHANCED CAMPAIGNS

This brings us to Enhanced Campaigns, a new feature that all AdWords customers were automatically opted into in July 2013.

The major feature of the Enhanced Campaign platform is that advertisers now set a single bid for their keywords and then modify that bid based on certain targeting rules. For instance, you may decide to pay more for mobile searchers located within 10 miles of your store.

Sounds great, right? But it might not be. There are some serious pitfalls that await the unwary advertiser.

- By default, you are automatically opted into all devices: desktop, tablet, and mobile.
- Your spend will increase. If you've implemented a budget cap (see Chapter 25 on why this isn't a great idea), it's likely your campaign will be throttled in an unintended fashion.
- You now need to implement an advertising strategy for all devices. The same ads that work on desktop and tablets are not likely to be as effective on cell phones.
- Your desktop/tablet and mobile campaigns are now linked. If you want to raise your bid for a keyword on desktop, you will also be raising it for mobile.

Fortunately, if you understand how Enhanced Campaign settings work, you can work around most of these limitations.

Enhanced Campaign Settings

To access the targeting options for your AdWords campaign, navigate to the "Settings" tab within AdWords. Immediately underneath the tabs, you will find four buttons that include the options "Locations," "Ad Schedule," and "Devices." These options are described next.

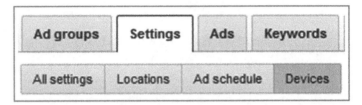

FIGURE 29–13. How to access Enhanced Campaign targeting options.

Devices

The Devices page allows you to modify your bids based on the type of device the searcher is using. For instance, if you want to reduce your bids on mobile devices by 25 percent, click once in the "Bid adj." column in the row that reads "Mobile devices with full browsers" (Figure 29-14). Enter your bid modifier in the popup that appears (Figure 29-15 on page 276).

Device	Bid adj. [?]
Computers	
Mobile devices with full browsers	- 25%
Tablets with full browsers	
Total	

FIGURE 29-14. The Devices page allows you to adjust bids based upon device type.

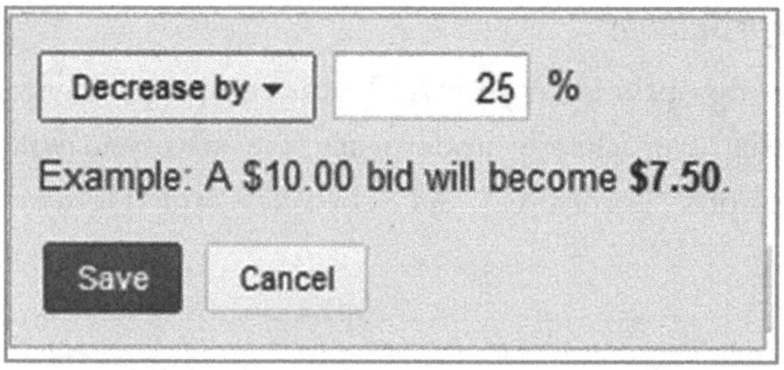

FIGURE 29–15. Applying a bid modifier.

Locations

The Locations page allows you to specify particular countries or metropolitan regions in which to display your ads. You can also modify your bids based on the physical location of the searcher.

By default, you can target countries and cities with a simple search.

FIGURE 29–16. Enhanced Campaign Location settings.

However, more advanced targeting options are available by clicking on the "Advanced Search" link. This screen (Figure 29–17) allows you to specify a radius around particular locations or target specific addresses that you've included in your ads via location extensions.

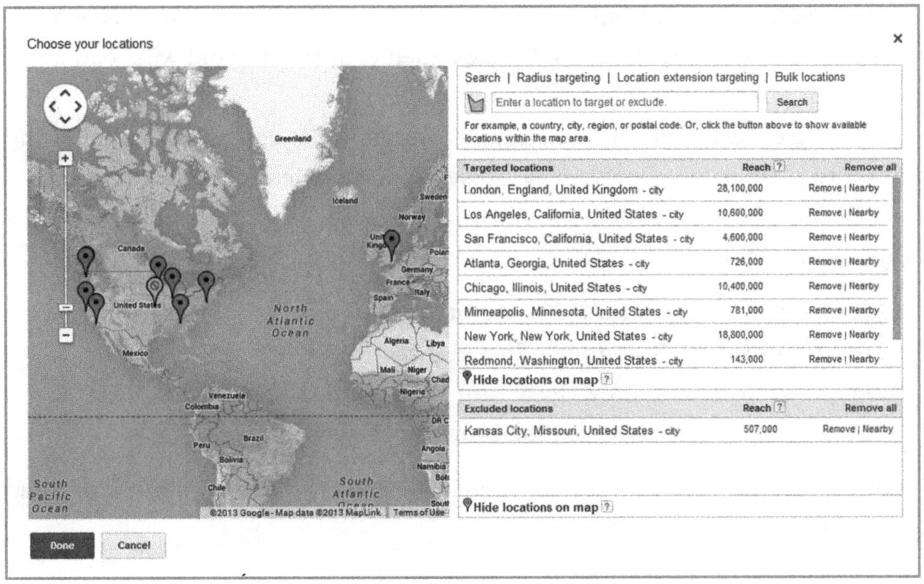

FIGURE 29–17. Advanced location settings

The ability to target your ads based on location is a very powerful feature and probably the best thing about the Enhanced Campaign platform. With it, you can turn off your ads in locations where they generate significant costs but little in the way of sales. For instance, our ads do well in London, but most of our traffic (and costs) are generated elsewhere in the United Kingdom. With location settings, we can now turn off those ads and cut down on wasted spend.

As with devices, you can apply a bid modifier to adjust your bids upward or downward based upon location.

Ad Schedule

This page allows you to modify your bids based on the time of day (see Chapter 27). Most advertisers won't need it, but if you do, note that it allows you to adjust placements based on the time only in the time zone you declared when you set up your AdWords account. If you'd like to adjust your ad placements in different time zones, you'll need to set up separate AdWords accounts for each.

HOW BID MODIFIERS WORK

The rules that you set for location, ad schedule, and device will be combined with your base bid for each keyword to produce a new modified bid.

For instance, if you set a bid modifier of +25 percent for ads shown in New York and a bid modifier of -25 percent for mobile ads, then your starting bid will be modified by 93.75 percent (1.25 x .75).

This is best illustrated with an example. Suppose that you apply the following bid modifiers to a campaign containing a single keyword, "Mercedes ML350," which has a bid price of $10.00. Furthermore, assume that this AdWords account has been set up in Chicago (Central Standard Time).

- Location: "United States" +25 percent
- Location: "United Kingdom" –25 percent
- Ad Schedule: 12AM- 6AM (local time zone only) –100 percent
- Devices: Mobile devices with full browsers –80 percent

Your actual bid prices for a few different scenarios will be computed as shown in Figure 29–18.

Keyword	Base Bid	Location	Time	Device	Actual Bid
Mercedes ML350	$10.00	Chicago (+25%)	8 A.M. CST	Tablet	$12.50
Mercedes ML350	$10.00	United Kingdom	3 A.M. CST / 9 A.M. GMT (–100%)	Desktop	Ad not shown
Mercedes ML350	$10.00	New York (+25%)	6 P.M. EST	Mobile (-80%)	$2.50

FIGURE 29–18. Effects of hypothetical bid -modification rules.

The Downside of Bid Modifiers

As you can see, it's easy to get in trouble because in a real-world campaign, it is virtually impossible to predict what your final bid prices will be. This is especially true with Ad Schedule modifiers, because they are based upon the time zone of your AdWords account, not the time zone of the searcher. In the example above, a search conducted in London during normal business hours would not trigger an ad because the time in Chicago is 3 A.M., when ads are turned off.

Another drawback is that your mobile and desktop/laptop campaigns are now coupled together, when they really shouldn't be. If you are manually optimizing specific keywords in order to maximize your impression share (per the instructions given in Chapter 21), this makes your job a lot harder. In order to edge out other advertisers, you need to tweak your bids up and down as necessary. However, when you do so, you'll now be adjusting them on mobile as well.

Fortunately, there's a simple solution. Create one campaign for desktop and laptop devices, and set your bid modifier for mobile devices to –100 percent. Then set up a second campaign for mobile devices, setting your bid modifier for desktops and tablets to –100 percent. (That assumes you want to target mobile devices. If you don't want to, then you need only a single campaign.)

Most advertisers will find that there's not a statistical difference between desktop and tablet campaigns, which is why I recommend that you combine them. If your business really does require a separate campaign for tablet devices (for instance, if you are selling an iPad app), then you can split that out into a separate campaign as well.

OUR EXPERIENCE WITH ENHANCED CAMPAIGNS

Jon Morris, CEO, Rise Interactive
Noam Dorros, Paid Search Expert

Google's Enhanced Campaigns marked one of the biggest changes that the AdWords system has seen to date. In making this change, Google hoped to provide additional benefits to consumers and marketers. For consumers, the new campaigns provide more context and an increased ability to take action when they see an ad. Marketers are offered a seamless way to reach their target audience at the right time and place. Understanding the features of Enhanced Campaigns is critical in making your search campaigns successful.

Some of those key features include:

Device Targeting—By default, your keywords now serve ads on all three devices (desktop, tablet, mobile). You can use separate campaigns to target mobile and desktop/tablet individually; however, desktop and tablet are now grouped together, with no ability to separate bids.

Bid Multiplier—Because each keyword now targets to all three devices, enhanced campaigns use a campaign-level "bid multiplier" to manage bids between desktop/tablet and mobile, with the range for bidding being -100 percent to 300 percent for mobile. If you want to turn off a particular device, use a setting of "–100%."

Bid Parameters—You can now adjust your keyword bids based on location and time of day.

OUR EXPERIENCE WITH ENHANCED CAMPAIGNS, CONTINUED

Ad Extensions—Advertisers can now schedule ad extensions to show only on certain days and times, allowing users to show a more appropriate ad and ad extension based on users' context and device.

We found that Enhanced Campaigns offered several key advanages:

Easier to Manage—The ability to set up a single campaign for all devices makes for more manageable accounts.

Cross-Device Conversion Tracking—Said to be on the horizon, this feature will help show users' conversion paths across devices.

More Powerful Targeting—You can now adjust bids based on day, location, or device.

Mobile Reporting—All advanced call metrics and reporting are now free.

The drastic change to Adwords caused many advertisers to develop a love-hate relationship with the platform. Below are several pain points that marketers have noted since the commencement of Enhanced Campaigns:

Day Parting—Day parting has become more complex and less user friendly.

Lack of Flexibility with Bid Multipliers—The ability to adjust at the ad group level is not yet available. Additionally, the lack of a big multiplier for tablets has been problematic.

Increased CPCs—Now that Google is essentially forcing everyone into the mobile game, CPCs have increased in that arena.

Mobile Campaigns—There is no longer an ability to create mobile-only campaigns, which is ultimately a loss of control for advertisers. Advertisers were forced to switch their strategies in order to accommodate the desktop/tablet targeting.

Minus a few bumps along the way, Enhanced Campaigns have not drastically altered our strategy toward optimization and daily management. There have been areas of lost control and efficiency of performance as such. The hope is that as Google continues to answer the cries of advertisers, Enhanced Campaigns will ultimately prove beneficial for all parties involved.

MOBILE ADS ON BING

With all of the complexity associated with AdWords Enhanced Campaigns, you may find it refreshing to hear that targeting mobile searchers on the Yahoo! Bing Network is dramatically simpler. To do so, you set up a campaign in the usual way. But when you get to the "Targeting Options" form, click "Device," then "Smartphones and other mobile devices with full browsers" (Figure 29–19). You can then set bids for your mobile keywords separately, just as you used to be able to do with AdWords.

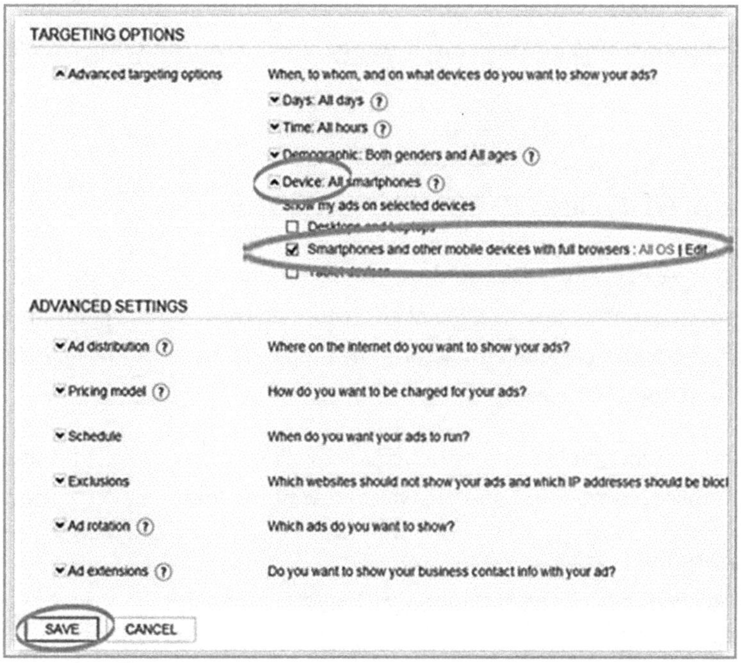

FIGURE 29–19. Setting up mobile ads on Bing.

COMPARING MOBILE ADS ON GOOGLE AND BING

We've found that there are clearly more mobile impressions available on Google. In the month of July, we estimated 2.8 billion impressions for Google and only about 350 million on Bing (12 percent of Google's).

However, Bing makes up quite a bit of the gap in clickthrough rate. For some reason, clickthrough rates for mobile ads on Bing appear to be much higher than on AdWords (Figure 29–20 on page 282).

	Google	Bing
Desktop	3.3%	1.5%
Mobile	2.3%	3.9%

FIGURE 29–20. A comparison of desktop and mobile clickthrough rates on Google and Bing. (*Source*: AdGooroo, July 2013)

When you factor this in, Bing mobile traffic runs at about 20 percent of Google's on average and much higher in certain categories where Bing is strong (Business, Legal, and Education).

If mobile plays a role in your search campaign, it's worth taking a look at Bing.

MOBILE ADVERTISING RECOMMENDATIONS

Mobile paid search traffic runs at about 10 percent the rate of desktop/tablet devices and requires a lot of effort to manage well. By default, most advertisers should opt out of mobile by setting the bid adjustment for "Mobile devices with full browsers" to –100 percent.

You should consider mobile ads only if you are willing to pay up for placement in one of the top three positions *and* you fall within one of the following categories:

- Automotive (particularly local dealers)
- Retailers (especially local retailers who offer coupons)
- Travel
- Mobile apps
- Lifestyle and Entertainment
- Small local business

If you do target mobile searchers, manage your desktop and tablet ads in a separate campaign from your mobile ads. Do this by using the Devices page (Settings > Devices) to set your mobile and desktop/laptop bid modifiers to -100 percent in each campaign, respectively.

- Use the Locations settings (Settings > Locations) to turn off ads in unproductive locales.
- Avoid using the Ad Schedule options unless absolutely necessary.

Chapter 30

Conclusion

I hope that as you've read this book (and possibly reworked an existing pay-per-click campaign) that you come to understand that the methods I recommend are a far cry from the seat-of-the-pants way most pay-per-click campaigns are run. They aren't based on the latest fads (which I largely ignore and you should, too) but rather on hard data and quantitative evidence.

I've shown you dozens of easy and often not-at-all obvious techniques you can use as part of your daily management routine. The benefits of this disciplined approach are immense. Individually, they eliminate many of the small slippages that reduce the effectiveness of most advertisers' campaigns. Together, they have a compounding effect that will ensure that few (if any) competitors will come close to getting results anywhere near as good as yours.

Here's to standing out from the crowd,

—Rich

About the Author

An internet marketer for more than 15 years, Richard Stokes is the founder and CEO of AdGooroo, a leading provider of search marketing intelligence. Prior to founding AdGooroo, Richard was a senior technology executive at Publicis Groupe/Leo Burnett. He has a BS in computer engineering from the University of Illinois and an MBA in entrepreneurship and technology management from the Kellogg Graduate School of Management (Northwestern University). Richard is a regular speaker on search marketing topics and is certified as a conversion optimization professional.

Index

A

Acquisio, 144
ad auctions, 58
ad copy, 161–185. *See also* ad
   copy optimization
   abbreviations in, 171
   accuracy in, 171
   action words in, 167
   ad spend levels, 181
   ampersands in, 166
   brand names in, 168
   calls to action in, 17,
      165, 188, 190–196
   capitalizing every word
      in, 167–168
   company names in, 172
   copy length, 208
   coverage in, 181
   exclamation points in,
      164–165
   free offerings in, 165
   lead capturing from, 168
   numbers in, 164
   "official site" in, 166
   optimizing. *See* ad copy
      optimization
   position and, 48–51,
      56–58, 65–68, 157–
      160, 181

price quotes in, 166
promises in, 172
quality scores and,
   40–41. *See also* quality scores
superlatives, using in, 172
trademarks in, 166–167
visitor perspective in,
   162–163
writing, 167–175
ad copy optimization. *See
   also* ad copy
   Ad Extensions in, 176–
      180, 280
   campaign setup and, 124
   common mistakes in,
      169–176
   copying successful con-
      cepts from other
      ads, 180–182
   defined, 161
   ineffective, 40–41
   placeholder copy, 138
   spend levels of ads, 181
   split-testing ads, 163–
      164, 180–185, 204,
      207
   visitor perspective and,
      162–163

writing good ad copy,
   167–175. *See also* ad
   copy
Ad Extensions, 176–180,
   280
ad groups, 124–127, 137–
   142
ad position, 48–51, 56–58,
   65–68, 157–160, 181
ad quality scores. *See* quality
   scores
AdGooroo, xviii, xix
AdGooroo Industry Insight,
   112–115, 239–240
AdGooroo's SEM Insight,
   42, 113–114
advertising media, 21–24
AdWords, xvii, 20–24,
   58–60, 74–76, 260
Adwords, 1
AdWords bid simulator, 68
AdWords Enhanced
   Campaign, 274–280
AdWords quality scores,
   74–76. *See also* quality
   scores
AdWords reports, 78–79,
   249–251
AdWords Select, 58, 72